ROUTLEDGE

New York & London

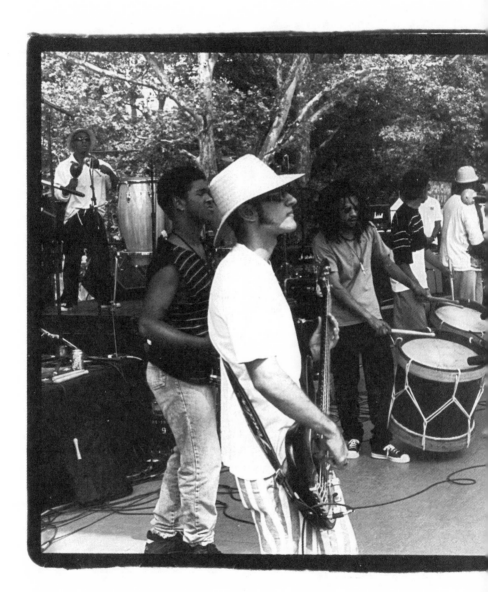

edited by

Charles A. Perrone
& Christopher Dunn

BRAZILIAN POPULAR
MUSIC & GLOBALIZATION

Published in 2002 by
Routledge
29 West 35th Street
New York, NY 10001

Published in Great Britain by
Routledge
11 New Fetter Lane
London EC4P 4EE

Originally published in 2001 by the University Press of Florida.
Reprinted by arrangement with the authors.
First Routledge paperback edition, 2002.
Copyright © 2001 by the Board of Regents of the State of Florida

Routledge is an imprint of the Taylor & Francis Group.
Printed in the United States of America on 250 year-life acid-free paper.

A somewhat abridged version of the essay "Carmen Mirandadada" (chapter 2) by
Caetano Veloso appeared in the New York Times on October 21, 1991. The present
version is a translation by Robert Myers and Charles A. Perrone of the text that
appeared in Folha de São Paulo on October 22, 1991, with emendations requested by
the author.

Song and translation copyrights appear on pages 273–75, a continuation of this
copyright page.

Title page illustration: Chico Science & Nação Zumbi, Central Park Summer Stage,
New York, 1995. Photo © by Jack Vartoogian.

07 06 05 04 03 02 01 6 5 4 3 2 1

Library of Congress Cataloging-in-Publication Data:

Brazilian popular music & globalization / edited by Charles A. Perrone and Christopher Dunn.
    p. cm.
    Includes bibliographical and discographical references and index.
    isbn 0-415-93695-0
    1. Popular music—Brazil—History and criticism. 2. Globalization. I. Title: Brazilian
popular music and globalization. II. Perrone, Charles. A. III. Dunn, Christopher, 1964–

ML3487.B7 B76 2001
781.64'0981—dc21

                                                                            2001019960

Contents

Illustrations

Preface

The year 2000 held special significance for Brazil, the largest country of the Southern Hemisphere. Besides celebrating the advent of a new millennium, the nation commemorated the quincentennial of the arrival of a fleet led by Pedro Álvares Cabral on the shores of what would become the only Portuguese colony in the Americas, later named Brazil. Like many artists and intellectuals before him, contemporary Brazilian singer-songwriter Caetano Veloso is intrigued by parallels between his land and the United States. In *Verdade tropical* he writes: "Brazil is the other giant of America, the other melting pot of races and cultures, the other promised paradise for European and Asian immigrants, the Other." And yet North Americans know notoriously little about the "other giant of America." Popular music in Brazil has done much to reflect and ponder this incognizance. Such critiques are part of a process that has generated models for engaging critically and creatively with the musical cultures of other nations, especially those that have exercised disproportionate influence in Brazil during the twentieth century. This book seeks to contribute to the dissemination of knowledge about Brazil and its popular music, exploring myriad ways in which it has been articulated in a global context.

Like many other collections of essays, the present volume can trace its origins to an academic congress. The final result here, however, goes far beyond a series of conference papers on a common theme; it emerges from subsequent initiatives, felicitous coincidences, exercises in cooperative international relations, and the persistence of key players. John Murphy had the initial idea of having a session on evolution and changes in Brazilian song and dance music at BRASA IV, Brazilian Identity and Globalization, the fourth international congress of the Brazilian Studies Association, which was held November 12–15, 1997, in Washington, D.C. The panel "Dialectics of Internationalization in Brazilian Popular Music" was further conceptualized, co-organized, and moderated by Charles A. Perrone. Christopher Dunn and Fred Moehn were essential to the success of the session, before, during, and after the presentations themselves. Because of a quirk in scheduling, the sequence of papers and roundtable was able to continue past the originally designated seventy-five minutes and to become a virtual double session, allowing presenters to expound somewhat more freely, and members of the audience to engage them in lively discussion in a way too often rendered impossible within the constraints of conference organization. Even before the noon-hour call to luncheon brought the session to a close, colleagues in attendance noted the timeliness of the general topic, the warm reception of the studies, the interest in debate, and the strong potential for a related collective publication. Before the end of the conference, several other participants approached the co-organizers with similar impressions. Other variously titled sessions at BRASA focusing on globalization and culture featured papers that could have formed a third session of the panel with "popular music" actually in the title; presenters of two such papers, Liv Sovik and Piers Armstrong, ended up contributing essays to this collection.

The urge to bring together scholarship sharing a concern with transnational aspects of Brazilian popular music grew with each suggestion during BRASA IV and in the weeks and months following the event. Camillo Penna was especially encouraging regarding development of a book proposal. Livio Sansone (a native of Italy, who studied in Europe and works in Brazil) was unable to attend the D.C. meeting because of other professional obligations, but contact with him and an initiative he had co-organized at UFBA, the Federal University of Bahia at Salvador, provided the opportunities necessary to undertake and bring to fruition an inter- and transnational endeavor. Before moving to Rio de Janeiro, Sansone led a graduate program called S.A.M.B.A. (Sócio-Antropologia da Música Bahiana [Social Anthropology of Music in Bahia]). A Cor da Bahia [The color of bahia]—a related program of research and training on racial relations, culture, and black identity in Bahia—worked together with that group to produce, with the support of the Ford Foundation, a volume of essays titled *Ritmos em trânsito* [Rhythms in Transit]. Coedited by Sansone and Jocélio Teles dos Santos, this title is cited numerous times in the present essays. The contributions of Ari Lima and Osmundo Pinho here emerge from work first published in Portuguese there. Their new formulations, as well as those by research fellows Antônio Godi and Milton Moura, were translated for this book by contributor John Harvey, with additional editing by the coeditors. Two colleagues at the home institutions of the coeditors, Larry Crook and Idelber Avelar, were especially generous in their contributions of original studies to this collection after an initial core had been established. Finally, we are privileged to have the scintillating article written by Caetano Veloso, the "intellectual pop star" who has been a leading name in Brazilian song for more than thirty years and who has deservedly become an internationally recognized and lauded performer and writer.

There are many people to thank for their editorial suggestions or assistance in obtaining bibliography, discography, and other information, materials, and permissions. Authors have thanked specific individuals in the notes that follow each chapter. We would like to express gratitude to the following academic colleagues, researchers, artists, and professionals: Martha Tupinambá de Ulhôa, Hermano Vianna, Zuza Homem de Mello, Jairo Severiano, Carlos Calado, José Ramos Tinhorão, Tom Zé, Carlos Diegues, Teresa de Souza, Bias Arrudão, Ana Vidotti, Nelson Vieira, Luiz Valente, Randal Johnson, and T. M. Scruggs. We also recognize all the songwriters, lyricists, music publishers, photographers, production companies, and agencies who have authorized use of lyrics or illustrations (see pp. 273–75). Susan Fernandez and Amy Gorelick of the University Press of Florida were helpful and encouraging throughout the editorial process. We thank Adolph and Naydja Bynum for their New Orleans hospitality during the most intense organizational phase in the spring of 1999. We are especially grateful to Regina Rheda and Alyse Ntube Njenge for their patience, generosity, and companionship during this period.

We are particularly indebted to the Center for Latin American Studies at the University of Florida under the direction of Charles H. Wood, and the Roger Thayer Stone Center for Latin American Studies at Tulane University under the direction of Thomas Reese, for providing funds to support the production of this book. Almost since its inception, Gene Yeager, the associate director of the Stone Center, endorsed the project and offered sage advice.

The title of the introductory chapter of this collection comes from a Brazilian song of the late 1950s that has both been quite well liked at home and traveled the globe. The literal translation of the phrase "Chiclete com banana" is "Chiclets [chewing gum] with bananas," which provides ample opportunity for observation and analysis, as will be seen in the chapter. The Portuguese connector *com* establishes a convenient and timely link, since it naturally suggests the surge of dot.com activity in the late 1990s. The Internet, of course, has had a tremendous impact on transnational flows of music and information about music, increasingly so as we begin the twenty-first century. Brazil has participated energetically in digital aspects of cultural communication, and as far as proliferation of Web sites is concerned, popular music has been one of the areas with greatest Internet coverage. In addition to the Web site for this book (see link at www.latam.ufl.edu/publications) and the URLs cited in the articles, readers are directed to a comprehensive site dedicated to Brazilian popular music (www.thebraziliansound.com), which contains links of many different kinds related to this topic. With the aid of standard search engines, readers will easily find numerous other Web sites about artists and trends discussed here. As the new millennium advances, such sites may come and go but the objects of interest will not cease to grow. As with any writing about music, finally, we hope these pages will inspire listeners to be readers, and readers to be listeners as well.

Charles A. Perrone and Christopher Dunn

Brazilian Popular Music and Globalization

Chiclete com banana

Eu só boto bebop no meu samba
Quando o Tio Sam tocar o tamborim
Quando ele pegar no pandeiro e no
    zabumba
Quando ele aprender que o samba
    não é rumba
Aí então eu vou misturar Miami com
    Copacabana
Chiclete eu misturo com banana
E o meu samba vai ficar assim:
bop-be-bop-be-bop
Eu quero ver a confusão
bop-be-bop-be-bop
Olha aí o samba-rock meu irmão
É mas em compensação
Eu quero ver um boogie-woogie
De pandeiro e violão
Eu quero ver o Tio Sam de frigideira
Numa batucada brasileira

Chiclets with Bananas

I'll only put bebop in my samba
When Uncle Sam plays the *tamborim*
When he grabs a *pandeiro* and a
    zabumba
When he learns that samba isn't
    rumba
Then I'll mix Miami with
    Copacabana
I'll mix chewing gum with bananas
And my samba will turn out like this:
bop-be-bop-be-bop
I want to see the confusion
bop-be-bop-be-bop
Hey, brother, check out the samba-rock
Yeah, but on the other hand
I want to see a boogie-woogie
With *pandeiro* and guitar
I want to see Uncle Sam with a frying pan
In a Brazilian percussion jam

Brazilian music . . . is the most
efficient means of the worldwide
affirmation of the Portuguese
language, so many are the admirers
who were conquered by the
sonorous magic of the word sung in
the Brazilian way.
—Caetano Veloso, *Verdade tropical*

ONE

"Chiclete com Banana"
Internationalization in Brazilian Popular Music

Charles A. Perrone and Christopher Dunn

Spanning a continent, Brazil has a diverse and vast musical system with a complex history. In varied manifestations, popular music stands out as a particularly powerful mode of expressive culture there. With respect to production and circulation of goods, Brazil is one of the world's six largest musical markets. Artistically, the Brazilian contribution to modern urban popular music is, in a certain sense, immeasurable. Since the formative years of the late nineteenth century, questions of foreign influence and international relations have been part of Brazilian popular music, having emerged with greater force in public discourse in decades of authoritarian rule. On the domestic front, song and dance music have been sensitive registers of the construction of national identity since the regime of Getúlio Vargas (1930–1945), when musical diplomacy, influx from abroad, especially the United States, and responses to Brazilian musical products first concerned thinkers and makers of popular music in a more appreciable fashion. Since the 1940s and the heyday of the well-known Carmen Miranda, the sounds of Brazil have enjoyed high levels of international exposure and consumer interest, most notably with the bossa nova movement of the early 1960s. In the final three decades of the twentieth century, analysts of Brazilian musical phenomena at home and abroad—including journalists, independent scholars, academics, and articulate musicians—regularly pondered, at times with evident anxiety, cultural importation and export quality. Debates initiated decades ago are reinvigorated as new musical styles emerge and evolve. Whether focused on the era of radio or the age of the Internet, discussions of urban popular music in Brazil inevitably involve in some way interhemispheric soundings, the interplay of the local and the global, a multifaceted dynamic of internationalization.

As used in the original conceptualization of the present collection, and in the title of this introductory chapter, the term *internationalization* encompasses several different aspects of the production and consumption of popular music. One primary sense is mimesis or stylistic imitation, whether in relatively unaltered local versions of foreign forms (e.g., rock 'n' roll), selective applications and adaptations thereof, or appropriations of the exogenous. While the most frequent association here is with the hegemonic models of Anglo-American pop, Brazilian adoptions and uses of African, Caribbean, and other diasporic elements have created particularly interesting circumstances. These varied musical dialects and dialectics may involve purposeful hybridizations and regionalist retentions alike. As for marketing and appreciation of endogenous material elsewhere, Brazil— home to samba, bossa nova, and subsequent forms with international presence— has a nuanced relationship to the central industrialized nations quite unlike that of any other peripheral country. As all nations of the world since the advent of electronic mass media, Brazil has been faced with unrelenting cultural penetration via sound recording and film. But like few others, Brazil has built a system of its own and has contributed to and participated in musical commerce and exchanges across oceans and borders, having received special recognition in communities of musicians worldwide. Varied facets of internationalization involve and give rise to significant links and relationships, both in the media of transmission themselves (radio, television, cinema, sound recording, Internet) and in creative and critical responses to a series of inputs. Such questions are naturally considered in the context of one of the most compelling issues in cultural criticism at the turn of the millennium: globalization. Its sources, repercussions, local manifestations, and worldwide meanings all impinge on an integral comprehension of contemporary musical phenomena in Brazil. Without pretense to any comprehensive coverage, the studies brought together here under the rubrics of internationalization and globalization explore how Brazilian artists and audiences have negotiated meanings in a spectrum of musical situations involving extradomestic factors, how (geo)political circumstances may mediate musical communication, how the transnational increasingly affects the national in musical realms, and how Brazilian production has achieved projection abroad. While looking back to the decades of the 1930s–1950s, the essays consider more closely groundbreaking developments in the 1960s, and especially variations, in the last two decades of the twentieth century, of African-Brazilian musical discourse in Salvador, Bahia, and innovations in Brazil's northeastern region.

A Song for All Seasons

Indeed, the point of departure of this collection is a song closely tied to the northeast. The title of the present introduction and the lyric that serves as an extended epigraph come from a 1959 song that captures and synthesizes in unassuming fashion several long-standing concerns of musicians, critics, and listeners of Brazilian popular music with regard to internationalization. The composition as a whole—the musical character and textual fabric—and its numerous implementations have rich resonances and open windows onto a series of issues relating to the scope of the studies presented here.

"Chiclete com banana" is most identified with singer-songwriter Jackson do Pandeiro (1919–1982). This stage name derives from that of Jack Perry, an actor in western cowboy films shown extensively in Brazil. The English appellation may suggest the tendency of peoples of the periphery to seek a measure of legitimacy or prestige through linguistic association with the center, as well as the inescapable hemispheric impact of U.S.-American entertainment media. Yet the nominal combination also reveals a characteristic local creativity, as Jackson is joined with *pandeiro*, the designation of the skinned tambourine fundamental to the execution of both samba, centered in Rio de Janeiro, and the equivalent genre in the artist's home region of the northeast, the *côco*, performance of which first distinguished him. One of the most flamboyant personalities in the history of

Brazilian music, Jackson do Pandeiro was known, in fact, for crossing traditional material of the northeast with samba, in a kind of interregional act of hybridity within a diverse and enormous country. In his own rendering of "Chiclete com banana," for instance, he underpins the samba with a northeastern *forró* pattern on the *zabumba* (Brazilian bass drum), an instrument usually associated with northeastern forms.[1] The chorus Jackson do Pandeiro leads in the transitional section of the song, in turn, manages to embody both the essential percussivity of the basic genres and the feel of vocal backings in new types of international pop music. Subsequently, the rendition of singer-songwriter Gilberto Gil reflects both a harmonic sophistication prominent in much Brazilian popular music since the advent of bossa nova, as well as the inquisitive retrospection found in Tropicália or *tropicalismo* [Tropicalism], which queried universality in popular music in unique and controversial ways. The leader of that celebrated movement, Caetano Veloso, once commented that the "American spirit in Jackson is very pronounced" and that "'Chiclete com banana' is a manifesto of this new style."[2] During the late-1960s heyday of the Tropicalists, the song's theme also inspired leading playwright Augusto Boal to stage "Chiclete e banana," a musical show with textual interludes that critiqued uneven relations of foreign (Anglo-American) and national popular musics in Brazil.[3] Less than twenty years later, in the Afro-Brazilian capital of Brazil, Salvador da Bahia, an ensemble blending regional rhythms and electrified pop information, and offering pointedly market-conscious versions of traditional and traditionally derived material, began to achieve surprising success with the name Chiclete com Banana. And at the turn of the decade of the 1990s, Jackson do Pandeiro's recording of the diverting and inspirational song was featured in a compilation of music of the Brazilian northeast organized by David Byrne, a leading U.S.-American rock star.[4] This sponsorship insured wide exposure and distribution of the foreign-theme collection, thus inserting the track into debates that have occupied considerable attention in recent popular-music studies.

The author of the manifesto-like "Chiclete com banana" continues to inspire producers and musicians. An impressive lineup of long-established and recently emerged artists recorded a special tribute to him: *Jackson do Pandeiro revisto e sampleado* [revisited and sampled]. Lenine, who hails from the northeastern state of Pernambuco, opens and closes the homage. The title of the first composition is "Jack Soul Brasileiro," which phonetically approximates the purposeful phrase "já que sou brasileiro" [Since I am Brazilian], as well as the name of the honored artist, while also suggesting his pioneering role in engaging a dialectic of the international (soul) and the national (*brasileiro*).[5] At the end of this funky cut-time mix, Lenine samples Jackson do Pandeiro's recording "Cantiga do sapo" [Chant of the toad] and sings the first stanza of "Chiclete com banana," thereby reinscribing the song once again into a contemporary interregional and international context.

This series of associations previews key themes explored in the sequence of essays that follow. A closer look at the text of "Chiclete com banana" will reveal further both the unusual crystallization the composition comprises and a web of issues with which students of Brazilian popular music necessarily grapple. The north-south encounter of musical realities, which echoes several historically relevant songs from the 1940s, is clear in the citation of respective genres (bebop, samba) and in the assertion of a fusion that actually would take place years after the original release of this song: samba-rock. The key attitude is contained in the playful appeal to reciprocity, which implies lack of awareness on the part of "Uncle Sam" of a distinctive productive Other, Brazil. Further implications include cultural imperialism, the pragmatic might of U.S.-American industry that may result in one-way flows of information, and an oppositionality that current cultural analysts are often eager to identify in subaltern expressions. The choice of "Chiclets" to represent U.S. interests is ironic in that it is the brand name of a product made from a raw material taken from Mesoamerica and commodified by a U.S.-American company for worldwide distribution, as well as the generic name for chewing gum in Brazil. "Banana" is a classic icon of Latin American underdevelopment and political instability (cf. the coinage "banana republic"), comprising for some as well a phallic symbol of the Latin lover. This common fruit has had a place in the Brazilian musical imaginary since the humorous *carnaval* march "Yes, nós temos bananas" [Yes, we have bananas] (Ribeiro-Barros, 1937), a retort to the Roaring Twenties tune "Yes, We Have No Bananas" (Silver-Cohn, 1923), which was used in a Broadway show, traveled the world, and eventually helped to shape primitive, simplistic show-biz representations of such places as Brazil.

The comic thrust of "Chiclete com banana" and a certain slapstick tone convene in the polyvalence of the word *confusão* [confusion], which can signify, in both Portuguese and English, beyond a mental state and inability to distinguish well or choose between related things, the act or effect of mixing, merger, blend, commixture, resultant disarray, and, in Brazil, tumult and noise. This last connotation suggests a new energetic symbiotic soundscape. In English, *confusion* may further connote overthrow, curiously hinting at a reversal of power relations. With these and other allusions and reverberations in sound and word, "Chiclete com banana" points to and departs in different directions that the essayists here explore.

Popular-Music Studies

The present volume seeks to contribute to multi- and interdisciplinary Brazilian studies and to popular-music studies, both of which grew considerably in stature in Europe and the United States in the last decade of the twentieth century. Caught between the historical prestige of classical or art music and the established legitimacy of folklore (whether through language/literature, anthropology, or ethnomusicology), popular music as an object of analysis has struggled for decades to attain due acceptance in the academy. In the 1950s and 1960s, when respectability was especially hard to come by, early North American scholarship on popular music naturally focused primarily on rock and jazz. As prejudices were overcome, the scope of musical studies expanded in the 1970s to give broader consideration to commercial/mass-mediated musics, though the non-Western world was largely overlooked. Gerard Béhague's seminal article on bossa nova and Tropicalism (1973) was one of only two articles on Latin American musics in the journal of the society for the study of ethnomusicology in the 1970s.[6] In that decade, the two most important books related to Spanish American/Brazilian popular musics in international perspective were John Storm Roberts's studies of African forms in the Americas and of the influence of Latin musics in the United States.[7] The 1980s mark a substantial expansion in popular-music studies in general and in Latin American varieties in particular. With the founding of the International Association for the Study of Popular Music (IASPM) came the seminal journal *Popular Music*, which did a Latin American feature issue and has consistently tried to maintain a global perspective.[8] *Studies in Latin American Popular Culture*, also founded in the early 1980s, has included numerous articles on urban popular musics. The most important serial, in this respect, has been *Latin American Music Review/ Revista de música latinoamericana*, which publishes studies of art music and folk traditions, as well as of urban popular music, especially Brazilian.[9] During the late-1980s transition from phonographic to laser technology, curricular coverage of popular music began to widen as general interest in international music grew.

Global Pop

The 1990s saw a remarkable proliferation of articles and books, both academic and journalistic, which probe diverse genres, styles, and systems of international popular music. These studies have focused on urban, cosmopolitan, and transnational products, instead of more conventional objects of ethnomusicological study, traditional sacred and secular folk musics.[10] Several recent titles broach the theoretical, cultural, and ethical issues involved in consuming and/or writing about international popular musics in general, while others provide compelling models for historicized and contextualized study of Latin American and Caribbean varieties in particular.[11]

Scholarship has accompanied the commercial growth in Europe and North America of international (largely Third World) musics in general, and Brazilian popular music in particular. During the last two decades of the twentieth century, the music market in the United States diversified considerably and there emerged a substantial market for so-called "world music," a problematic category that flattens out a diverse panoply of musical practices into a vague, yet readily marketable label.[12] This new category allowed for the marketing of Brazilian popular music outside of jazz, its typical channel of international distribution since the success of bossa nova. North American interest in "world music" is focused especially on the popular musics of Africa, Latin America, and the Caribbean, which have achieved unprecedented exposure in broadcast media, especially via such vehicles as the weekly syndicated radio program "Afropop Worldwide," initiated in 1986. Many public and community radio stations around the country feature "world music" or Afropop shows, and a good number carry Brazilian programs.[13] Major retail outlets, specialty shops, and on-line vendors have made an increasingly wider selection of Brazilian and other international musics available to consumers in the United States. The frequency of relevant articles in the print media and the number of Internet sites concerning the popular musics of Brazil housed outside the country also attest to the breadth of interest. Brazilian musical figures have used the Internet wisely to disseminate information and promote their products around the world. Some maintain sophisticated multilingual Web sites. Perhaps the greatest enthusiast in this regard is Gilberto Gil, as evidenced by his vast and richly documented Web site and by his composition "Pela Internet" [On the Internet], a clever parody of the first recorded samba, "Pelo telefone." In his song, Gil uses the Web as a vehicle to maintain contact with "homes in Nepal" and "bars in Gabon," to send e-mail to Calcutta, to establish a hot link to a site in Helsinki, and to "promote a debate" among a "group of fans from Connecticut."[14]

The essays presented in this collection, while not bound by any theoretical approach, seek to locate Brazilian phenomena within larger debates about the shifting meanings of popular musics as they circulate through established and emerging domains of global capitalism. How does Brazilian popular music relate to the catch-all category of "world music"? How have Brazilian musicians negotiated the contested terrains of cultural authenticity within local, national, and international realms? How and why have they appropriated musical styles from abroad? What historical trajectories has Brazilian popular music followed within a context of international cultural flow and exchange?

The Emergence of Brazilian Musical Genres

Internationalization concerns the development and evolution of Brazilian popular music since the second half of the nineteenth century. The relationship of the system of national forms to European and American models is fundamental. Indeed, a leading authority on popular-music studies in Brazil finds it as important to organize the history of the genres of what she calls "popular Brazilian music" vis-à-vis "foreign music" ("adapted" or "unaltered") as it is to distinguish the "popular" from the "erudite" and the "folkloric."[15] While a detailed recapitulation and examination of such a history lies well beyond the scope of this introduction, it will be worthwhile to highlight in successive periods some of the ways in which the foreign has been processed musically in Brazil and things Brazilian have been sent to the shores of Europe and North America. The first genres of national urban popular music in the late eighteenth and early nineteenth centuries, the *lundu* and the *modinha*, emerged, respectively, from Afro-Brazilian culture and Portuguese lyricism. In the 1870s, Brazilian dancers and musicians altered the major European models of the era—polka, mazurka, schottische—to produce what was called tango (not to be confused with Argentine tango), and, in more vivacious versions, the first "national" dance: *maxixe* [mah-she'-she]. This form was performed widely in the theaters of Rio de Janeiro, was exported to Europe, and led to the genre known as samba. Hispanic input (e.g., *contradanza, habanera*) also helped inform early national music, notably the *tango brasileiro* and piano composition. A most significant aspect of the definition of new musical styles in this period is the interaction of black and white musicians.

The modern samba, the genre that would come to represent Brazil internally and abroad, began to develop in the 1910s in Rio de Janeiro, mostly as a type of music for *carnaval*. It was rooted in the *batuque* (a generic term for Afro-Brazilian music making dominated by percussion), which became increasingly prevalent in Rio de Janeiro following the abolition of slavery in 1888 and the influx of migrating ex-slaves, especially from Bahia. It is thought that samba first took shape as a distinct genre in locales in central Rio. Festive occasions at private homes provided a haven for musicians to avoid police repression during a time when much of the Eurocentric elite was still hostile to and fearful of black expressive culture. The *carnaval* hit of 1917, "Pelo telefone" [On the telephone], the first song to be officially registered as a samba, was likely a collective composition.

As samba gradually gained acceptance outside Afro-Brazilian communities, many of the early innovators of urban samba found work in orchestras that played for musical revues and silent films, utilizing scores of ragtime and early jazz. In 1922, one of the most important early groups, Os Oito Batutas (a multiracial group that featured the master composer-musician Pixinguinha) spent six months in Paris, where they interacted with touring jazz bands from the United States, which they would subsequently emulate in terms of ensemble structure and repertoire. Most of the musical combos active in Rio during the 1920s adopted the appellation jazz band, even though they performed local genres such as samba, *maxixe*, and instrumental *choro*. Recordings of samba later in the decade were inevitably affected by the presence in Brazil of personnel from abroad, as the European-controlled recording companies (e.g., British Odeon) employed studio orchestras largely composed of foreign musicians and directors, and the recording engineers were all German, English, or North American.[16] In the 1920s, a second basic genre of *carnaval* music known as the *marchinha* took on a modern form. The context of its development is markedly internationalized, as described in a definitive chronology of Brazil's urban popular music:

> Unlike the samba, a mestizo product resulting from the fusion of European melody and harmony with Afro-Brazilian rhythm, the *marchinha* is a descendant of the polka-march, which incorporates some characteristics of the Portuguese march and of certain American rhythms in fashion at the time. Indeed, the post–World War I period is marked by an overwhelming expansion of the popular music of the United States, which begins to influence not only Brazilian music but that

of the entire Western world. Our environment was invaded by a series of dances and American musical genres, such as the shimmy, the charleston, the black-bottom, and principally the foxtrot, which would inspire, still in the 1920s, the first Brazilian foxes.[17]

The emergence and solidification of *marchinha* and samba dovetailed with *modernismo*, a broad cultural movement involving literature, concert music, and fine arts, which was formally launched in 1922, the year radio was installed in Brazil. *Modernismo* fractured into several distinct, if not opposing, groups with various artistic, ideological, and regional concerns.[18] The modernists were generally committed to the renovation of Brazilian arts by exploring and exalting the popular foundations of national culture while selectively appropriating international aesthetic models and techniques. Vanguardist provocateur Oswald de Andrade authored a celebrated manifesto calling for a "poetry of export" that would allow Brazil to make a distinctive intervention in the sphere of international letters. In this project, popular culture would provide an imagined reservoir of native originality that could be "mined" by cosmopolitan artists.[19] A second manifesto by Oswald would form the basis of *antropofagia* [anthropophagy, or cultural cannibalism], a program that inspired artists and theorists throughout the twentieth century, as seen in several chapters here.

By the late 1920s, urban samba had received enthusiastic endorsements from sectors of the Brazilian cultural elite, including the young sociologist Gilberto Freyre, composer Heitor Villa-Lobos, and Mário de Andrade, a leader of *modernismo* on both literary and musical fronts. For nationalist thinkers, samba represented well Brazil's *mestiço* culture, based on African and European miscegenation (unlike other Latin American mestizo identities that foregrounded the indigenous element). Freyre, for example, fancied samba as an uncontaminated expression of the emerging "real Brazil" that had been obscured by Eurocentrism among elites. Hermano Vianna has argued that the relationship between such intellectuals and samba musicians was essential to the eventual consecration of samba as the musical expression of the nation.[20]

The Golden Age of Samba and Musical Diplomacy

A central concept of the second phase of *modernismo* in the 1930s was *brasilidade* [Brazilianness], which found extensive artistic expression and functioned as an ideology of national identity transcending differences of class, race, and region.[21] The decade witnessed both a surge of cultural nationalism and a flourishing in popular music. Soon after the rise to power of the nationalist and populist leader Getúlio Vargas in 1930, samba would gain its status as the premier genre of Brazilian popular music. Since this period, samba has been intrinsically associated with *brasilidade*. Musicians from black working-class neighborhoods in Rio benefited from the growing popularity of the genre among the middle class and often participated in efforts to legitimize and institutionalize it. The nationalist moorings of samba were often endorsed by its composers. The most renowned songwriter of this golden age, Noel Rosa (1910–1937), criticized Hollywood talking films for popularizing foreign-language expressions in Brazil. In "Não tem tradução" [No translation], he satirized such local cosmopolitan pretensions while affirming the linguistic and cultural authenticity of Rio's hillside slums, largely inhabited by blacks. The song concludes:

> Amor, lá no morro é amor pra chuchu
> As rimas do samba não são "I love you"
> E esse negócio de "alô, alô boy, alô Johnny"
> Só pode ser conversa de telefone
>
> [Up on the hill, there's lots of love
> The rhymes of samba aren't "I love you"
> And that business of "Hello, Johnny boy"
> Can only be a bunch of talk on the telephone]

Such caustic positioning aside, the film industry would subsequently prove to be a powerful vehicle for disseminating stylized Brazilian popular music throughout the world.

The Vargas regime established numerous links with the sphere of popular music, some with notable international implications. In the early 1930s, for instance, popular musicians accompanied an ambassadorial mission to Argentina. A few years later, singing sensation Carmen Miranda would record "O samba e o tango," an early example of Latin American fraternity sung in a mixture of Portuguese and Spanish.[22] Afro-Brazilian composer-performers were rarely given the chance to record or perform on live radio shows, yet they were occasionally called upon to perform the role of national cultural emissaries. In 1936, the state-operated Radio Nacional set up a shortwave broadcast from the Mangueira

Samba School to Germany, at a time when some officials in the Vargas government were openly sympathetic to the Nazi regime. A similar broadcast was made
to fascist Italy. During Vargas's authoritarian Estado Novo [New state] (1937–
1945), makers of samba were mobilized to sing the praises of a unified, harmoni-
ous, and hard-working nation. In his efforts to consolidate further the regime, to
seek cohesion through popular culture, and to formalize his co-optation of artists, Vargas ordered the fortification of the Departamento de Imprensa e Propa-
ganda (DIP), which would exercise institutional control over the press and entertainment media, promoting dissemination of determined images of the country
at home and abroad. In 1942 this department oversaw the mounting of a super
radio-transmission tower—one of the five largest in the world at the time—to
broadcast to Europe and North America. National music was instrumental in
the plan to win over listeners in Brazil and abroad. In a public pronouncement,
the director of the state radio operation asserted: "It is the voice of Brazil that will
speak to the world, to tell civilized peoples of the universe what is being done
here for the benefit of civilization. It is Brazilian music that will be broadcast to
the far corners of the globe, exhibiting all its beauty and splendor."[23]

On the cultural wing of the Good Neighbor Policy (Washington's courting of
the nations of the hemisphere to attract markets and support in the World War II
effort), Brazilian popular music was favored and had an impact in the United
States, and considerable new amounts of music from Hollywood and Broadway
flowed into Brazil. In pragmatic terms, what most galvanized the interest of Brazilian musicians in 1939 was the government selection of a team of players to
represent Brazil at the World's Fair in New York. In 1940 a U.S. ship brought the
All-American Youth Orchestra to Rio, where dozens of "the most authentic"
samba compositions were arranged and recorded, resulting in the series *Native
Brazilian Music* (Columbia Records). In the early 1940s, samba enjoyed a vogue
in the United States similar to that of the conga and ballroom rumba of Cuba.
Texts and photos accompanying a 1942 set of discs by the Copacabana Orchestra
of Frank Marti (who had been sent by the Brazilian government to Europe as
early as 1925 to show off Brazilian music) described this "new dance rage of
America," perhaps an exaggeration but a sure sign of presence. This same year,
Orson Welles, who had filmed *carnaval* in Rio for the unfinished Brazil-spot-
light film *It's All True*, did a series of CBS Pan-American radio broadcasts from
New York in which he presented Latin American nations, notably Brazil. In the
November 15 broadcast of "Hello Americans" he discussed the "deep music"

of samba, making a point to distinguish it from jazz and rumba for his North American listeners.[24] His guest for this broadcast was the celebrated film and stage star Carmen Miranda (1909–1955), truly an influential voice in North America.

Miranda, a media star in Brazil since the early 1930s, came to Broadway contracted by a private-sector impresario and supported by both Vargas and the U.S. Department of State. In the account of one distinguished chronicler, the nationalistic fervor that her trip inspired was naïve because the invitation was linked to Good Neighbor developments and because the music that the flamboyant artist and her band would have to play did not reflect musical realities in Brazil.[25] In critical and public reception of Miranda in Brazil after 1938, the authenticity of the music she purveyed was often at issue. President Vargas himself met with her before she departed to urge that she take her own band and that they display musical honesty. After Miranda had spent a year in the United States, she received a cold and negative response when she performed in Rio, the primary complaint being that she had taken on foreign characteristics. This occurrence inspired the song "Disseram que voltei americanizada" [They said I came back Americanized], in which she defends herself and her Brazilianness. Whatever her treatment back home, she was regularly referred to in the Brazilian press as "ambassadress of Brazilian popular music." Her stage and film performances made the first major impression of Brazilian music in North America. In his segment of this volume, Caetano Veloso explores the wider meanings of Miranda for the musical movement he headed and for the country at large. A leading popular-music critic in Brazil rightly notes that Miranda was a "Brazilian icon in the scene of planetary pop" who "preceded the pop stars of the video clip era adding image and sound still in the pre-history of multimedia" and "embodied as no one else the myth of tropical exuberance."[26] Miranda's appearances in a series of Latin-theme films certainly raise of a number of issues regarding ethnicity, representation, appropriation of subaltern expressions, and the cultural and geopolitical designs of Hollywood and Washington in the 1940s.[27]

The self-celebration encouraged by the Vargas government led to one of the nation's trademark compositions, Ary Barroso's "Aquarela do Brasil" [Watercolor of Brazil, "Brazil," 1939], which spawned the sub-genre *samba-exaltação* [samba-exaltation], characterized lyrically by romantic patriotism and musically by long, involved melodies and grandiose arrangements. This last feature would be in keeping with a 1940s vogue in upper/middle-class Brazilian ballrooms: the North

American big-band sound. Barroso's best known song also fulfilled a role in the Good Neighbor Policy, as it was used in *Saludos Amigos* (*Alô Amigos*), Walt Disney's first Latin American cartoon adventure (1943). This experiment was followed by *The Three Caballeros* (1945), also featuring the wily Brazilian parrot, Zé Carioca. Both were supposedly designed to embody a spirit of friendship and understanding and have been subject to keen analysis.[28] The song "Brazil" was recorded by leading artists of the day in North America, Bing Crosby and Xavier Cugat, and registered millions of executions in the space of two years.

Several Brazilian songwriters took note of the official interest in the popular music of the land. The most clever musical response to the U.S.-Brazil connection was "Boogie woogie na favela" (Denis Brean, 1945), a samba commentary on the invasion of U.S.-American music that referred to a hypothetical presence in the shantytowns, imprecisely calling boogie-woogie "the new dance that forms part of the Good Neighbor Policy." In a similar vein, "O samba que agora vai" [The samba that's leaving now] (Pedro Caetano, 1946) speculates about changes in a samba that "no longer talks about bread and banana/and only takes off for Miami from Copacabana." The best-known samba of this type is "Brasil pandeiro" (Assis Valente, 1941), which was composed for Carmen Miranda. She, however, declined to add the song to her repertory, perhaps concerned with the irreverence of the lyric. The energetic tune, which begins in the mode of samba-exaltation ("It's time for these bronze-skinned people to demonstrate their value!"), inspired one of the most respected critics of Brazilian popular music to call it "the epic poem of the Brazilian race" and a "challenge to the rest of the world."[29] The pertinent humorous declarations include: "I want to see Uncle Sam playing *pandeiro* for every one to dance samba . . . Uncle Sam wants to get to know our *batucada*/he says the Bahian sauce improved his dish . . . In the White House he's danced *batucada* with Mammy and Pappy. . ." All three songs inevitably echo in the subsequent lyric of "Chiclete com banana" at the end of the following decade.

Another landmark Brazilian recording with transnational connections was "Copacabana" (Barros-Ribeiro), originally composed at the behest of a U.S.-American impresario planning to open a thematic club in New York. The song was recorded (1946) in Brazil by Dick Farney, stage name of Farnésio Dutra, a crooner with a very strong interest in North American ballad, who had previously declined to sing in Portuguese. Offering a wholly new arrangement for the time, with diversified instrumentation and no typical percussion instruments of

Cover of sheet music for North American version of "Aquarela do Brasil,"
© Disney Enterprises Inc.

the samba battery, this rendering inaugurated a new tendency in urban popular music more attuned to the cosmopolitan aspirations of residents of Rio's beachfront districts. As one observer put it, "for the ascendant middle class of the post-war years, already attracted to and conquered by the American way of life seen in films, that 'Copacabana' was equal to a revelation. It was as if our prosaic everyday values suddenly took on airs of distinction by being sung à la Bing Crosby."[30] Such stylizations were a prelude to the emergence of an internationally influenced and influential Brazilian musical style.

Bossa Nova, Home and Abroad

The most extensive international musical interplay occurred with the bossa nova movement of the late 1950s and 1960s. In many ways, bossa nova is linked to what historian Thomas Skidmore has called "the years of confidence" during the presidency of Juscelino Kubitschek (1956–1960), who had promised "fifty years' progress in five" and then undertook to build the utopian, futuristic capital of Brasilia on the high plains of central Brazil.[31] Like the vanguard of *poesia concreta*, or concrete poetry, which gave Brazil recognition abroad, and the architectural concept of Brasilia, the new musical reality was related to the cultural logic of developmentalism.[32] Concrete poet and critic Augusto de Campos later would argue that with bossa nova Brazil "began to export finished products to the world instead of raw material (exotic rhythms)."[33] For his part, José Ramos Tinhorão perceived alienation and capitulation to foreign interests in bossa nova. He also availed himself of metaphors of industrial development when he sarcastically compared the new music to the assembly of foreign cars masquerading as national products.[34]

Bossa nova was created with ample U.S.-American influence, jazz musicians adopted the form, many Brazilians operated in the United States, and unusual commercial successes ensued, albeit with notable transformations. From varying angles, chronicles and interpretations of contemporary Brazilian popular music have been concerned with—beyond its musical characteristics per se—the origins, evolution, and social stratification of this manner of performance and composition. The reserved character of bossa nova contrasted sharply with the dominant middle-class taste of the 1950s. The variant of vocal samba known as *samba-canção* had been affected by the Cuban *bolero*, popularized via New York, and, as seen above, by the North American ballad. Most Brazilian crooners sought a loud, dramatic, relatively simple style. Bossa nova presented sambas and original material in a mollified, understated, and sophisticated fashion. There is considerable debate about the extent of U.S.-American influence in this new approach, which has been referred to, in a convenient but inadequate simplification, as a cross of samba and jazz. It has been suggested that the deep roots of the movement are in the 1953–1954 recordings of saxophonist Bud Shank and guitarist Laurindo Almeida, though Almeida's playing does not display the syncopated plucking and altered chords characteristic of bossa nova nor do the tracks have any defining percussion parts. For his part, the acknowledged creator of the foundational stance, singer-guitarist João Gilberto, speaks of admiration for the delicate attack of such jazz musicians as Chet Baker and Gerry Mulligan. The feel of "cool jazz," notably in the work of Miles Davis, also had a substantial impact on Brazilian players and arrangers in 1958–1959.

The musically centered film *Black Orpheus* (1959), considered here in the chapter by Charles Perrone, introduced a wide international audience to samba and incipient bossa nova. The arrival of the new Brazilian sound in the United States can be ascribed to the interest and promotion of serious musicians and enthusiasts. The export/import of bossa nova also began with a diplomatic mission: while on a goodwill tour in 1961, guitarist Charlie Byrd heard the music that was flourishing in Rio de Janeiro. His subsequent versions of "jazz-samba" in Washington, D.C., sparked immediate and intense interest, leading to his seminal recordings with Stan Getz. In 1962, an entourage of musicians from Brazil played a historic engagement at Carnegie Hall, an event that touched off a veritable explosion of bossa nova recordings and, to the surprise of xenophobic producers, of sales. Numerous Brazilians were signed to record, and dozens of bossa nova theme albums were made by jazzmen, often in conjunction with a Brazilian headliner. Getz and Gilberto's "The Girl from Ipanema" (Jobim-Morais-Gimbell, 1963) made a showing on the pop charts never before achieved by a foreign song. It was highly unusual for a music of non-U.S. origin in the jazz category to achieve the mass popularity of pop music. Professional fraternity was soon lost in commercialism, and the international exchange was debased in many eyes. There was no process of gradual assimilation of musical concepts by composers and performers. Instead, the style was exploited for quick turnaround in hastily conceived jazz albums and in thoughtless pop renditions. Even though it was *not* dance music, promoters tried to make of bossa nova another dance craze, complete with schools and shoe styles. Falsehoods were propagated in such songs as "Blame It on the Bossa Nova," in the voice of Edie Gormé, and "Bossa Nova Baby," recorded by Elvis Presley and Tippy and the Clovers. In view of such treatments, the music critic of *Saturday Review* called industrial bossa nova-ization: "one of the worst blights of commercialism ever to be inflicted on popular art."[35] In the wake of the pop phenomenon, Brazilian Sérgio Mendes abandoned jazz formats and formed easy-listening ensembles (e.g., Brazil 66) that maintained tenuous affinities with Brazilian beginnings. In the jazz realm, however, bossa nova remained a constant. Antônio Carlos Jobim (1927–1994) became one of the most frequently recorded jazz composers and achieved world-wide recognition.[36] João Gilberto continued to make occasional international performances into the 1990s, celebrating the fortieth anniversary of the birth of his style with 1998 appearances in the United States as well. Many of these episodes in entertainment history resonate with implications about musical ideologies, inter-American relations, and appropriation, and suggest some of the rationale for skepticism expressed about the international success of bossa nova.

Cultural Controversy in the Sixties

Just as bossa nova was enjoying popularity overseas in the early 1960s, emerging artists in Brazil were growing dissatisfied with the cosmopolitanism and urbane romanticism of most bossa nova. Young musicians yearned for greater interaction with the expressive cultures of the masses. New outlooks are reflected in the joco-serious song "Influência do jazz" (Carlos Lyra, 1962), a "musically enacted obituary for the traditional samba," seen to be harmed by mixing and modernizing.[37] This second phase of bossa nova roughly coincided with the presidency (1961–1964) of João Goulart, who promised sweeping changes in Brazilian society. It was a time of extensive political and cultural activism on the left. Some argued that Brazilian underdevelopment was directly caused by dependency on foreign capital and imported consumer goods and that the consumption of cultural products from abroad contributed to the political alienation of the people. Nationalist and populist artists and critics thus regarded Anglo-American cultural products with suspicion, if not antagonism. Such attitudes were exacerbated by the U.S.-backed coup of April 1, 1964. The military regime moved quickly to suppress labor movements, students activists, and radical cultural movements. The right-wing government was regarded by some on the left as a passing aberration, the elite's last-ditch attempt to maintain the status quo in the face of an impending social revolution. Despite official repression, left-wing artists and intellectuals were able to create a lively "nationalist-participatory" protest culture. Critic Roberto Schwarz later claimed that the left maintained cultural hegemony for nearly five years after the military coup.[38] In March 1968, a hard-line faction assumed control and dissolved the Congress, suspended habeas corpus, and instituted blanket censorship. This situation sent several leading figures of popular music into exile, where they encountered even more new ideas, and, together with other musical emigrés, established a post-bossa presence abroad.[39]

During the period immediately following the 1964 coup, the field of popular music became polarized between cultural nationalists who sought to defend and promote "authentic" Brazilian popular music (known simply as MPB, for Música Popular Brasileira), and the Jovem Guarda [Young guard], a homegrown rock movement led by Roberto Carlos, who would later rival Julio Iglesias in the international market for música romântica.[40] The nationalist left regarded the Jovem Guarda as politically and culturally removed from Brazilian reality. The early MPB camp objected especially to the use of electric instruments in Brazilian music, just as orthodox folk-music fans jeered Bob Dylan for using an electric guitar at the Newport Folk Festival of 1965. The Jovem Guarda and international pop maintained a strong presence on urban Brazilian airwaves, but the MPB approach dominated a series of popular-music festivals in São Paulo and Rio de Janeiro that marked the epoch of the late 1960s. The final rounds of these annual competitions were televised live before studio audiences composed primarily of middle-class students and professionals with populist sympathies. While the initial cycles of these events had a clear national focus, another round was organized as the International Song Festival. At a 1967 festival, two young musicians from Bahia, Caetano Veloso and Gilberto Gil, introduced what they called *som universal* [universal sound], which combined Brazilian themes and rhythms with electric instrumentation. Gil and Veloso were soon leading the insurgent movement of Tropicalism, which critiqued orthodox cultural nationalism and renovated Brazilian song by creatively engaging with vanguardist experimentation and international countercultures. The Tropicalists' landmark group concept album, *Tropicália ou panis et circensis* (1968) has been hailed as a unique artistic document and as the Brazilian equivalent to the Beatles' historic *Sgt. Pepper's Lonely Hearts Club Band*.

Taking cues from the radical iconoclast Oswald de Andrade and his proposal of *antropofagia*, or aesthetic anthropophagy, the Tropicalists aggressively devoured foreign information and styles, especially rock, but also tango, bolero, and mambo. "The idea of 'cultural cannibalism' fit us, the Tropicalists, like a glove. We were 'eating' the Beatles and Jimi Hendrix," Veloso writes in his memoirs of this period, *Verdade tropical* [Tropical truth].[41] It is interesting to note that the idea for this literary project was originally proposed by a publisher in New York who had read Veloso's piece on Carmen Miranda. After initially declining the offer, Veloso agreed to write the memoir precisely in order to "value and situate the experience of Brazilian popular music in global terms" (510). Unlike bossa nova, however, the Tropicália of Veloso and associates was not readily exportable, likely because it bore too much resemblance to Anglo-American pop for jazz audiences to appreciate it. In the late 1990s, curiously, post-rock artists and fans in the United States and United Kingdom discovered Tropicalist recordings, including, beyond the early work of the two leaders, the zany rock of Os Mutantes, the ethereal mezzo-soprano of Gal Costa, and the quirky experimentalism of Tom Zé, who performed in the United States and Brazil in 1999 with the Chicago-based band Tortoise. A Brazilian cultural scholar has noted that U.S. and European cognoscenti regard Tropicália not as an exotic curio of "world music," but rather as a "vanguard school" within the history of international pop/rock.[42] Indeed, pop innovator Beck has expressed a sense of eerie pleasure at the discovery of Os Mutantes and their combinatory experimentations with sound that predate his own collage aesthetic by three decades.[43]

In Brazil and abroad, the Tropicalist movement has been the focus of renewed academic, journalistic, and popular interest. In this volume, Christopher Dunn reads the Tropicalist experience and subsequent work of Gil and Veloso in light of emergent Afro-diasporic cultural formations. Liv Sovik, in turn, theorizes polemics surrounding Veloso, arguing that the Tropicalist paradigm has become hegemonic within the context of globalization. John Harvey, for his part, examines shifts in North American countercultural profiles and a related enthusiasm for the decentered ironic pastiches of Tropicalist music.

Tom Zé is an unusual case of internationalization in Brazilian popular music. Following the dénouement of Tropicalism, this foundational figure slipped into obscurity as he continued to push the limits of pop experimentalism. While looking for material for a samba compilation in the late 1980s, David Byrne happened upon Tom Zé's music. Byrne's label released an anthology of Tom Zé's 1970s work and a subsequent album of new material, both of which received critical acclaim. In another U.S. release, *Fabrication Defect* (1998), Tom Zé proposes insurgent forms of music making that selectively plagiarize material from national and international sources, a strategy he calls *estética do arrastão* [dragnet aesthetics]. In the liner notes to the album, he writes that Third World subjects are like "androids" who serve as cheap labor for "First World bosses," but also contain inherent "defects" that allow for creative agency and resistance.[44] His project stands out as a radical attempt within popular music to theorize the asymmetries of economic and cultural power in a global context.

After the Sixties

In the 1970s, internationalization of Brazilian popular music took different forms, several of which have attracted the attention of scholars. Input into mainstream popular music came from regional founts, rock, soul, disco, African musics, and various other sources. The Clube da Esquina [Corner club] music collective in Minas Gerais, led by the well-known Milton Nascimento, acknowledged debts to the Beatles while affirming local identity. The symptomatic song "Para Lennon e McCartney" (Nascimento-M. Borges-F. Brant) refers to being from South America, Minas Gerais, and the world as well as to a western (cowboy) side of the artist.[45] In the course of the decade, a few artists associated with the MPB trend released albums in the United States. A particularly well-received work was Wayne Shorter's *Native Dancer* (1975), which showcased Milton Nascimento. Brazilian percussionists made many contributions to jazz and fusion ensembles; some of them relocated permanently to the United States and marked a presence in jazz history. In Europe, Brazilian instrumentalists and singers have become an expected part of performance circuits. The thirty-second Montreux Jazz Festival (1998), tellingly, commemorated twenty years of Brazilian music with special sessions including Gil and a cast from the northeast.

There was a newsworthy resurgence of Brazilian popular music in North America in the 1980s. A phenomenon dubbed Brazilian Wave occurred in all areas of the industry (recording, broadcasting, performance, publishing, media coverage).[46] Unlike the 1960s epoch of bossa nova, when a manner of interpretation became generic and was pursued by all participants, the 1980s brought variety. While bossa nova had operated with stylistic homogeneity, Brazilian Wave was defined by heterogeneity, the only overall common ground being national origin. This umbrella term covers instrumental music as well as singer-songwriters like Veloso, Ivan Lins, and Djavan, whose diverse repertories show electric-acoustic alternance, modern samba, hybrid post-bossa sounds, regional rhythms, and rock. By the turn of the decade of the 1990s, now fully within the context of the "world-beat" or world-music trends, North American listeners began to be exposed to compilations and series of traditional musics, MPB, and neo-Afro-Bahian repertories discussed below.[47]

In an accommodating view, Brazilian Wave would also encompass the brief appearance of *lambada* (a dance music with popular origins in northern Brazil), which was packaged and marketed by French producers in the late 1980s. With a multimillion-dollar campaign, *lambada* became an immediate megasuccess in Europe and around Latin America, including Brazil, where further consumption was encouraged by the dance music's international showing. In 1990, a similar blitz took place in the United States. Guilbault refers to *lambada* as one of the "rare cases [in which] the emergence of world musics on the international market [can] be said to be tributary to the blind acceptance or/and promotion of something different by the dominant media."[48] Sensational press accounts of the history and uses of the "sensual" dance and music have been balanced by informed research.[49]

A contemporaneous case pointedly relevant to the question of internationalization is Veloso's last album in the 1980s, which was coproduced by Brazilian-bred musician Arto Lindsay in New York. *Estrangeiro* [Foreigner, or stranger] naturally alludes to Camus' novel *The Stranger* and explores several transnational and diasporic themes. The work travels over the topos of the estranged Latin American artist in the metropolis, but a Brazilian focus remains central. The opening recitative of the title track contains contrasting impressions of noted outsiders (Paul Gaugin, Cole Porter, Claude Lévi-Strauss) of Rio's Guanabara Bay, a national symbol. The oneiric lyric contests touristic images and constructs a persona at odds with conventional interpretations of the city, the nation, and its guiding values. At the end of the song, Veloso intones in English, "some may like a soft Brazilian singer, but I've given up all attempts at perfection," which paraphrases a line from the jacket of *Bringing It All Back Home*, one of Bob Dylan's landmark LPs.[50] This reprise aligns Veloso with Dylan against conservative criticism and the establishment, but also undermines common notions about Brazilian song abroad (that is, suave bossa nova). In this unsettling and "foreign" song, Veloso is ironically "bringing it all back home," affirming an individual stream in the context of U.S. Brazilian Wave or of xenophobic sentiment in Brazil. The hard-edged guitar arrangement of the song is functionally inte-

Posters for international appearances of Milton Nascimento. Courtesy of Quilombo Criação e Produção, 1988.

grated, highlighting a poetics of sight and sound that implies real-life musical practices like rock.

A major aspect of international impact in Brazilian popular music in the 1980s was rock. Following the flirtations with Anglo-American rock 'n' roll and subsequent variations in the 1960s and 1970s, there flourished a full-fledged movement in the 1980s. With a wide array of styles (largely based on foreign models), all the behavioral (e.g., show-biz antics), nominal (group names, titles), and sartorial trappings associated with British and North American sources, and a well-developed media circuit, the cultural presence of rock was prominent, the commercial side comprising a major boom. Indeed, middle-class, and to some extent working-class, interest in the mid-to late 1980s was electric rock, as measured by the preferences of the younger generation in radio airplay, record sales, and performance circuits. Perhaps the single most important event in this regard was the Rock in Rio Festival in 1985, when Brazilian Rock (sometimes referred to as "BRock") came of age. This seven-day megaconcert featured international headliners as well as Brazilian acts such as Lulu Santos, Paralamas do Sucesso, and Erasmo Carlos. Rock in Rio occurred as Brazil prepared to return to civilian governance after twenty-one years of military rule.

The ascent of rock raised anew issues of generational aesthetic reception, of the ideologies of popular music (especially in contrast to 1960s song), and of the relationship between centers of cultural hegemony and the periphery. Brazil's rockers, as their counterparts elsewhere, have always confronted questions of originality and cultural authenticity. Since the late 1950s, when they were first perceived as inappropriate Yankee youth rebellion, rock styles have received apprehensive responses from the musical establishment in Brazil. Eighties editorials and interviews from a pro-rock standpoint often seemed to feel obliged to include "justifications" of the use of rock. If those who hailed rock as the natural music for their urbanized and media-aware generation could indeed avoid the issue of copying, and whatever the ultimate degree of stylistic independence, Brazil's consumption of homebred rock had, and continues to have, peculiar nationalist implications. After decades of competition with foreign musics— from jazz band, *chanson*, Broadway, UK pop, and the like—the celebration of local rock meant increased attention for a *national* item. Purchases of Brazilian rock came to guarantee that national product would surpass foreign product in sales of sound recordings. Composed, performed, and recorded in Brazil, new rock created its own idioms, idols, and paradigms, thus complicating the notion of cultural alienation via music.

Rock is clearly a major player across Latin America, but, as has been noted with respect to widespread *rock en español*, the tendency of analysts is to shy away from this fact, and studies of Latin American popular music have rarely concerned rock.[51] This is quite true in Brazil, which, by virtue of its size and musical diversity, has the largest rock scene in the region. Relative to the quantities of rock, it has been quite understudied in Spanish American and Brazilian contexts.[52] In what remains one of the most cogent general studies of rock, Peter Wicke makes clear that it involves an irrational "sensory-motor intensity," an "immediate perceptual intensity," and "quasi-ritualistic employment of technology."[53] When investigating the spread of rock in Brazil, or other Third World nations, one could ponder how the "magic electricity" of rock might relate, for makers and consumers, to images of industrial or technological potency associated with the First World. One could further ask how the "intensities" to which Wicke refers may be universal, transcending national and ideological boundaries. If rock in any language has physical properties unprecedented in human history, the practice of the music in Brazil will be understood in the contexts of evolving cultural codes, local social anatomy, and unavoidable historical factors.

One of the most curious manifestations of internationalization in Brazilian music is Phoenix-based Sepultura, a heavy-metal band originally from Belo

Horizonte, Minas Gerais. Its apocalyptic brand of "death metal" has attracted legions of fans throughout the world. Indeed, Sepultura is the most successful Brazilian group in the international music market since Sérgio Mendes and Brazil '66.[54] It is tempting to regard this band as an anomaly—some might say as the protagonist of a cautionary tale about the extreme Americanization of Brazilian music—but the group is symptomatic of the complexity of urban Brazil, which sustains a wide variety of youth subcultures. This band sings in English and enjoys an international fan base, yet has also evidenced concern for Brazilian history and culture. Sepultura's album *Roots* (1996), for instance, contains songs with Afro-Brazilian percussion about the decimation of Amerindian populations and the horrors of the slave trade. This work has attracted the attention of popular-music scholars abroad.[55] The band's founder, Max Cavalera, left in 1997 to form Soulfly, a similar group that has also delved into Brazilian themes and rhythms. His custom-made green guitar bears the distinctive design of the Brazilian flag. Soulfly's debut album features a heavy-metal version of Jorge Ben's celebrated "Ponta de lança africano (Umbabarauma)," as well as original compositions (e.g., "Quilombo," "Bumba") that pay homage to runaway slaves and others who resisted violence and exploitation in Brazil.[56] Idelber Avelar, who hails from Belo Horizonte, the epicenter of Brazilian heavy metal, offers personal and theoretical reflections here on the vexed relationship between *metaleiros* in his homeland and consecrated icons of regional and national identity within the MPB canon, represented by Minas Gerais's favorite son, Milton Nascimento.

Brazil and the African Diaspora

As various currents of rock were being explored by mostly white, middle-class urban youth, parallel movements inspired by the worldwide circulation of musical cultures of the African diaspora had an equally significant impact on the mostly black, working-class youth of major urban centers in Brazil. In this respect, developments in Afro-Brazilian music may be located within a global phenomenon described by George Lipsitz: "The diasporic conversation within hip hop, Afrobeat, jazz, and many other Black musical forms provides a powerful illustration of the potential for contemporary commercialized leisure to carry images, ideas, and icons of enormous political importance between cultures."[57] In *The Black Atlantic*, his landmark study on diasporic cultural exchange, Paul

Gilroy claims a special role for black popular music in the international dissemination of cultural values and political imperatives that respond to comparable histories of racial inequality and neocolonialism throughout Africa and its diaspora in Europe and the Americas.[58] Given the expansive scope and title of Gilroy's project, it is remarkable how little space he dedicates to transatlantic exchanges involving Afro-Brazilians, Afro-Cubans, Afro-Haitians, and other non-Anglophone diasporic Africans. Nevertheless, Gilroy is correct in assigning particular importance to the transnational status of soul, funk, hip-hop, and reggae. The last three decades of the twentieth century saw an extraordinary proliferation of African-American and Jamaican musical cultures in Brazil and their subsequent reconfiguration according to local contexts.[59]

To discuss the significance of these distinct but related movements, it is necessary to recall the historical importance of Brazil's most representative musical genre, samba, in defining and expressing national identity. Samba has been implicated historically in making hegemonic the ideology (or myth) of racial democracy in both official and popular discourses. The effect of that myth is to deflect race-conscious dissent. Still, some samba composers and performers have made expressions of black pride and racial protest on occasion. Afro-Brazilian artists who explicitly questioned, rejected, or sought to demythify the notion of racial democracy were vulnerable to severe critiques on the grounds that they were racist and anti-Brazilian. Such was the case in the mid-1970s when Afro-Brazilians began to appropriate the music, dances, and visual styles of the African-American soul and funk countercultures. These phenomena in Brazil first centered on weekend dances held in social clubs and samba schools in Rio's working-class North Zone, with enthusiasts primarily consuming U.S. recordings of predisco soul and funk. However, there were notable local funk-samba fusion bands, such as Banda Black Rio, as well as soul singers such as Tim Maia (1942–1998), who learned his craft during a residence in the United States. Despite the repressive atmosphere under military rule, disenfranchised Rio youth, inspired by African-American political and cultural mobilization, formed a movement called Black Rio. The activity was quickly reproduced in São Paulo and other major Brazilian cities.

The soul tendency faded in the early 1980s, but social functions based on funk music continued to proliferate. Among the insights of the study by Livio Sansone here, such dances are seen to provide opportunities for predominantly black working-class youth to construct social identities and participate in an international black counterculture. In the course of the 1990s, funk encountered predictable rejection by the establishment, but nonconfrontational and pop-inflected funk and hip-hop were assimilated into the mainstream media, with local artists often appearing together with international guests on television.[60]

In the 1990s, São Paulo emerged as the most vibrant site of the Brazilian rap movement. Several groups have appropriated the performance codes, sartorial accouterments, and hand signs of L.A.-style gangsta rap. The leading rap formation, Racionais MC, recorded "Periferia é periferia (em qualquer lugar)" [Peripheries are peripheries (anywhere)], which pointedly situates the poverty and violence of metropolitan São Paulo in global perspective. Print and electronic media, such as fanzines and the Brazilian version of "Yo! MTV Raps," document the local rap scene while keeping followers abreast of developments in the United States. The stylistic and gestural vocabulary of Brazilian rap may almost suggest an unmediated transference of practices in New York and Los Angeles. However, global youth cultures like hip-hop are constantly reinterpreted and reinvented according to local contexts. Even an esteemed defender of nationalist positions in popular music found some consolation in the idea that local rap is merely an updated version of *embolada*, a rapid-fire sung verse form from the rural northeast.[61]

The case of Brazilian reggae is somewhat different, of course, because the model music is from a peripheral country. Tropicalist leaders Veloso and Gil, ever attentive to other musical discourses, were in London when rock-steady artists of Jamaica were developing a new sound called reggae, which was almost simultaneously taken to London by emigrés. Brazilian uses of the genre are encompassed within larger structures of Afro-Brazilian sociocultural organization and of syncretism in commercial popular music. Chapters here by Osmundo Pinho and Antonio Godi demonstrate in depth the significance of reggae for black youth in Salvador. For the most part, Bahian reggae artists shunned the uptempo dance-hall style, which had eclipsed roots reggae in Jamaica in the 1980s, and remained committed to the politically charged origins of Bob Marley, Peter Tosh, and Jimmy Cliff. Reggae musicians from the south have been more open to change. In Brazil, as elsewhere in the developing world, reggae first emerged as a contestatory music of black liberation before entering the mainstream. The foremost Rio-based group, Cidade Negra, began as a "protest" group and, after commercial success, recorded with Jamaican dance-hall star Shabba Ranks and with Gabriel o Pensador [the thinker], a celebrated Brazilian rapper. The vocalist of that ensemble, Toni Garrido, was chosen to play the lead role in *Orfeu* (1999), also examined here; the heterogeneity of musical practice in the present-day *favela* resounds on the film's sound track.

African-American soul-funk and Jamaican reggae also contributed to the formation of the musical ensembles and community-based organizations called *blocos afro*, which articulated new social concerns within the context of *carnaval*.[62] Although these groups are regarded as a specifically Bahian phenomenon, they evidence acute awareness of political and cultural movements in Africa and the diaspora. As Milton Moura illustrates in his essay here, Afro-Bahian *carnaval* groupings have elaborated on claims to African and Third World allegiances since the nineteenth century. In the mid-1980s, then-musical director of the prominent *bloco afro* Olodum, Mestre Neguinho do Samba, hybridized *samba-reggae*, which accompanied *carnaval* theme songs about Cuba, Egypt, Madagascar, and Ethiopia.[63] In the 1990s, no other *bloco afro* has embraced cultural globalization, particularly the category of world music, with more enthusiasm than Olodum. Since a watershed recording with Paul Simon (*Rhythm of the Saints*, 1990), the group has done several tours of Europe, North America, and Japan, and has collaborated with such well-known figures as Michael Jackson and Spike Lee.[64] The directors of Olodum have been especially shrewd in promoting their organization by cultivating a relationship with the international press, collaborating with nongovernmental organizations, and launching a Web site on the Internet. Piers Armstrong considers such elements in his exploration here of the rhetoric and internal structures of Olodum.

These vibrant innovations of the late 1980s paved the way for the formation and repertory choices of pop bands in Salvador that enjoyed local and national success producing radio-friendly covers of *bloco afro carnaval* songs. After a tour with David Byrne in 1989, the Afro-Bahian performer Margareth Menezes achieved international note with a cover of "Elejibô" by the erstwhile *bloco afro* Araketu. This was a key moment for the international marketing of new Afro-Bahian popular music, which would be labeled *axé music*. This moniker suggests a calculated bid for recognition in the world-music market by appropriating the Yoruba term for "life-giving force" as an adjective and the English noun. In the early 1990s, some of the *blocos afro* began to alter their original voice-drum format and to add electric instrumentation, largely in order to compete in the national and international markets for *axé music*. The manager of Araketu, the *bloco afro* that pioneered this move, defended her group from accusations of inauthenticity with references to cosmopolitan African modernity: "Even in Africa popular music is being universalized by mixing elements of Caribbean, European, and North American music. We want to de-mystify this search for African roots that some groups pursue."[65] These examples suggest the degree to which notions of cultural authenticity, political efficacy, and racial identity in contemporary Afro-Bahian music are mediated by increasingly globalized practices and discourses.

The most significant innovator of the Bahian music scene in the 1990s was Carlinhos Brown, the founder and director of Timbalada, a percussion-dominated ensemble that has enjoyed local and international success. Unlike the *blocos afro*, Carlinhos Brown and Timbalada avoid racial protest and explicit appeals to Pan-African political solidarity. Rather, as seen in the analysis by Ari Lima here, they have created an original sound and visual aesthetic based on notions of *baianidade* [Bahianness] aligned with the expressive cultures of "globalized black youth" without referencing the specific struggles of black communities in Brazil or abroad.

In the early 1990s in Recife, Pernambuco, there emerged a vibrant cultural activity known as *movimento mangue*. The musical arm—known as *mangue beat* or *mangue bit*, mangrove beat or bit, as in computer terminology—coalesced around the seminal band Chico Science & Nação Zumbi (CSNZ), which fused traditional forms with funk, rap, and heavy metal. The movement's iconography features a marsh-dwelling crab with brains, emphasizing native subaltern intelligence, and a parabolic antenna stuck in the mud, which suggests a purposefully unresolved dialectic between the social reality of the mangrove shantytowns of metropolitan Recife and a deterritorialized, technologically informed sensibility. While most Brazilian rock of the 1980s was beholden to metropolitan models, *mangue beat* privileged regional difference, a strategy first pursued by the Tropicalists in the 1960s. After sending their first album to music festivals and promoters abroad, CSNZ was contracted by Sony Music and successfully marketed as "world music." The group subsequently appeared at the Montreux Jazz Festival, the Central Park Summer Stage (which led to a lengthy feature on National Public Radio), and CBGBs, a key site of the New York underground rock scene.[66] New scholarship focuses on the symbiotic relationship of tradition and modernity in CSNZ and other groups in Pernambuco.[67] In his essay here, Larry Crook explores the evolution of identity and repertory of Afro-Pernambucan *maracatu* ensembles and the specific contribution of CSNZ. John Murphy then discusses local-global interplay in the formation and expressions of Mestre Ambrósio, a sextet that utilizes pop information to enliven regional heritage. Finally, Fred Moehn highlights the example of CSNZ, alongside that of others such as Carlinhos Brown and Rio-based funk diva Fernanda Abreu, in his considerations of hyperaware transnational aesthetics.

Brazilian Popular Music at the Turn of the Millennium

Despite perennial anxieties and complaints in Brazil that multinationals exert excessive influence over consumption and that the power of international pop stars undermines local musical production, the Brazilian music market is, in fact, dominated by national acts. In 1995, for example, Roberto Carlos sold 1.5 million units in Brazil compared to Michael Jackson's 110,000. All genres included, national product accounted for up to 70 percent of unit sales of sound recordings in 1998, and all the top-ten sellers were Brazilian acts.[68] Even MPB artists, who generally appeal to a narrower audience, regularly outsell leading foreign artists. Except for the United States and Japan, Brazil consumes a greater percentage of national music than any other country with a major music market.[69] Furthermore, the Brazilian music recording and marketing complex is increasingly less confined to the cultural and economic centers of Rio de Janeiro and São Paulo. There are thriving regional markets throughout the country for *música sertaneja*, the Brazilian analog to country music, which outsells MPB three to one. Bahian pop music, especially *axé music*, dominates the local airwaves and record sales, yet sells relatively little in the south. According to a 1990 report, top regional artists sell more in their respective local markets than most nationally recognized artists sell in the whole country.[70] By no means, then, is Brazilian music overwhelmed by supposedly homogenizing economic and cultural forces from dominant nations. Ownership of Brazilian subsidiaries of multinational entertainment corporations is another question.

Among others, Arjun Appadurai has argued that globalization does not entail the cultural homogenization of the world.[71] In the case of Brazilian popular music, increased exposure to musical products and cultural styles from abroad has generated an ever-expanding panoply of hybrids without necessarily effacing more traditional styles, perhaps even encouraging them. Indeed, the history of Brazilian popular music during the last half of the twentieth century attests to what Néstor García Canclini has called "cultural reconversion," a process by which local cultural practices are reelaborated and amplified using the tools of modernity.[72] Access to these tools, of course, is not democratized, but marginalized urban communities in Brazil have been remarkably successful in maximizing media resources in order to intervene in local, national, and international cultural production.

Following a major fiscal crisis in the early 1990s, Brazil witnessed for the first time in its history substantial emigration to destinations in the United States and Europe. In the final decades of the twentieth century, Brazilian immigrant communities were established in greater New York, New England, Florida, and capital cities throughout Europe. In the Rio *carnaval* of 1999, the samba school Império Serrano paid homage to Brazilian emigrés with the theme "Uma rua chamada Brasil" [A street called Brazil], referring to Forty-sixth Street, the commercial center of Little Brazil in New York City. The theme song proclaimed: "Vi o jeito brasileiro na Grande Maçã/Há esperanças de um novo amanhã" [I saw Brazilian ways in the Big Apple/There is hope for a new future].[73] Following behind floats bearing popular icons such as Superman and official symbols of the United States, Império Serrano paraded wearing red, white, and blue and waving stylized American flags. This performative choice suggests a reduction in anxiety about U.S. cultural and economic influences in Brazil, as well as the development of transnational allegiances and identities among Brazilians who live abroad.[74]

As for North American perceptions of Brazil, decades after Jackson do Pandeiro's injunctions in "Chiclete com banana," most still do not distinguish samba from rumba, but information about and consumption of Brazilian popular music have reached unprecedented levels. For their part, Brazilians from south to north continue to incorporate everything from be-bop to hip-hop into evolving musical forms. There is no question that the flow from abroad, especially the United States, is much greater to Brazil than vice versa, but Brazilian musical creativity may more than compensate for economic disadvantage. The constant influx of musical information from abroad has proved to be not only musically fruitful in so many ways but useful as well for reflections on cultural practice, social concerns, modernity, nationality, and globalization.

Notes

1. On the traditions and legacies of the region, see Larry N. Crook, "Brazil Northeast," in *The Garland Encyclopedia of World Music*, vol. 2, *South America, Mexico, Central America, and the Caribbean* (New York: Garland Publishing, 1998), 323–339. Other entries pertinent to material discussed here are "Popular Music, Brazil," "Brazil: Afro-American," and "Brazil: Southeast."

2. Christopher Dunn, "The Tropicalista Rebellion: A Conversation with Caetano Veloso," *Transition* 70, vol. 6, no. 2 (1996), 128. Cited later in text.

3. The material for the production at Teatro Arena was selected in conjunction with musical researcher and writer José Ramos Tinhorão (cf. references to his work below). These compositions refer especially to the post–World War II period of U.S.-American supremacy, when sentimental Hispanic music was in vogue, but also refer to the Big Stick policy and previous events. Three of the titles contain the word "America." The sound track of the show was recorded as *Teatro Arena de São Paulo apresenta Chiclete & Banana* (Beverly BLP 9006, 1969).

4. *Forró Etc.* (Warner-Sire-Luaka Bop 9 26323, 1991), number three in the Brazil Classics series cited in note 47. "Chiclete com banana" is there attributed to Gordurinha and Castilho. The latter is Almira Castilho, the first wife of Jackson do Pandeiro (real name José Gomes Filho). His (co)compositions were registered in her name after 1959. The song was first recorded by Odete Amaral, 78 rpm Polydor 258 (Gordurinha-José Gomes), March 2, 1958. The second recording was by Jackson do Pandeiro himself, 78 rpm Columbia 3097 (Gordurinha-José Gomes), in November 1959. The third recording was by the coauthor himself, Gordurinha, 78 rpm 17 756 Continental (attributed to him alone), December 1959. A fourth version was done by northeastern vocalist Carmelia Alves, 78 rpm Mocambo 15376 (Gordurinha-Castilho), 1962. The song was rerecorded by Jackson do Pandeiro (Philips 632930, 1970) and by Gilberto Gil (Philips 6349034, 1972). Thanks are due to Jairo Severiano for assistance with this information.

5. "Jack Soul Brasileiro" is the first track on Various, *Jackson do Pandeiro revisto e sampleado* (BMG 7432155241, 1999), produced by Maurício Valladares; it is reprised on Lenine, *Na pressão* (BMG 7432171076, 1999). It first appeared on Fernanda Abreu, *Raio X* (EMI Odeon 859283-2, 1997), with guest appearance by Lenine.

6. Gerard Béhague, "Bossa and Bossas: Recent Changes in Brazilian Popular Music," *Ethnomusicology* vol. 17, no. 2 (1973), 209–233. A follow-up article appeared as "Brazilian Musical Values of the 1960s and 1970s: Popular Urban Music from Bossa Nova to Tropicália," *Journal of Popular Culture* 13 (Winter 1980), 437–452.

7. John Storm Roberts, *Black Music of Two Worlds* (New York: Praeger, 1972); and *The Latin Tinge: The Impact of Latin American Music on the United States* (Oxford: Oxford University Press, 1979). A revised edition of the former (New York: Schirmer Books, 1998) discusses recent developments in Brazil considered here.

8. The relevant annotated discobibliography is Charles A. Perrone, "Sources and Resources Brazil," *Popular Music* vol. 6, no. 2 (1987), 219–226. With respect to the conceptualization of popular music in the age of globalization and Latin American case

studies, a fundamental publication was the special issue of *the world of music* (Journal of the International Institute for Traditional Music), vol. 35, no. 2 (1993), subtitled "The Politics and Aesthetics of 'World Music,'" guest editors Veit Erlmann and Deborah Pacini Hernández. The former contributed a theoretical overview, "The Politics and Aesthetics of Transnational Musics," and the latter a Hispanic Caribbean perspective.

9. Gerard Béhague, founder and general editor, first issue 1981. For pertinent materials on topics discussed here, see Charles A. Perrone, "An Annotated Inter-Disciplinary Bibliography and Discography of Brazilian Popular Music," *Latin American Music Review* vol.7, no. 2 (Winter 1986), 302–340. For a historicized update, see Charles A. Perrone and Larry N. Crook, *Folk and Popular Music of Brazil* (Albuquerque: Latin American Institute, 1997), in the New Brazilian Curriculum Guide Specialized Bibliography, Series II.

10. *The Chronicle of Higher Education* of May 1, 1998, listed nearly forty recent titles in popular-music studies published by academic presses. Nearly half of these books deal with musical cultures outside of Europe and the United States.

11. In addition to studies cited below, a most pertinent example is Timothy Taylor, *Global Pop: World Music, World Markets* (New York: Routledge, 1997). Within the context of the African diaspora, migration, and music, notable new titles include Gage Averill, *A Day for the Hunter, A Day for the Prey: Popular Music and Power in Haiti* (Chicago: University of Chicago Press, 1997); Paul Austerlitz, *Merengue: Dominican Music and Dominican Identity* (Philadelphia: Temple University Press, 1997); and Robin Moore, *Nationalizing Blackness: Afrocubanismo and Artistic Revolution in Havana, 1920–1940* (Pittsburgh: University of Pittsburgh Press, 1997).

12. The category of "world music" was established by small, independent record labels in England that were having a difficult time marketing their international releases through conventional categories (e.g., rock, folk, jazz). See the introduction to *World Music: The Rough Guide* (London: The Rough Guides, 1994). Updated theoretical studies include Jocelyn Guilbault, "Interpreting World Music: A Challenge in Theory and Practice," *Popular Music* vol. 16, no.1 (1997), 31–44; and Veit Erlmann, "The Aesthetics of the Global Imagination: Reflections on World Music in the 1990s," *Public Culture* 8 (1996), 467–487. The difficulties of the term "world music" are discussed by David Byrne, *New York Times*, October 3, 1999. He begins: "I hate world music. That's probably one of the perverse reasons I have been asked to write about it. The term is a catchall that commonly refers to non-Western music of any and all sorts, popular music, traditional music and even classical music. It's a marketing as well as a pseudomusical term—and a name for a bin in the record store signifying stuff that doesn't belong anywhere else in the store. What's in that bin ranges from the most blatantly commercial music produced by a country, like Hindi film music . . . to the ultra-sophisticated, super-cosmopolitan art-pop of Brazil."

13. The Boston-based publication *Bossa: Brazilian Jazz World Guide* regularly lists radio shows and performances of Brazilian popular music in North America along with reviews and feature articles with translated song texts.

14. Gilberto Gil, "Pela Internet" on *Quanta* (WEA 06301864, 1997) and *Quanta Live*

(Atlantic 92807, 1998). Both his trilingual Web site and the equally comprehensive site of Caetano Veloso are engineered by André Vallias.

15. Martha Tupinambá de Ulhôa, "Nova história, velhos sons: notas para ouvir e pensar a música brasileira popular," *Debates: cadernos do programa de pós-graduação em música* 1 (1997), 78–101.

16. Sérgio Cabral, *A MPB na era do rádio* (São Paulo: Editora Moderna, 1996), 22. Cabral cited again below, note 23.

17. Jairo Severiano and Zuza Homem de Mello, vol. 1, *A canção no tempo, 85 anos de músicas brasileiras* (São Paulo: Editora 34, 1998), 49.

18. On the extensive bibliography on Brazilian modernism, see Charles A. Perrone, *Seven Faces: Brazilian Poetry Since Modernism* (Durham, N.C.: Duke University Press, 1996), chapter 1, cited below by title.

19. Oswald de Andrade, "Manifesto da Poesia Pau-Brasil" (1924). See trans. Stella de Sá Rego, "Manifesto of Pau-Brasil Poetry," *Latin American Literary Review* vol.14, no. 27 (1986), 184–187.

20. Hermano Vianna, *The Mystery of Samba: Popular Music and National Identity in Brazil* (Chapel Hill: University of North Carolina Press, 1999).

21. There is a rich bibliography on modern Brazilian national identity. Two indispensable Brazilian sources are Carlos Guilherme Mota, *Ideologia da cultura brasileira* (São Paulo: Editora Ática, 1977) and Renato Ortiz, *Cultura brasileira e identidade nacional* (São Paulo: Brasiliense, 1985). On *brasilidade* and the ever-relevant myth of racial democracy, see Thomas Skidmore, *Black into White: Race and Nationality in Brazilian Thought*, 2nd ed. (Durham, N.C.: Duke University Press, 1994).

22. The 1937 song by Amado Regis was reprised by Caetano Veloso on *Fina estampa en vivo* (Polygram 314528918, 1995), a project built around Hispanic content.

23. Quoted by Cabral, 82. On this period—especially on the discourse of samba in Noel Rosa, Ataulfo Alves, and Ary Barroso—see Lisa Shaw, *The Social History of the Brazilian Samba* (Brookfield, Vt.: Ashgate, 1998).

24. Orson Welles and Peter Bogdonavich, *This Is Orson Welles* (London: Harper and Collins, 1993), 374. The 1998 film *Tudo é Brasil* by Rogério Sganzerla, third of a series of experimental films exploring Welles's intriguing stay in Brazil and enduring filmic legacy, reproduces much of this radio broadcast in the original English. On Orson Welles in Brazil, his role as cultural translator, and the centrality of music in his film project, see Robert Stam, "Orson Welles, Brazil, and the Power of Blackness," in *Perspectives on Orson Welles*, ed. Morris Beja (New York: G. K. Hall Co., 1995), 219–244 (originally 1989); and *Tropical Multiculturalism: A Comparative History of Race in Brazilian Cinema and Culture* (Durham, N.C.: Duke University Press, 1997), 107–133.

25. José Ramos Tinhorão, *O samba que agora vai: a farsa da música popular no exterior* (Rio de Janeiro: JCM, 1969), 45 ff.

26. Tárik de Souza, "Carmen Miranda: a trajetória," liner notes to CD box *Carmen Miranda* (BMG 7432152774, 1997). On the international implications of the star's

career, see Ana Rita Mendonça, *Carmen Miranda foi a Washington* (Rio de Janeiro: Record, 1999).

27. See Ana M. López, "Are All Latins from Manhattan? Hollywood, Ethnography, and Cultural Colonialism," in *Mediating Two Worlds*, ed. López and John King (London: BFI, 1993), as well as the Helen Solberg film *Bananas Is My Business* (1995).

28. See Julianne Burton, "Don (Juanito) Duck and the Imperial Patriarchal Unconscious: Disney Studios, the Good Neighbor Policy, and the Packaging of Latin America," in *Nationalisms and Sexualities*, ed. Andrew Parker et al. (New York and London: Routledge, 1992), 21–41; and José Piedra, "Donald Duck Discovers America/O Pato Donald descobre as Américas," *Lusitania* vol. 1, no. 4, n/d [c.1991], 119–129.

29. Ary Vasconcelos, introduction to *Assis Valente*, fascicle of *História da música popular brasileira: grandes compositores* (São Paulo: Abril Cultural, 1982), 2.

30. Luiz Carlos Saroldi and Sonia V. Moreira, *Radio nacional: o Brasil em sintonia* (Rio de Janeiro: FUNARTE, 1988), 67–68.

31. Thomas Skidmore, *Politics in Brazil, 1930–1964: An Experiment in Democracy* (New York: Oxford University Press), 164.

32. On Brasilia, see James Holston, *The Modernist City* (Chicago: University of Chicago Press, 1989); on concrete poetry and related sources, see Perrone, *Seven Faces*, chapter 2.

33. Augusto de Campos et al., *Balanço da bossa e outras bossas* (São Paulo: Perspectiva, 1974), 143.

34. José Ramos Tinhorão, *Música popular: um tema em debate* (Rio de Janeiro: JCM, 1966), 36. The critic's expressions of disdain for jazz and its role in the creation of bossa nova relate to what Vianna uncovered in *The Mystery of Samba*. Gilberto Freyre, one of the elite intellectuals who celebrated samba as a vibrant expression of the "real Brazil," detested jazz when he first heard it in New York and later expressed anxiety over its influence in Brazil (60–62).

35. Robert Farris Thompson, "Bossa Nova from the Source," *Saturday Review* July 11, 1964, 42–43. See also Gene Lees, "Bossa Nova: Anatomy of a Travesty," *Downbeat* November 8, 1962, 62.

36. There was a worldwide flood of press accounts, live homages, and recordings soon after Jobim's death. For English-language historical criticism focused on this figure, see Suzel Ana Reily, "Tom Jobim and the Bossa Nova Era," *Popular Music* vol. 15, no. 1 (1996), 1–16.

37. David Treece, "Guns and Roses: Bossa Nova and Brazil's Music of Popular Protest, 1958–68," *Popular Music* vol.16, no. 1 (1997), 16.

38. Roberto Schwarz, "Culture and Politics in Brazil," in *Misplaced Ideas: Essays on Brazilian Culture*, ed. and trans. John Gledson (New York: Verso, 1992), 127.

39. Brazil's leading news magazine reported on the considerable number of Brazilian musicians residing abroad at the beginning of the 1970s, contrasting the penetration of foreign music with the export of Brazilian artists to Europe and North America; "As

duas invasões da música brasileira," *Veja* March 11, 1970, 56–63; cited below by article title.

40. For a nuanced class analysis of the Jovem Guarda and MPB, see Martha de Ulhôa Carvalho, "Tupi or not Tupi MPB: Popular Music and Identity in Brazil," in *The Brazilian Puzzle: Culture on the Borderlands of the Western World*, ed. David Hess and Roberto DaMatta (New York: Columbia University Press, 1995), 159–179.

41. Caetano Veloso, *Verdade tropical* (São Paulo: Companhia das Letras, 1997), 247. Next quote in text.

42. Hermano Vianna, "A epifania tropicalista," *Folha de São Paulo—Mais!* September 19, 1999.

43. Jackson Griffith, "Boogaloo with Beck," *Pulse!* 188 (December 1999), 81.

44. Tom Zé, *Fabrication Defect* (Warner-Luaka Bop 9 46953, 1998). This recording was followed by a remix album by a series of U.S. post-rock groups: *Postmodern Platos* (Luaka Bop PRO CD 9561, 1999). See also note 47.

45. Recorded on *Milton* (EMI Odeon 064 422900D, 1970). For a more complete account of this song, the overall repertory, and the foundations of MPB, see Charles A. Perrone, *Masters of Contemporary Brazilian Song: MPB 1965–1985* (Austin: University of Texas Press, 1989).

46. For a comprehensive press account, see Chris McGowan et al., "The Brazilian Wave Comes Ashore," *Billboard* vol. 99, no. 45 (November 7, 1987), B1–32.

47. The David Byrne series Brazil Classics also included the MPB of *Beleza tropical* (Warner Sire-Luaka Bop 9 25805, 1988), *O samba* (Warner Sire Luaka Bop 9 26019, 1989), *Beleza tropical 2* (Warner-Luaka Bop 46275, 1998), and two albums by Tom Zé, *Massive Hits: The Best of Tom Zé* (Warner Sire-Luaka Bop 9 26396, 1991) and *The Return of Tom Zé: The Hips of Tradition* (Warner-Luaka Bop 9 45118, 1992).

48. Jocelyn Guilbault, "On Redefining the 'Local' Through World Music," *the world of music* vol. 35, no. 2 (1993), 38.

49. See the account in Chris McGowan and Ricardo Pessanha, 2nd expanded ed., *The Brazilian Sound: Samba, Bossa Nova and the Popular Music of Brazil* (Philadelphia: Temple University Press, 1998), cited below by authors. See also the final chapter in José Ramos Tinhorão, 6th ed., *Pequena história da música popular: da modinha à lambada* (São Paulo: Art, 1991).

50. Caetano Veloso, *Estrangeiro* (Polygram 838 297, 1989); Bob Dylan, *Bringing It All Back Home* (Columbia CS 9128, n/d [1965]). For further contextualizations, see Charles A. Perrone, "Os Outros Românticos: Signs of Life in Lyric (-) Song & Dance (-) Music," *Brazil in the Eighties*, in the series *Los Ensayistas*, Georgia Series on Hispanic Thought, 28–29 (1990), 179–197.

51. Deborah Pacini Hernández, "Amalgamating Musics: Popular Music and Cultural Hybridity in the Americas," keynote address at Rhythms of Culture conference, University of Michigan, March 23, 1997.

52. Studies of the Brazilian case include Charles A. Perrone, "Changing of the Guard: Questions and Contrasts of Brazilian Rock Phenomena," *Studies in Latin American Popular Culture* 9 (1990), 65–83; Angelica Madeira, "Rhythm and Irreverence

(notes about the rock music movement in Brasilia)," *Popular Music and Society* vol.15, no. 4 (1991), 57–70; and Stephen Walden, *"Brasilidade:* Brazilian *Rock Nacional* in the Context of National Cultural Identity," dissertation, University of Georgia, 1996. Among the few rock publications in Brazil of academic origin, see Antônio Marcus Alves de Souza, *Cultura rock e arte de massa* (Rio de Janeiro: Diadorim, 1995); Goli Guerreiro, *Retratos de uma tribo urbana: rock brasileiro* (Salvador: Centro Editorial e Didático da UFBA, 1994); and Patrícia Farias, "Sobre rock, jornais e Brasil," Occasional Papers 45, Centro Interdisciplinar de Estudos Contemporâneos, UFRJ, 1993.

53. Peter Wicke, "Rock Music: A Musical-Aesthetic Study," *Popular Music* 2 (1983), 222, 226, 229.

54. McGowan and Pessanha, 199. Mendes's group was formed in Los Angeles, included non-Brazilians, and performed much material with little relation to tradition.

55. Keith Harris, "'Roots'?: The Relationship between the Global and the Local within the Global Extreme Metal Scene," *Popular Music* vol. 19, no. 1 (2000), 13–30.

56. Soulfly, n/t (Roadrunner 8748, 1998). A decade after inclusion on Byrne's *Beleza tropical* compilation, Ben's funk-samba was used in the United States in a nationally broadcast commercial for Intel computer chips. It had also been covered by Arto Lindsay and Peter Scherer, Ambitious Lovers, *Lust* (Elektra 60981, 1991).

57. George Lipsitz, *Dangerous Crossroads: Popular Music, Postmodernism and the Poetics of Place* (London: Verso, 1994), 27.

58. Paul Gilroy, *The Black Atlantic: Modernity and Double Consciousness* (Cambridge, Mass.: Harvard University Press, 1993), 76.

59. There are two excellent Brazilian volumes of essays on these cultural complexes: *Abalando os anos 90: funk e hip-hop. Globalização, violência e estilo cultural,* ed. Micael Hershmann (Rio de Janeiro: Rocco, 1997); and *Ritmos em trânsito: sócio-antropologia da música baiana,* ed. Livio Sansone and Jocélio Teles dos Santos (São Paulo: Dynamis Editorial; Salvador: Programa A Cor da Bahia e Projeto S.A.M.B.A., 1997). Both cited below by title. See also the pioneering study by Hermano Vianna, *O mundo funk carioca* (Rio de Janeiro: Jorge Zahar Editor, 1988).

60. See George Yúdice, "The Funkification of Rio," in *Microphone Fiends: Youth Music and Youth Culture,* ed. Tricia Rose and Andrew Ross (New York: Routledge, 1994), 193–217.

61. José Ramos Tinhorão, "O inimigo da MPB está de volta," *Folha de São Paulo-Ilustrada,* February 14, 1998.

62. Brazilian bibliography on the new Afro-Bahian *carnaval* is cited in the several essays concerning Bahia in this volume. An early English-language source was Christopher Dunn, "Afro-Bahian Carnival: A Stage for Protest," *Afro-Hispanic Review* vol. 11, nos. 1–3 (1992), 11–20.

63. See Larry Crook, "Black Consciousness, *Samba-Reggae,* and the Re-Africanization of Bahian Carnival Music in Brazil," *the world of music* vol. 35, no. 2 (1993), 90–108; Livio Sansone, "The New Blacks from Bahia: Local and Global in Afro-Bahia," *Identities* vol. 3, no. 4 (1997), 457–492; and Gerard Béhague, "La afinidad caribeña de la música popular en Bahía," *Del Caribe* 19 (1992), 87–92.

64. See Petra Schraeber, "Música negra nos tempos de globalização: produção musical e *management* da identidade étnica—o caso do Olodum," in *Ritmos em trânsito*, 145–160. In the context of black activism, see João Jorge Santos Rodrigues, "Olodum and the Black Struggle in Brazil," in *Black Brazil: Culture, Identity, and Social Mobilization*, ed. Larry Crook and Randal Johnson (Los Angeles: UCLA Latin American Center, 2000), 43–51.

65. Vera Lacerda quoted by Goli Guerreiro, "Um mapa em preto e branco da música da Bahia: territorialização e mestiçagem no meio musical de Salvador (1987/1997)," in *Ritmos em trânsito*, 107. New Afro-Bahian popular music is one of the focuses of a Brazil special issue of *The Beat* vol. 10, no. 2 (1991).

66. See the interview with Chico Science on the Web site of Brazilian Music up to Date, www.uptodate.com.br. On September 23, 1996, National Public Radio's "All Things Considered" broadcast "Cutting Edge Brazilian Band Remains True to Its Roots," byline by Daisann Mc Lane; see her earlier "Mucking Up," *Village Voice* July 11, 1995, 60 for a view from the popular press, as well as Chuck Eddy, "Chico Science, 1996–1997," *Village Voice* February 18, 1997, 65.

67. See Philip Galinsky, "'Maracatu Atômico': Tradition, Modernity, and Postmodernity in the *Mangue* Movement and 'New Music Scene' of Recife, Pernambuco, Brazil," Ph.D. dissertation, Wesleyan University, 1999.

68. "MPB entra na era industrial," *Folha de São Paulo-Mais!* April 12, 1998, 5.

69. In the 1990 survey year, Brazilian music constituted 66 percent of all music sales in the country compared with Japanese music constituting 74 percent of music sales in Japan, American music sales at 69 percent in the United States, British music sales at 61 percent in the UK, French music sales at 45 percent in France, and Italian music sales at 39 percent in Italy. Paul Rutten, "Local Popular Music on the National and International Markets," *Cultural Studies* vol. 5, no. 3 (1991), 294–305. In 1969, the Brazilian recording industry reported that 47 percent of records pressed in Brazil were of foreign music. "As duas invasões," 56.

70. "Os santos da terra," *Veja* September 12, 1990, 86–88.

71. Arjun Appadurai, *Modernity at Large: Cultural Dimensions of Globalization* (Minneapolis: University of Minnesota Press, 1997), 17.

72. Néstor García Canclini, *Hybrid Cultures: Strategies for Entering and Exiting Modernity* (Minneapolis: University of Minnesota Press, 1995).

73. José Carlos Sebe Bom Meihy, "Considerações em torno de um samba," *The Brasilians* vol. 28, no. 292 (January–February 1999), 10. On communities, see Maxine Margolis, *Little Brazil: An Ethnography of Brazilian Immigrants in New York City* (Princeton: Princeton University Press, 1992).

74. A U.S.-based Brazilian scholar indeed postulates new configurations in the musical minds of Brazilian music makers and consumers; see Cristina Magaldi, "Adopting Imports: New Images and Alliances in Brazilian Popular Music," *Popular Music* vol. 18, no. 3 (1999), 309–330. The cover of this issue reproduces a CD cover of the Brazilian rap group Racionais MC.

TWO

Carmen Mirandadada

Caetano Veloso

For the generation of Brazilians who reached adolescence in the late 1950s and became adults at the height of the Brazilian military dictatorship and the international wave of counterculture—my generation—Carmen Miranda was first a cause for a mixture of pride and shame and later a symbol of the intellectual violence with which we wanted to face our reality, of the merciless gaze we wanted to cast upon ourselves.

Carmen Miranda died in 1955. In 1957, the recordings she made before she came to the United States in 1939 sounded archaic to our ears, and those she made in the United States seemed ridiculous: "Chica chica boom chic," "Cuanto le gusta," and "South American Way" were the opposite of our craving for good taste and national identity. We were listening to female vocalists who have perhaps never been heard of here [in the United States] but who to us seemed—and in some ways indeed were—superior to her: Ângela Maria, Nora Ney, Elza Soares, Maysa. We could almost sense the advent of bossa nova. Yet

Carmen Miranda, ca. 1940. Courtesy of FUNARTE, São Paulo.

Carmen had become one of the formative personalities of postwar American life, influencing not only fashion but the gestures of a generation. Nowadays we are fascinated when we find her cited in Wittgenstein's biography as one of his favorites. In the late 1950s, however, it carried considerable weight simply to know that she was the only Brazilian artist recognized worldwide, and to hear our elders reiterate "not undeservedly so." We kept our pride about her to ourselves, which is not so different from the way we react when we hear the name of Pelé outside Brazil or see the drum band Olodum playing with Paul Simon in Central Park for hundreds of thousands. In a country that doesn't figure in the news section of the big dailies of the First World unless a catastrophe befalls its people or something ridiculous happens to its leaders, everyone can get excited about such things. But as we were more inclined to see Carmen Miranda's grotesqueness instead of her grace, and we weren't mature enough to ponder her fate, the easiest and most frequent attitude was simply to ignore her. This wasn't difficult in a country that, unlike Argentina, doesn't usually keep its mass figures alive in memory, be they political leaders or popular singers.

Nevertheless, in 1967 Carmen Miranda reappeared as a central figure in our aesthetic concerns. A movement that came to be known as *tropicalismo* appropriated her as one of its principal signs, capitalizing on the discomfort that her name and the evocation of her gestures could create as a provocation to revitalize the minds that had to traverse an epoch of inebriation with political and aesthetic utopias, in a country in search of its place in modernity while under a military dictatorship. That movement derived its title from an installation by the visual artist Hélio Oiticica, found inspiration in some of the images of the film *Terra em transe (Land in Anguish)* by Glauber Rocha (1967), and dialogued with the theater of José Celso Martinez Correa, but was mainly concentrated in popular music. The song-manifesto "Tropicália," homonymous with Oiticica's work, closes with the exhortation: "Carmen Miranda da-da dada." We had discovered that she was both our caricature and our x ray, and we began to take notice of the destiny of that woman: she was a typical girl from Rio, born in Portugal, who, using a blatantly vulgar though elegant stylization of the clothes characteristic of a *baiana* [woman from Bahia], had conquered the world and become the highest-paid woman entertainer in the United States. Today there are Latin female stars living in the United States and working for the masses of resident Latins. Carmen conquered "white" America as no other South American had ever done or ever would. She was the only representative of South

America who was universally readable, and it is exactly because of this quality that self-parody became her inescapable prison. It was, therefore, easy for us to understand the profound depression she experienced in the 1950s, the abuse of pills, the destruction of her life. Even today, to write these words about her is something painful and difficult for me. Today, anything associated with Brazilian music in America—or with any music from the Southern Hemisphere in the Northern—makes us think of Carmen Miranda. And to think of her is to think about the complexity of this relationship: Olodum on Paul Simon's album, the collection of Tom Zé's experimental sambas released by David Byrne, Naná Vasconcelos and Egberto Gismonti, Sting and Raoni, Tania Maria, Djavan and Manhattan Transfer, the cult of Milton Nascimento. She is always present.

When bossa nova burst on the scene in the United States—in other words, the world—we felt that Brazil had finally exported a highly refined quality product. But the fact that the style had been inaugurated by a single off the *Getz / Gilberto* album—"The Girl from Ipanema" sung beautifully in English by Astrud Gilberto—creates the impression of a cool-jazz Carmen Miranda. Not only does Astrud's voice spring like a luscious fruit from Tom Jobim's dense harmonies, the character praised in the song, the girl from Ipanema, seems to be wearing fruit on her head. This image is not contrived, it is in the air. Recently, on the night of a gala benefit for the Rain Forest Foundation, emceed by Sting and starring Jobim himself, there was a rumor backstage that when Tom and his band played the Ipanema song, Elton John would appear dressed like Carmen Miranda, or at least wearing one of those turbans full of bananas or umbrellas. It didn't happen. But only, they say, because Elton and Sting weren't sure if Tom (and the audience) would take kindly to such kidding. But it is revealing that the rumor should have gone around there. She is always present. Airto shaking traditional Brazilian trinkets in Miles Davis's band in 1971. Flora Purim and Chick Corea.

She is always present also because there is, as the Tropicalists soon had to consider, beyond the extraordinary character of her destiny, the quality of her art. Before she became the international *falsa baiana* [fake Bahian woman], well before assuming a position as the goddess of camp (indeed the image of endless bananas coming out of the top of her head, created by Busby Berkeley with his tendency to produce visions of mystical ecstasy, is the confirmation of a deity), Carmen Miranda had already left in Brazil abundant evidence of her reinvention of samba. Later, after bossa nova had matured and been exported, when Tom Jobim had joined the greatest songwriters of the century and Sérgio Mendes had found the best way to get Brazilian musicality into the international market—

after all that had been made possible by the magic of the great sorcerer João Gilberto, our most profound adventure—Carmen's old records no longer sounded like antiquities. A collection of these recordings was released on CD in Brazil several months ago (it wouldn't be a bad idea for the same thing to happen here in the United States). Her dexterous and spontaneous style treats the dazzling repertory superbly. The agility of diction and the sense of humor tossed into the rhythm are marks of a nimble mind from which we had much to learn. In the recording of "Adeus batucada," a prophetic samba by Synval Silva (who was her chauffeur and showed himself to be an extraordinary songwriter), Carmen Miranda bids farewell to her companions in the samba circles, saying "eu vou deixar todo mundo, valorizando a batucada" [I'm going to leave everyone praising the samba beat]. It is one of the most beautiful sambas ever written in Brazil. The song ended up echoing in another years later, written in retaliation for the icy reception she received from the crowd at the Cassino da Urca nightclub in Rio during her first performance after her success in the United States: "Disseram que voltei americanizada" [They said I came back Americanized; Peixoto-Paiva, 1940]. It is a good-humored settling of scores with the Rio public and critics who resented her adulteration of Brazilian rhythms. American musicians had difficulty adapting to them and, in their impatience, perhaps did not pay proper attention, inevitably giving them a Cuban rendering. There were many stylistic snags in her performances because, being a singer from the only Portuguese-speaking country in Latin America, she had been chosen to represent the set of Spanish-speaking communities. Today, after bossa nova and Milton Nascimento, one can at least count on American musicians to attempt to capture the peculiarity of the music of Brazil. In Carmen's day it was enough to make a percussive din that was recognizably Latin and Negroid. But she had insisted on bringing the musicians of Bando da Lua with her and she represented less the adulteration alleged by her critics than a pioneering role in a history that is still unfolding and that today seems more fascinating than ever: the history of the relationship between the very rich music of a very poor country and musicians and audiences from the rest of the world. A history whose least curious episode is not this chapter, given that its author wrote the Tropicalist song that ends with the name of Carmen, with Miranda echoing in dada. It is from this singular perspective that one seeks to observe the critical turn around that led us to discover the charms of the old Brazilian recordings of Carmen Miranda and the dignity that predominates in her American discography. She made more and better samba here than we were willing to admit.

The Brazilian poet Oswald de Andrade, of the modernist movement of 1922, once said, "My country suffers from cosmic incompetence." Carmen seemed somehow free of this curse. What strikes us when we look at her films today is the definition in the movements, the hand-eye coordination, the extreme clarity and polish of her gestures. Years after the pearl of Oswald de Andrade, Hanna Arendt would refer to the disparity between poor and rich countries exactly in the area of competence. Much of what comes out of Brazil is notable for its magic, its mystery, its joy; very little for its competence. When I'm asked why Carmen Miranda pleased Americans as much as she did, I answer I don't know. But I still wonder whether her great vocation for the finished product, her ability to design extremely stylized samba dancing as though creating a cartoon character, might not have been the decisive factor in her popularity. "Competence" is a word that well defines the American way of evaluating things. Carmen excelled in this area. Gal Costa, Maria Bethania, Margareth Menezes are true Bahian women and great artists of joy and mystery. Carmen Miranda's gestural style, however, finds expression in the vocal style of Elis Regina: high definition in attacking the notes, clarity in the phrasing, and the pitch of a computer—competence. Perhaps the United States today isn't as enthralled by this quality; perhaps people here have a less healthy naïveté about technological progress than in the 1940s and 1950s: to go to Japan is to make one think about this. As for Brazil, there were those who said that surrealism was the only realism possible in Latin America, since everyday life in misery is surreal. We the Tropicalists, in a period when the highbrows and lowbrows caroused together to the consternation of some middle-brows, believed that dada had more to do with us than surrealism; it was the unaestheticized unconscious, the nonexplanation of the inexplicable. It was also the opposite of binding ourselves to a formalized absurdity, and it was the choice, above all, of liberty as a fundamental theme. Clearly we weren't dadaists. We were a handful of kids from Bahia, the children of bossa nova, who were interested in 1960s English neo-rock 'n' roll. Some of us had gone to college. After we moved to São Paulo, we went on to have a good rapport with Augusto and Haroldo de Campos, leaders of the mid-1950s movement of concrete poetry. They suggested to us the parallel between dada and surrealism, which we used as I described above. Today, as the early-century avant-garde is being questioned, among other things, for having attracted semiliterate hordes who produce mass culture, we look back without shame and without pride. We just smile happily when we hear Marisa Monte singing a song of Carmen's, accompanying it with

Caetano Veloso and band, "Prenda Minha" tour, 1998. Photo by Paulo Macedo.

a very subtle reproduction of her gestures. And we find nothing in our own recordings that is comparable to the best recordings of Carmen Miranda from the 1930s.

I was in exile in London in 1971 when I first saw that well-known photograph in which Carmen unwittingly appears with her sex in view. I was reminded of the first Portuguese who, arriving in Brazil and seeing the Indians naked, noted in a letter to the king of Portugal that "they don't cover their shame" (that is, genitals). In sixteenth-century Portuguese it was common to refer to the *pudenda* as "shame." I thought it particularly significant that our representative should have been the only one among all the figures of the Olympus of Hollywood to show her "shame" and that she should have done it inadvertently, innocently. "Shame" is a word that echoes in this chapter from the very first paragraph, but such a sight caused more pride in me than embarrassment. In the arms of Cesar Romero, with a pure Hollywood smile on her lips, surrounded by glitter full of intention and control, everything about and around her seemed obscene next to the innocence of her sex.

The lighting, the set, the pose, the fantasy were Carmen Miranda. Her exposed sex was dada.

Mitologia no samba, amor . . .
E o samba do negro Orfeu
tem um retorno triunfal

[Mythology in samba, love. . .
and the samba of the black man Orfeu
has a triumphant return]
—G.R.E.S. Viradouro, 1998

THREE

Myth, Melopeia, and Mimesis
Black Orpheus, Orfeu, and Internationalization
in Brazilian Popular Music

Charles A. Perrone

Orfeu negro (*Black Orpheus*), the 1959 film of French director Marcel Camus, although not a Brazilian production, has wielded a tremendous influence on the construction of Brazil's image abroad. Forty years after its release, that cinematic success remains a fundamental point of reference for any discussion of perceptions of Brazil in other countries. As one team of observers has clearly explained, the film "has almost certainly been seen by more non-Brazilians than any other film shot in that country and is likely to have provided a first introduction to Brazilian culture for more Europeans and North Americans than any other art work."[1] With respect to Brazilian popular music, a key instance in its attainment of global reach, and in the process of locating its historical place in the international arena, is constituted in *Black Orpheus*. The widespread effects of the land-mark film are confirmed in the testimony of a prestigious contemporary singer-songwriter of Brazil with extensive foreign experience, Caetano Veloso:

> When we arrived in London in 1969, record-company executives, hippies, and intellectuals, everyone we met, without exception, referred enthusiastically to *Black Orpheus* as soon as they were informed that we were Brazilians . . . Even today there are endless repetitions of narratives of discovery of Brazil by foreigners (rock singers, first-rate novelists, French sociologists, actresses, debutantes), all marked by the unforgettable film of Marcel Camus.[2]

In addition to lending his acumen to an understanding of the impact of the film outside Brazil, Veloso has now become a significant participant in the series of Orpheus-related works in the Brazilian arts. Carlos Diegues has realized a longtime ambition to make a national film version of the Greek myth trans-planted to Rio de Janeiro. Veloso, for his part, acted as musical director of the new film (1999), titled simply *Orfeu*. In a felicitous coincidence, the Viradouro Samba School had chosen Orfeu as its theme for the 1998 Carnival, and Diegues filmed and integrated scenes of its rehearsals and the parade itself. The performance of the samba school and Diegues's cinematic effort are the latest chapters in an Orphic adventure in Brazil that began with a stage play by the renowned poet-diplomat-songwriter Vinícius de Morais. His drama was the frame of reference for the screenplay of *Black Orpheus* and became the foundation of *Orfeu*. The outlook of the Brazilian director and the new original sound track both inevitably reflect on the legacy of Camus' film and its musical significance. The unfolding and overlappings of the roles and goals of players in this Orphic thread in the fabric of contemporary Brazilian culture—in fictive narratives, real-life revelry, and communication media—reveal different levels of mythification and re-sponses that have multinational currency.

The force and enduring appeal of *Black Orpheus* in the international domain are undeniable. They derive in great part from its presentations of the landscape and popular culture of Rio de Janeiro, especially music. Given the Orphic themes of inspiration and their concrete realizations in this film, music can be regarded as its central pillar. However, no study has examined in detail musical aspects of *Black Orpheus*. The present chapter concerns the functions of music in the filmic diegesis, as well as some pragmatic considerations of its projections. The film is structured around instrumental sounds, vocals, and performative material that reconstitute mythemes of the Orpheus legends and that are, inevitably, seen to represent real-world expressive behaviors alike. Such perceptions invite reflection on the use of archetypal and actual sources. In terms of aesthetic pleasure, identifications of mythical allusions help illuminate musical moments and motifs. In addition, given the extensive levels of exposure the film has given Brazilian popular music worldwide, the percussion-dominated music making and instances of song in the film should be interpreted with specific attention to historical conjuncture. Seeing how the dynamism of sound fields and the *melopeia* (melodious poetic rhythm) of sung texts are integrated and contextualized in the film helps further to uncover the senses of its enactments of emotivity in individuals and collectivities. And with respect to the *mimesis* of musical narrative, the generic functions and "authenticity" of the music also merit scrutiny for a practical comprehension of the film, which, with its sound track, became its own point of reference in the evolution of contemporary popular music. Any full grasp of *Black Orpheus* begins with its mythical foundations and Brazilian origins.

The Artistic Heritage

The legends of Orpheus comprise a centuries-long continuum in Western art and one of the deepest reservoirs in the Western mind. These are tapped by the film in compelling fashion through sound and image. Camus reconfigures the hero's tragic loss of his beloved Eurydice during Carnival in a black shantytown and the streets of Rio de Janeiro proper. As Stam underscores, the film established a strong association, in international consciousness, among Brazil, blackness, and Carnival.[3] The setting is taken from *Orfeu da Conceição* [Orpheus from Conception], the dramatic text by Morais, written in 1953 and staged, with singular historical importance, in 1956. Material and ideological aspects of the play are also relevant to the film, and their respective public treatments relate intimately. Performance and musicality in *Orfeu da Conceição* and *Black Orpheus* both directly concern issues of race and critical reception, which have been the object of specific analyses.[4] Both the theatrical production and the classical framework resonate meaningfully in the modern cinematic versions.

Orpheus represents a rich symbolic legacy and a potent frame of dramatic and filmic reference. He embodies, genealogically, both regal character and the very essence of musicality, whether epical or lyrical. In ancient Greek texts and myriad cultural expressions over the centuries, Orpheus has been endowed with exceptional powers of performative enchantment. He may stand for the ultimate power of music, or the failure of musical enlightenment.

In myth, Orpheus was depicted as a native of Thrace, though he may even have been a real historical figure, as mentions of him appear in documents from the sixth century B.C. He was the son of Apollo (or of the king of Thrace) and his wife Calliope, who was the muse of epic poetry. Orpheus was a shaman and a magician, but above all a unique musician, who sang and played the lyre with such power that he could alter the course of nature. He married Eurydice, who died from a snakebite soon after their marriage. With the lyre that Apollo himself had given him, he tried to console himself by filling the valleys with beautiful sound, but to no avail. Still grief stricken, Orpheus descended to the underworld to search for Eurydice. There he implored Pluto and the keepers of Hades to allow him to take her back to the world of the living. They were convinced—and here lies the proof of the power of Orpheus—by his magical song. She was allowed to return with him on the condition that he not look back to see if she was following until their ascent was complete. Unable to bear the burden of doubt, he did look back to see if Eurydice was there, and he lost her forever. Upon his return to the world, the attractive Orpheus now shunned women, which infuriated the Maenads (or Bacchants, the female followers of Dionysius), who set upon him and tore him to pieces by a river. As his head floated downstream, it kept on singing and making prophesy, and his lyre kept on sounding. In this way is established the permanence of music and the continuity of the enterprise of music, which remains a fundamental part of the legend.[5]

In the domain of music, Orpheus is perhaps the prime symbol in Western history and tradition. In the Baroque period (1600–1760s), Orpheus became the patron saint of opera. The first musical drama was, in fact, Monteverdi's *L'Orfeo* (early seventeenth century). Elizabeth Newby summarizes the centrality of Orpheus references:

> In the most basic terms, the legends of Orpheus symbolize the power of musical ethos. The complex of Orphic stories tells that music can reverse the laws of nature, assuage the gods of the dead, and mitigate the torments of Hades. . . . Depending on where one finds oneself in the history of Western musical speculation, Orpheus may be seen either as the quintessential poet-musician, whose artistic talent stands for the ultimate power of musical affect, or as an illustrious

failure, whose musical, intellectual, and moral limitations serve as a lesson for those who would follow in his footsteps in pursuit of musical enlightenment. . . . the myth stands as one of the central symbolic statements in the history of Western musical philosophy for man's search for a definition of the meaning and function of music.[6]

If in musical philosophy all who have viewed Orpheus (e.g., empiricists, idealists et al.) have seen a profound mix of sound and verse, he has been no less celebrated in the visual arts—painting, lithography, sculpture—in representations spanning the ages and notably diverse in the twentieth century.[7]

The inspiration for the work that led to the films *Black Orpheus* and *Orfeu*, according to the dramatist, was both literary and musical. With the reading of a neoclassical version of the legend fresh in his mind, Morais heard a *batucada* [percussion session] and "began to think about the life of the blacks on the hillside and to Hellenicize their life."[8] He transposed an outline of the Orphean story to a *favela* and composed a musical play in which a Carnival ball serves as the hell to which Orpheus descends. The making of *Orfeu da Conceição* brought together, beyond the specialized and groundbreaking all-black cast, the diverse talents of the poet-playwright, the designer architect Oscar Niemeyer, the artist Carlos Scliar as "visual advisor," and the young composer Antônio Carlos Jobim, who wrote the score and music for the songs. For popular music, the play proved to be, beyond the point of departure for the musically organized French film and the basis of the later Brazilian film, a spawning ground of bossa nova, as seen below. Moreover, the play was a historical opening up to the black voices of the shantytowns (cf. the 1962 song " A voz do morro" [The voice of the hillside] by Jobim and Morais), as well as a preview of the Brazilian musical theatre of the 1960s and 1970s in such works as "Opinião," "Arena canta Zumbi," and "Gota d'água."[9] The guiding social concern of those works, though, is not to be found in Vinícius de Morais's play.

Black Orpheus: Film, Fantasy, and Fate

Though with *Black Orpheus* Camus did not pretend to make any social statements, his direction reflected significant involvement with marginalized African-Brazilian populations. He filmed hundreds of meters during the 1957 Carnival parade in Rio, and he later staged a small event of his own with a local supporting cast of several thousand. In relating a mythical love story, *Black*

Orpheus gives emphasis to festive practices and musical expressions from start to finish. It opens during final preparations for the official beginning of Carnival. The protagonist is a trolley-car conductor, singer-songwriter, and leader of a small samba school in a *favela* that overlooks the city proper. Orfeu is engaged to the stunning Mira, but he falls in love with a visitor from the countryside, Eurydice, whose eventual fatal misfortune in the midst of the revelry is due to a mistake of his. From this point on, the story comprises his attempts at recovering Eurydice. The jealous rage of Mira leads to the death of Orfeu back in the *favela* on the verge of sunrise. In the final scene, an enthusiastic young boy plays Orfeu's guitar as his pal and a young girl dance with joy.

After an initial wave of hopeful news and enthusiasm about Camus' film, reception in Brazil was largely negative. One nationalist objection concerned the wide distance and consequential differences between the final film version and the play by Morais, whose poeticity was lost in the view of many. Most detractors considered the cinematic approach to be overly "exotic," or even demeaning. In noting the foregrounding and centrality of the performative in the film, Stam's analysis articulates central objections: "*Black Orpheus* . . . registers the phenomenal surface of carnival—dance, rhythm, music, color, laughter—but does so ultimately in the service of a stereotypical and Eurocentric vision."[10] In his late teens, Veloso saw the film in Bahia. His youthful desire to be a film critic aside, his reaction to Camus is symptomatic and refers specifically to the question of musical quality in the service of uncomfortable representations:

> . . . the whole audience and I laughed and were ashamed of the bold inauthenticities that French filmmaker allowed himself in order to create a product of fascinating exoticism. The criticism that we Brazilians made of the film can be summarized in this way: How is it possible that the best and most genuine Brazilian musicians should have accepted to create masterpieces to adorn (and dignify) such deceit? (*Verdade tropical* 252)

It is particularly relevant to register the perspective of Carlos Diegues, for what he says both reflects a widely shared view and explains motivations for making a national film version of the story: "I detested Camus' film because it depicts the *favela* in an allegorical way, as a perfect society in which only death is bothersome."[11] In addition, Diegues accounts for the popularity of the film with historical factors: Cold War viewers were pleased to see the musicality and beauty of Rio, to experience something happy and utopian. Locally, what mattered was the social concern of the emerging trend in Brazilian film: "We were preparing Cinema Novo and for us that totally superficial spectacle, transforming the *favela* into a paradise, was inadmissible."[12] Another Brazilian director, contemplating the Palm d'Or that *Black Orpheus* garnered at the premier international film festival, said the film "won Cannes thanks to new Brazilian music," comments that ironically undercut the quality of the cinematography but verify the ultimate importance of the music.[13]

Veloso's insights into Carmen Miranda in his chapter in this volume may also relate usefully to *Black Orpheus*. The Brazilian Bombshell could generate both pride and shame for Brazilians. On the one hand, she was a sensational performer and international success onstage and in film. On the other hand, her act was often perceived as vulgar or exoticized. She had to sing all manner of pseudo-Brazilian material and, with her self-deprecating gestures, she did not necessarily convey mature ideas of the country. In similar fashion, *Black Orpheus*, while not strictly a national product, had inspired pride early on as an award-winning worldwide success that showcased the beauty of the nation's major city and transmitted a definite cultural vigor. The exotic exaggerations would comprise the shameful aspect. Part of Miranda's acceptance abroad, others have concluded, has to do with a certain "de-racialized reading" of the dress and music of Bahia.[14] As for the film, some critics were troubled because they perceived it to concentrate too heavily on the black underclass and/or Carnival as a pagan rite.

In addition to aesthetic and ideological subjects, critiques of *Black Orpheus* have involved some real-world issues of exploitation related to performance and music. In a section of *Unthinking Eurocentrism: Multiculturalism and the Media* dedicated to examination of "the burden of representation," Shohat and Stam consider the participation of minorities in the production apparatus of films. A notable case of Europeans using others can be found in the thousands of black Brazilians who staged an out-of-season Carnival for Camus' cameras with virtually no pay but who saw none of the millions of dollars that *Black Orpheus* generated worldwide.[15] Ramifications of compensation in this cinematic production can clearly be seen on a black-white axis, but they go further. First of all, the white Brazilian musicians who worked on *Black Orpheus* were also exploited. French producer Sacha Gordine did not want to use songs already written for *Orfeu da Conceição* in order to avoid paying royalties to Brazilian publishers. Instead, he commissioned new compositions that he would be able to publish as music editor and thereby claim half of revenue. The composer-lyricist team (Antônio Carlos Jobim—Vinícius de Morais) got only 10 percent on songs that proved to be extremely successful, as has been well documented.[16] Because of the status of the parties involved, this situation became part of the "mythology" or "folklore" in the community of musicians in Brazil.

Orphic Imperatives, Cinematic Scenes, Universal Success

The quality and power of the sound track of *Black Orpheus* have been remarked worldwide. However, the mythical rationale ultimately failed to convince most film critics outside of Brazil. To whatever degree the film is perceived to correspond to the foundational myth, the protagonist remains a lofty musical icon, and an appreciation of the film is enhanced by following allusions to the legend. Aspects of the myth are replayed in diegetic and specifically musical ways. If some find dramatic drawbacks in the film, the music, as had been the case with *Orfeu da Conceição*, may be thought to be all the more important. On another plane, while *Black Orpheus* is a love story and not a documentary or ethnographic film, it does make use of extensive geographical and musical realia, and an honest approach to the cinematic construction calls for both a functional understanding of the songs and for weighing music-related elements against their sources and contexts. While not specifically faulting music in his critique of Camus' film, renowned director Jean-Luc Godard did express concern with its "inauthenticity," a topic that naturally also affected Brazilian reception of the film, as Veloso's comments demonstrated.[17] The question of legitimacy should certainly be extended to music and Carnival, especially since *Black Orpheus* exposed so many people worldwide to Brazil (and since the film has, in fact, been used to illustrate aspects of Brazilian culture).

The film's music comprises full performances, where musicians are both seen and heard in action, and executions in the auditory dimension alone. The three basic types are: (1) *batucada*—percussion sessions with typical Brazilian membranophones and idiophones (e.g., *pandeiro, reco-reco, agogô, cuíca*) in groups of varying size; (2) instrumental versions, and (3) songs, usually with an individual voice. There are five compositions per se: "A felicidade" (Antônio Carlos Jobim-Vinícius de Morais), "Frevo," instrumental (Jobim), "O nosso amor" (Jobim-Morais), "Manhã de carnaval" (Luiz Bonfá-Antônio Maria), and "Samba de Orfeu," instrumental (Bonfá) (see texts in appendix following this chapter). One special segment features the voices and conga-type drums [*atabaques*] of an Afro-Brazilian spirit-possession rite. The generic percussion tracks permeate the film and relate directly to the practice of Carnival. The composed songs operate in particular situations, as seen below. Music—also encompassing such ambient noises as whistles, bird calls, and the hum of human voices—is a highly determinant presence.

The first phrase of the melody of the theme song "A felicidade" [Felicity] is heard over the opening frame, of an ancient frieze of a couple, and the last chord of the concluding composition, "Samba de Orfeu," resonates over the final frame, a wider-angle shot of the frieze that reveals a third countenance. At the outset, *batucada* begins simultaneously with shots of the *favela* and continues with the credits. With brief interludes dominated by dialogue, percussive music in different guises remains virtually constant—at levels of gain (volume) varying from soft, deep background to absolute, loud foreground—for nearly an hour. Overall, nonmusicalized moments of silence are rare. Sound editing, then, is very important in this film. Percussion tracks, songs, voices, and other ambient sound are overlaid and interlaced, a fabric that suggests raucous festivities but also the proximity of others in the *favela*, paths crossing, lives intersecting, and destinies intertwining.

The operative mythemes are both general or paradigmatic (in the category of music, and its command) and specific, tied to syntagms of the legend. The character of Orfeu is special: in the imagination of the boys who admire him, he makes the sun rise with his guitar; he charms women, an aspect that is strong in Morais's play and noted in Viradouro's *samba-enredo*; and as a samba-school leader and singer-songwriter, he is a facilitator of the reversals that Carnival brings. In a broader sense, Orfeu is a "magician" who represents a cultural force, as entire parts of society are moved by music at Carnival time in Rio. Some of the mythical angles or allusions are independent of place and race. A number of salient scenes mold the Orphic persona and practice. When the protagonist finishes his last workday before Carnival, recovering his guitar from the pawnshop takes precedence over getting an engagement ring. When he gives money to another customer who wants to pawn a gramophone, he is enabling revelry, and when the gramophone gets split in two (the cone being taken away and the fiancée Mira leaving the base of the record player behind), there is humorous foreshadowing of the couple's split and of Orfeu's eventual loss of power. Attention is focused on the instrument (the mythical lyre) at his humble house, where he shows the boys an inscription ("Orpheus is my master") and explains that there had been a master before him and that perhaps another would follow (thus setting up the conclusion). Also at the shack, one hears in passing that the cat is named Caruso. More pointedly, after Orfeu sings a new love song, "Manhã de carnaval," he realizes he has been overheard by Eurydice, with whom he exchanges names for the first time. Addressing her, he blends excerpts of the lyric into his speech, a vague explanation of the love story of the mythical couple. Taken with emotion, she says she remembers the words of the song but that it was their melody that she liked. This emphasis on what the Greeks called *melopeia* functions narratologically, as she is deflecting his advances at this early point by diverting attention away from the amorous lyric. Her comment further underscores the enchantment of sound, which transcends words, and connects with the film's final song, "Samba de Orfeu," whose vocal part comprises vocables, syllables without words. One of the boys performs the final song with the deceased Orfeu's "master" chordophone, assuming his role and accounting for the continuity of music, so fundamentally inscribed in the legend.

Beyond blending the mythical name with the characteristic Brazilian genre, the single upbeat performance of "Samba de Orfeu" is an act of closure. The lyrical song "Manhã de carnaval" (of which one hears only half of the lyric of the original composition) also figures only once, co-relating rather literally to the story line as an anticipation of the new love of the couple on the upcoming morning of Carnival. It also illustrates, in the fiction, the enchanting songwriting skills of Orfeu. He is not identified as the author of the key song "A felicidade," with its themes of fleeting felicity, the illusions of Carnival, and new love. Three-quarters of the song are heard in the first minutes of the film, but, in the English-language market release, it is difficult to make associations since no subtitles are provided. Translations are given when Orfeu serenades Eurydice with this song at dawn and makes, as interpreted by the boys who follow him, the sun rise. At this point, the most relevant amorous section of the lyric (the second bridge) is indeed sung. Near the end, as he carries her corpse up the hill, Orfeu sings, in subdued form, half of the first bridge, being cut short by the approaching Furies before he can pronounce melodically the end of Carnival. The complete lyric of the song shows the best musico-poetic self of the author.

As for Carnival music proper, there are two instances of composition. During the introduction to downtown Rio, "Frevo" is heard in the version of a uniformed marching band; it recurs near the tragic end as Orfeu lies prostrate in the dark street. This title designates a type of march typical in the northeastern city of

Recife. In the film scene it represents a manifestation of brass-band music that did constitute a greater presence in street carnival in the 1950s. The central seasonal tune is "O nosso amor," the theme song of Orfeu's neighborhood group. It is heard throughout in instrumental and vocal versions, outside homes in the *favela*, during the rehearsal of the samba school, in the streets during the parade. The simple lyric does no more than declare, anonymously, a mutual love, reflecting the Orpheus-Eurydice binomial. With this focus, the song would not qualify as a modern *samba-enredo*. In the early 1930s, the nascent samba schools did sing such simple tunes, but since the mid-1930s organization and officialization of Carnival in Rio, the sambas of schools have been structured around chosen themes. The annual hymns of the samba schools, especially since the Estado Novo (1938–1945), have usually been intricate and based on aspects of Brazilian history, with folklore and popular culture (including Carnival itself) eventually becoming conventional topics too. In this sense, "A felicidade"—with its references to preparations, dedication, and costumes—is actually closer to the accepted mold of *samba enredo*.

The overall depiction of Orfeu's neighborhood's participation in the larger structure of Carnival also merits comment. The film does show, beyond the suspension of normal public operations, many of the aspects involved in a samba school: for instance, a communal song, making of costumes and props, rehearsals, a coordinated parade, and the pursuit of a prize. There is a six-minute nonstop sequence of samba music and dance, which could be said to exemplify the emphasis on the exotic or to be a long illustration of the phenomenon of rehearsal. But in a larger sense, the film does not communicate the real organizational complexities and extended preparations of a samba school. Stam notes how "little of the creative work that goes into a samba school presentation" and of "the high degree of organization required" are made evident (*Tropical Multiculturalism* 176). For his part, Diegues, aware of the problems with setting in Camus' original film, made a conscious effort to bring his film production and the participating samba school together "so that everything would happen where the story really exists" (Mota).

In addition, the time frame of events in *Black Orpheus* is skewed, as the three (or four) days of Carnival are compressed into one (or the drama simply jumps over two or three days). The identity and level of the school, moreover, are not clear. Already in the late 1950s the city's many samba schools had been grouped into first and second divisions.[18] The film announces and shows footage of the two most historically important samba schools, Portela and Mangueira, the first- and third-place winners in 1957 when the French filmed the parade (unfortunately distant and badly illuminated). The scene in question further implies that their league includes Orfeu's school, which would more naturally be thought of as a smaller-scale, more grassroots guild (i.e., belonging to a lower division).

Despite such incongruencies, one of the filmic originalities of Camus' *Black Orpheus* certainly was, in a very general fashion, the use of Carnival. While the seasonal festivities vibrantly situate the enactment of a mythical love story, they are not the ultimate focus or theme. However that may be, and whatever intentions may be attributed to *Black Orpheus*, foreign gazes (and ears) inevitably fix on Carnival above all, with music maintaining prominence. With respect to the international audience, a notable illustration of the marketing campaign of Camus' film, its success, and the assumptions it makes about viewership and knowledge of Brazil, is the publication of a fictional version of the film.[19] In the French paperback, only three chapters are not wholly plot driven. The first one of these presents the space of the *favela*, while the second features and explains the centrality of Carnival. A third chapter tries to elucidate briefly local spirit-possession rituals in what is called *macumba*. The structure of *Black Orpheus* offers a parallel, for just as there is an extended clip of samba rehearsal, there is a six-minute segment in an African-Brazilian religious temple.

Within an ample festive contextualization, the film appropriates and displays a nonseasonal and spiritual aspect of traditional culture: ceremonies of *umbanda*. The musical dimension of this episode cannot be discussed separately from its religious function, which fits into the general mythical mood of the film. Orfeu searches for Eurydice at the Missing Persons Bureau in an eerie (almost infernal?) government building, which he exits by way of a spacious spiral staircase in a suggestion of a descent into hell. He is taken to a cult house guarded by a barking hound (Cerberus in the myth). Orfeu observes the ongoing ritual until a spirit possession takes place. To help with his own plight, he is told to sing— this is an appeal to his proverbial strength—and having entoned the melody of the initiates (not his own), he hears the voice of Eurydice. She, however, is lost because he does not heed the enjoinder not to look back. He accuses the medium-voice of deceit though it is his own lack of faith that seals the fate of Eurydice, as in the myth. As for real-world correspondences, the cult members, vestments, and music (vocalized *pontos de umbanda* with drum accompaniment) are genuine. The rites depicted in *Black Orpheus* also seem to be, except for the part that links with Orfeu, which wavers between a realistic and an artistic use. There is a wide spectrum of practices in the domain of *umbanda* in Rio, and while mediums generally receive divine spirits rather than souls of the dead, a Kardecist variety does involve personal problem solving and reception of spirits, including those of the recently deceased.[20]

The public domain voice-and-drum *pontos* of the ceremony figure on the historical sound track of *Black Orpheus*. While those items and the pervasive unattributed *batucada* are faithful reflections of specific realities, other manifestations require historical clarifications. It was seen, for instance, that "O nosso amor" is a reliable samba of its time but not as a *samba enredo*. The enchanting "Manhã de carnaval" can be thought of as a *samba-canção*, the sentimental lyrically oriented variety of the genre, in transition toward the bossa nova style that was emerging in Brazil in the late 1950s. In the concluding "Samba de Orfeu," the harmonies and guitar performance style (syncopated plucking of chords with altered tones) also hint at the new development in popular music. Yet the primary vehicle of stylistic innovation is the theme song "A felicidade," with its harmonic and melodic sophistication, relatively restrained vocal performance, and more nuanced guitar attack. The essential point here is one of disjunction: Bossa nova, as scholars have repeatedly emphasized, emerged not in the nearly exclusively African-Brazilian *favela* portrayed in the film but rather in the largely European-Brazilian beachfront district of Rio's southern zone, which has absolutely no part in the film.[21] It is the samba that represents a more "popular" genre, while the bossa nova would be a decidedly middle-class alternative.

While the making and marketing of Camus' film influenced popular music in Brazil and around the world, the line of developments, again, began with the play, for which the talents of Jobim and Vinícius were first brought together. *Orfeu da Conceição* featured the playwright's own "Valsa de Euridice," an oeuverture by Jobim, and four musical settings of texts. On this partnership, Morais affirmed that the play "was the point of departure of the bossa nova movement and bore the fruit . . . of nearly a hundred songs."[22] Of the songs from the play (which were recorded in 1957 on a 10-inch LP), "Se todos fossem iguais a você" ("Someone to light up my life") was the only commercial success. The incipient bossa nova sensibility expressed in the music of the drama developed further with the film tunes, composed by Jobim and Luiz Bonfá, who had played guitar in the play. The voice-over of "A felicidade" in the film was by Agostinho dos Santos, whose recording helped define, in one of the many narratives of origin, a certain style of accompaniment and therefore bossa nova.[23] In his own ascendance, Jobim cites the play as his major "internal" break and the film as his major international career opportunity.[24] Gordine's insistence on new songs for the film proved to be felicitous from the musical point of view, since it resulted in landmark compositions that gained Jobim and Bonfá international fame. It is claimed, for instance, that more than 700 recordings have been made of the latter's "Manhã de carnaval" ("Black Orpheus") in North America alone. In general terms, the "smashing success" of the film was instrumental in "putting bossa nova on the world map."[25] In this regard, the experience of jazz flautist Herbie Mann is exemplary: "Anyone who has seen *Black Orpheus* can surely recall the haunting, primal feelings the movie evoked and the music that counterpointed the dark, erotic story line. . . . When I left that theatre, however, my feelings about Brazil, its music, and music in general had been forever transformed. . . the movie seared Brazil forever in my being."[26] Stam (*Tropical Multiculturalism*, 177) further sees *Black Orpheus* as having paved the way not only for bossa nova but for *axé music* of the 1980s and 1990s.

Given fluctuations of information over the years, it is also useful to verify a few facts of the recording history of the songs of *Black Orpheus*. Antônio Maria wrote words for "Samba de Orfeu," but they were not used in the film; nor were the second verse of "Manhã de carnaval" and the lyric Morais wrote for "Frevo." In 1959, João Gilberto, whose vocal and guitar styles were the models for bossa nova, made two 78-rpm recordings, one with "Manhã de carnaval" and "Frevo" (no vocal) and another with "A felicidade" and "O nosso amor," which did much to popularize the songs. In 1962, well after the heyday of the film, he released a compact with all four tunes. This version of "A felicidade," the film's most enduring song, remains a memorable point of reference for two reasons. First, it stands out at home because the sound track of the film was never released in Brazil, although it has had successive releases in Europe, Japan, and North America.[27] Secondly, Gilberto's version of "A felicidade" features an ingenious arrangement in which the chorus is played to traditional samba accompaniment and the verses are played in his characteristic bossa nova style. This rendering thus both serves as a juxtapositional crystallization of a chapter in the history of urban popular music in Brazil and underscores one of the most important points to retain with respect to the musical material of *Black Orpheus*: the contrast of the fundamentally Afro-Brazilian samba rooted in Carnival and the emergent style that the film helped to disseminate.

Orfeu and the Difference of Space

In the years after Carmen Miranda, no single agent is as important as *Black Orpheus* in the internationalization of Brazilian music and imagery. In general and musical terms, Dieguess's *Orfeu* will inevitably be compared in criticism to its thematic predecessors in film. As for sound tracks and repercussions, historical conditions make it difficult to conceive of this Brazilian film as a whole, or of its sound track in particular, as being able to have an impact on musical spheres comparable, even in relative terms, to that of *Black Orpheus*. When it appeared, color movies and the LP format had not yet even been established definitively. The present context of end-of-the-century globalization, in turn, already implies incorporation and surpassing of a series of technologies involved in the transmission of sound and image (cassette tape, video, CD, Internet, and others), highly accelerated distribution of products, and massive exposure to cultural goods in and from center and periphery alike, specific cases of which may involve considerably less of what was once quite purposefully called "dependence" (e.g., given popular musics of Third World nations). Familiarity with samba and bossa nova is a given in markets of the industrialized world, and contemporary international and Afro-diasporic manifestations of pop music have increased significantly in Brazil. For its part, *Orfeu* quite effectively reflects this last aspect of cultural reality.

On another level, Dieguess's film relates to and calls into question the "myth" of Orpheus within the cinematic domain in several ways. It is, most obviously, another, alternative, filmic reading of the myth of Orpheus. But it also implicitly alludes to the de facto role of *Black Orpheus* as a vehicle of Brazilian culture in Europe, North America, and the rest of the world, notably with respect to music, given the role of Camus' film in the global growth of interest in the sounds of Brazil. The new Brazilian work further implies a challenge to the portrayal of the inhabitants of Rio's hillside shantytowns, to the mystification of a New World Other attributed to the French film. The making of *Orfeu* gives continuity to a twentieth-century cinematic mythification in a specifically Brazilian context, while simultaneously attempting a realist demystification of a certain decomplexified image of Brazil—encompassing general setting, Carnival, and musical representations—largely associated with the previous filmic depiction.

Though irretrievably aware of Rio's famed landscapes, Diegues presents a significantly different Brazil, counterposing the love story, local color, popular cre-

Toni Garrido (center) and Gabriel o Pensador (right) with rock star Lulu
Santos, 1998. Photo by Cristina Granato.

ativity, and innate musicality with certain antilyrical tendencies and unkind situations including domineering drug dealers, deadly weaponry, police invasions,
community confrontations, vulgar sexuality, and vigilante violence. Such hyper-
realism follows a suggestion of the source drama, as seen below, and makes a
tacit statement about the idealizations constructed in *Black Orpheus.* In general,
Camus displayed a mythifying urge, an impulse to beautify. Diegues wants to
head in another direction, tempering impressive views of Rio, the energy of
Carnival, and human beauty with dystopic elements on material and spiritual
planes.

Jean-Luc Godard was critical of Camus' lack of adventure and of the loss of
poetry. His above-cited complaint about inauthenticity also concerns choice of
locations and roles. Godard questions the director's knowledge of Rio and asks,
for example, why not use a jitney driver instead of a trolley-car conductor as
Camus did? He also suggests that Eurydice arrive at Rio's bayside downtown air-

port. There lurks an allusion to Godard's critique in Diegues's depiction of the tragic heroine's arrival in Rio, indeed by air, which is framed by the classic Orphean act of charming: women, the animals of nature, and the sun itself, which rises as he plays the guitar in inspired fashion.

The new Orphean film inexorably extends and expands upon received mythemes, doing so with a local focus that begins with the inclusion of the champion samba school. The archetypal connections in the production of *Orfeu* include touching on both Greek origins and constants of the contemporary urban imaginary, with the mediation of Viradouro's appearance involving elements of diverse character. In 1984 the state of Rio de Janeiro constructed the *sambódromo* [sambadrome], an enormous public parade ground with stadium-like seating, designed for the spectacle of the elaborate presentations of the first-division samba schools of the city's renowned Carnival. While the construction and determination of control of this site did not occur without controversy, the name given to the wide expanse at the end of the avenue is suggestive of social, cultural, and political functions associated with this architectonic spotlight of samba.[28] The name is Praça da Apoteose, or plaza of apotheosis. This Greek term has natural mythical overtones and specific meanings in the context of Carnival. In a literal sense, *apotheosis* connotes the culmination of the parade of each school, the ultimate point of the development (called evolution) of the thematic parade. On a next level, if a samba school is victorious (an expected result that occurs in *Orfeu* and *Black Orpheus* alike), *apotheosis* will refer to the moment of crowning glory, the exaltation to a superior status of the school, its songwriter(s) and its *samba-enredo*.

In another, less concrete sense, there is a degree of apotheosis in that very genre. As seen above, in the late 1930s the Vargas regime encouraged samba schools to derive their yearly themes from Brazilian history, its heroes, or landmarks. By the 1960s, folklore and moments of African-Brazilians' own history came to be established as common sources for theme-sambas. With the increased commercialization of Carnival in the late twentieth century, schools have increasingly chosen to exalt (or target) not only historical names or traditions but contemporary urban phenomena and current public personalities or media stars, including such figures as filmmaker Glauber Rocha (1983), best-selling crooner Roberto Carlos (1987), venerable novelist Jorge Amado (1988), and MPB [Música Popular Brasileira] artist Chico Buarque (1998). In such cases, samba schools do not just reflect an established point of reference but—through their deliberations, selections, and presentations—help to verify definitively the status of given artists as cultural icons, to create, in effect, new points of reference. In the recognition of something or someone as theme of a major samba school, there is an element of apotheotic christening in the realm of popular culture, an indication of the structure of thought in urban legend, an air of mythification in the popular imaginary. When the reigning champion G.R.E.S. (Samba School Recreation Guild) Viradouro performed the theme song "Orfeu, o negro do carnaval" (Gilberto Gomes, Mocotó, Gustavo P. C., Portugal, Dadinho) for *carnaval* 1997, it was paying homage to an artistic icon locally constituted in Morais's play and globally immortalized in the protagonist of *Black Orpheus*, whose musicality is alluded to in the *samba-enredo* via a citation of the lead song ("Tristeza não tem fim/ Felicidade sim"). The making and screening of *Orfeu*, necessarily, comprise further exaltation in this paradigm.

Music is also a crucial historical and cultural marker in *Orfeu*. Diegues, recognizing and assuming "the responsibility of creating another image of Brazil," set out "to make a film in solidarity with the *favela* culture of today,"[29] hence the effort to represent local utilizations of international pop culture. The film includes, beyond playback of Rio's own funk music, local reflections of trends in U.S. black-youth wardrobe, and characters named Be Happy and Maicol (i.e., Michael Jackson).[30] Diegues made a point of not using Camus' sound track in order to "make it clear that the film is not a remake of *Black Orpheus* but an updated version of the play."[31] Morais, after listing his dramatis personae, had added a playwright's note: "since popular slang plays a very important role here, and since people's language is extremely subject to change, if the play is staged, it should be adapted to its new conditions . . . always seeking to update the action as much as possible."[32] This guideline is heeded by Diegues, who, though pointedly using the opening and some other verses of the Brazilian play he admired (including a monologue of Orfeu recorded by Morais himself), sought out considerable assistance to compose a screenplay conceptually and linguistically consistent with the present.[33]

The filmmaker and the musical director extend the suggestion of adaptation to new conditions to musical language as well. *Orfeu* activates a three-part legacy in a varied scheme: (1) three songs from *Orfeu da Conceição* (instrumental versions of Morais's own valse and of another song done with Jobim, as well as the market success "Se todos fossem iguais a você"); (2) the two songs from *Black Orpheus* with highest international visibility ("Manhã de carnaval" and "A felicidade"); and (3) a pair of traditional sambas, "Cântico à natureza (primav-era)" [Song for nature (spring)] (Nelson Sargento-Jamelão, 1959), and, briefly, "Os cinco bailes na história do Rio" [Five dances in the history of Rio] (Silas de Oliveira-Dona Ivone Lara-Bacalhau, 1965), a theme song for Império Serrano school, which interested Veloso since it actually mentions Orfeu. This historical impulse echoes in the rich and exemplary *samba-enredo* that Veloso cocom-posed to anchor the sound track "História do carnaval carioca" [History of Rio Carnival] (see appendix). The new conditions include an original love lyric ("Eu sou você" [I am you], also by Veloso), but they are established above all by the presence of different registers of funk (rap, hip-hop, bass tracks), which enter the public soundscape, over radio and playback speakers, of present-day *favelas* in Rio and throughout the film.[34]

The use of this beat has a significant link to the samba school featured in *Orfeu*. Viradouro is known for staking out new territory, and the percussion di-rector Mestre Jorjão in particular has sought to innovate within the highly codi-fied and circumscribed practice that is Carnival samba. The arrangement of the composition that won first place in 1997 contained a wholly unexpected inter-lude: samba drums pounding out a beat characteristic of the local versions of hip-hop. This unheard-of gesture generated familiar commentary about cultural invasion and contextual appropriateness. Ultimately more relevant to the ques-tion of internationalization is how a samba school's awareness widens the terms of discussion. Hermano Vianna usefully interrelates the role of Olodum, the Bahian *bloco afro* that forged *samba-reggae* and later incorporated electronic pop data, with the samba's school's self-evaluation: "they say it's not funk, they prefer to defend an influence of Olodum. But Olodum itself has quite a bit of foreign influence. In sum, it is an international style of the transatlantic black diaspora."[35]

This angle on a local sounding of a globalized pulse inside a highly mediated tradition opens onto the centerpiece of the sound track of *Orfeu*. The second part of Veloso's *samba-enredo*, penned by rapper Gabriel o Pensador [the thinker], is emphatically rap and hip-hop in rhythm and language. The telling debate provoked by Viradouro's innovation surfaces in the film too, as a police-man explicitly questions and objects to the funk interlude in Orfeu's theme-song samba (toward the end, the superior officer even shoots out a loudspeaker play-ing local funk). From the viewpoint of "new conditions," the samba-school song in this beyond-traditional guise frees itself of unrealistic purity and, if you will, demystifies a rarely challenged given of Carnival music. The victory of the composition by the fictive hero of *Orfeu* is mimetic; it only confirms a real occurrence.

In any medium, an essential part of the Orphic is to assure the continuity of music as enchantment. In the oft-criticized last scene of *Black Orpheus*, the boy who had adulated the deceased hero assumes his role, plays his instrument to make the sun rise as he had, and inspires his young companions to dance gleefully. The penultimate sequence of *Orfeu* shows the inevitable death of the local hero at the hands of the Bacchants; the suggestion of continuity comes in a turn to the loud, colorful television broadcast of the performance of the victorious samba school led by Orfeu. Such a conclusion implies a different kind of carnivalesque apotheosis: the power of electronic media and their hold on popular vision. This episode of Brazilian song and film history, finally, illustrates how the complexity of popular music making in Brazil has grown since the recording of *Black Orpheus*, while celebrating within a universal reprise a mythical continuity in local soundscapes.

Notes

1. Peter Rist and Timothy Barnard, *South American Cinema: A Critical Filmography 1915–1994* (New York: Garland, 1996), 123.

2. Caetano Veloso, *Verdade tropical* (São Paulo: Companhia das Letras, 1997), 252; subsequently in text by author.

3. Robert Stam, "Samba, Candomblé, Quilombo: Black Performance and Brazilian Cinema," in *Cinemas of the Black Diaspora: Diversity, Dependence, and Oppositionality*, ed. Michael T. Martin (Detroit: Wayne State University Press, 1995), which looks specifically at Afro-Brazilian music and cinema, 284–291. Originally in *The Journal of Ethnic Studies* vol. 13, no. 3 (1985), 55–84.

4. See Robert Stam, *Tropical Multiculturalism: A Comparative History of Race in Brazilian Cinema and Culture* (Durham: Duke University Press, 1997), 166–177, cited below; and Charles A. Perrone, "Don't Look Back: Myths, Conceptions, and Receptions of *Black Orpheus*," *Studies in Latin American Popular Culture* 17 (1998), 155–177.

5. The principal source here is Walter A. Strauss, *Descent and Return: The Orphic Theme in Modern Literature* (Cambridge, Mass.: Harvard University Press, 1971). For psychological and philosophical variations in lyric from antiquity to the present (not including film), see also Elizabeth Henry, *Orpheus with His Lute: Poetry and the Renewal of Life* (Carbondale: Southern Illinois University Press, 1992).

6. Elizabeth A. Newby, *A Portrait of the Artist: The Legends of Orpheus and Their Use in Medieval and Renaissance Aesthetics* (New York: Garland, 1987), 2–3. A valuable

approach to musical Orphism, with awareness of the social character of music, is Wilfrid Mellers, *The Masks of Orpheus: Seven Stages in the Story of European Music* (Manchester: Manchester University Press, 1987).

7. For examples analyzed in literature, music, film (including French director Jean Cocteau's *Orphée*), and especially the visual arts, see Judith E. Bernstock, *Under the Spell of Orpheus: The Persistence of a Myth in Twentieth-Century Art* (Carbondale: Southern Illinois University Press, 1991).

8. Quoted by José Eduardo Homem de Mello, *Música Popular Brasileira* (São Paulo: USP-Melhoramentos, 1976), 59; cited below by author.

9. Luiz Tosta Paranhos, *Orfeu da Conceição (tragédia carioca)* (Rio de Janeiro: Editora José Olympio, 1980), 62–63. On "Opinião" and this current in the theatre, see Leslie Damasceno, *Cultural Space and Theatrical Conventions in the Works of Oduvaldo Vianna Filho* (Detroit: Wayne State University Press, 1996). As for Orpheus in Brazilian theatre, in October/November 1995, Rio director Haroldo da Costa reprised "Orfeu da Conceição," merging the original three acts into two and, tellingly, using the major songs from the Camus film. In September 1997, he brought the stage presentation to São Paulo.

10. Robert Stam, *Subversive Pleasures: Bakhtin, Cultural Criticism, and Film* (Baltimore: Johns Hopkins University Press, 1989), 138.

11. Quoted by Denise Mota, "Orfeu espera o carnaval de '98 chegar," *Folha de São Paulo*, September 20, 1997, *Ilustrada*, 4–5; cited below in text.

12. Quoted by Marcelo Bernardes, "Diegues quer ser cineasta popular brasileiro," *Estado de São Paulo*, September 4, 1997.

13. Paulo César Saraceni, *Por dentro do Cinema Novo: minha viagem* (Rio de Janeiro: Nova Fronteira, 1993), 45.

14. Camillo Penna, "Carmen Miranda: Sound-Images and Transcultural Translations," paper presented at BRASA IV conference, Brazilian Identity and Globalization, November 14, 1997.

15. Ella Shohat and Robert Stam, *Unthinking Eurocentrism: Multiculturalism and the Media* (New York: Routledge, 1994), 187; cited in next note.

16. Shohat and Stam cite (n. 218) the most widely respected history of bossa nova, Ruy Castro, *Chega de saudade: a história e as histórias da bossa nova* (São Paulo: Companhia das Letras, 1990); see also Mello, 86.

17. Jean-Luc Godard, "Le Brésil vu de Billancourt," *Cahiers du cinéma* vol. 17, no. 97 (1959); reprint (New York: AMS Press, 1971), 59–60; cited below by author in text.

18. Sérgio Cabral, *As escolas de samba do Rio de Janeiro* (Rio de Janeiro: Lumiar, 1996), 392 ff.

19. Violante do Canto, *Orfeu negro* [fiction] (São Paulo: IBRASA, 1961); trans. of idem (Paris: Séghers, 1959).

20. Diana De G. Brown, *Umbanda: Religion and Politics in Urban Brazil* (Ann Arbor: University of Michigan Research Press, 1986), esp. 20. While Camus' presentation is sensitive for its time, the imposition or loose integration of the myth leaves the scene open to associations with otherworldly irrationality, or an infernal black magic.

Given Orfeu's protests of deceit, one might ask whether the *umbanda* episode can be read as a rejection of African-Brazilian religion. I am grateful to Manuel Vásquez for his advice on this subject.

21. On the history of Carnival samba and the social territory of bossa nova, see José Ramos Tinhorão, *Pequena história da música popular: da modinha à lambada*, 6th ed. (São Paulo: Art Editora, 1991).

22. Vinícius de Morais, preface to *Orfeu da Conceição (tragédia carioca)*, 2nd ed. (Rio de Janeiro: Editora Dois Amigos, 1967), 2; cited below as preface.

23. João Carlos Pecci, *Vinicius sem ponto final*, 2nd ed. (São Paulo: Saraiva, 1994), 260.

24. Quoted by Mello, 17; see also Suzel Ana Reily, "Tom Jobim and the Bossa Nova Era," *Popular Music* vol.15, no. 1 (1996), 8.

25. Chris McGowan and Ricardo Pessanha, *The Brazilian Sound: Samba Bossa Nova and the Popular Music of Brazil*, 2nd expanded ed. (Philadelphia: Temple University Press, 1997), 94.

26. Liner notes to Trio da Paz, *Black Orpheus*. Mann was one of numerous jazz musicians to tour Brazil in the early 1960s and to bring bossa nova back to the United States. The U.S. release of the sound track (which has a few studio selections not actually in the film) calls the music early bossa, neglecting the other genres.

27. The LP was released in several different countries with different notes and cover art; see all the latter at the following Web site: http://www.kudpc.kyoto-u.ac.jp/~yasuoka/Bonfa/Orfeu.html

28. See Roberto M. Moura, *Carnaval: da Redentora à Praça do Apocalipse* (Rio de Janeiro: Zahar, 1986), 79 ff.

29. Quoted by Hugo Sukman, "Não temos mais o direito à inocência," *O globo*, February 22, 1998.

30. The resonance of the theme of Orpheus in film in Brazilian cultural consciousness is also evident in a 1996 *crônica* by Luis Fernando Veríssimo, "Orfeu novo," *Jornal do Brasil*, February 7, 1996, sparked by the visit of superstar Michael Jackson to a *favela* in Rio de Janeiro to film scenes of the music video "They Don't Care About Us" that would also include Olodum in Bahia.

31. Quoted by Maria Lucia Rangel, "A segunda vinda de Orfeu," *Bravo!*, May 1998, 93.

32. Preface, 17. See also his liner notes to the play's sound track.

33. The script was cosigned by anthropologist Hermano Vianna, with subsequent collaborations by poet-novelist Paulo Lins (*City of God*), theatre specialist Hamilton Vaz Pereira, and *favela* sociologist João Emanuel Carneiro.

34. A current sensibility is further shaped on the sound track CD with the addition of two funk-inflected radio remixes. However, unlike *Black Orpheus*, with its emphasis on *batucada*, scenes of *Orfeu* present conventional orchestral variations on themes drawn from the lead songs.

35. Quoted by Pedro Butcher, "Um Orfeu revisitado," *Jornal do Brasil*, October 5, 1997.

Discography

Gilberto, João. *Interpreta Tom Jobim*. EMI Odeon 31 C 052 422005, n/d (ca. 1978).
———. *O mito*. EMI Odeon 31 C 164 791115, 1988.
Trio da Paz. *Black Orpheus*. Kokopelli Records 1299, 1994.
Various. Sound track *Black Orpheus*. Fontana SRF 67520, n/d (ca. 1960).
Various. *Sambas de enredo '98*. BMG 7432153593–2, 1998.
Various. Sound track *Orfeu da Conceição*. EMI Odeon MODB 3056, n/d (1956).
Veloso, Caetano, Toni Garrido et al. Sound track *Orfeu*. Natasha 292.105, 1999.

Appendix

A felicidade

(Antônio Carlos Jobim-Vinícius de Morais)

[Felicity]

Tristeza não tem fim	Sadness has no end
Felicidade sim	Happiness does
A felicidade é como a pluma	Happiness is like a feather
Que o vento vai levando pelo ar	that the wind leads through the air
Voa tão leve, mas tem a vida breve	It flies so light, but its life is brief
Precisa que haja vento sem parar	It needs wind without end
A felicidade é como a gota	Happiness is like a drop
De orvalho numa pétala de flor	Of dew on a flower's petal
Brilha tranqüila, depois de leve oscila	It shines tranquil, after light it wavers
E cai como uma lágrima de amor	And falls like a tear of love
A felicidade do pobre parece	The happiness of the poor seems
A grande ilusão do carnaval	to be the grand illusion of Carnival
A gente trabalha o ano inteiro	People work the whole year long
Por um momento de sonho	To dream for a moment
Pra fazer a fantasia	To make the costume of
De rei ou de pirata ou jardineira	A king, a pirate, a gardener
E tudo se acabar na quarta feira	For all to be over on (Ash) Wednesday
A minha felicidade está sonhando	My happiness is dreaming
Nos olhos da minha namorada	of the eyes of my girlfriend
É como esta noite passando passando	It's like this night passing, passing
Em busca da madrugada	In search of dawn
Falem baixo por favor	Speak softly please
Pra que ela acorde alegre com o dia	So she will awake happily with the day
Oferecendo beijos de amor	Offering kisses of love

Frevo, instrumental (Antônio Carlos Jobim)

O nosso amor (Jobim-Morais)

O nosso amor vai ser assim
Eu pra você, você pra mim
Tristeza, eu não quero nunca mais
Vou fazer você feliz
Vou querer viver em paz

[Our love]

Our love will be this way
Me for you, you for me
Sadness, I want it never more
I will make you happy
I'm going to want to live in peace

Manhã de carnaval (Luiz Bonfá-Antônio Maria)   **[Morning of Carnival]**

Manhã tão bonita manhã
Na vida uma nova canção
Cantando só teus olhos
Teu riso tuas mãos
Pois há de haver o dia em que virás

Morning, such a beautiful morning
A new song in life
Singing only of your eyes
Your laugh your hands
For there will be a day when you
    come

Das cordas do meu violão
que só teu amor procurou
Vem uma voz
Falar dos beijos
Perdidos nos lábios teus

From the strings of my guitar
That only your love sought
A voice comes
To speak of the kisses
Lost in your lips

Canta o meu coração
A alegria voltou
Tão feliz a manhã desse amor

My heart sings
Joy has come back
So happy the morning of this love

Manhã tão bonita manhã
De um dia feliz que chegou
O sol no céu surgiu
E em cada cor brilhou
Voltou o sonho então ao coração

Morning, such a beautiful morning
Of a happy day that arrived
The sun came out in the sky
And in every color shined
Dreams then came back to the heart

Depois deste dia feliz
Não sei se outro dia haverá
Em nossa manhã
Tão bela afinal
Manhã de carnaval

After this happy day
I don't know if there'll be another day
In our morning
So pretty after all
Morning of Carnival

Samba de Orfeu, instrumental (Luiz Bonfá) [Orpheus' samba]

História do carnaval carioca   [History of Carnival in Rio]
(Veloso–Gabriel o Pensador)

Nosso carnaval	Our Carnival
É filho dos rituais das bacantes	Was born of the rituals of the Bacchants
Do coro das tragédias gregas	Of the choruses of Greek tragedies
Das religiões afro-negras	Of the black Afro religions
Das procissões portuguesas católicas	Of the Portuguese Catholic processions
E não tem rival	And it has no rival
"Manhã tão bonita manhã"	Morning, such a beautiful morning
Quando o rancho acabou de passar	When the second line had passed
E deixou no ar um aceno	And left in the air a waving
Ao passado e ao amanhã	at the past and at tomorrow
"Ô Abre Alas"	Hey, make way
Ainda somos do Rosa de Ouro	We're still the Golden Rose [show]
O carnaval da cidade é o tesouro	The city's Carnival is the treasure
que nunca ninguém nos pode roubar	That no one can ever steal from us
(Não rouba não)	(No, you can't do that)
Pois no Estácio	'Cause in the Estacio [district]
Famoso reduto de gente bamba	Famous hangout of hep cats
Nasceu a primeira escola de samba	The first samba school was born
que é rancho, é sociedade, e é cordão	It's a second line, a corporation, a krewe
Quando Hilário saiu	When [founder] Hilario came out
Lá da Pedra do Sal	From Salt Rock [locale]
Rei de Ouros surgiu	The King of Diamonds [group] was born
É carnaval	It's Carnival
O nosso carnaval vai ferver	Our Carnival is going to be hot
Vai fazer o morro descer	It'll make folks come down the hill
Vai fazer o asfalto tremer	It'll make the asphalt shake
Pra ficar legal	To be cool
Tem que ter o quê?	You gotta have what?
Tem que ter bateria (demorou)	You gotta have drums (took a while)
Tem que ter harmonia (demorou)	You gotta have harmony (took a while)
Tem que ter fantasia (demorou)	You gotta have a costume (took a while)
Tem que ter alegria (demorou)	You gotta have happiness (took a while)
E dança, pula, canta, fala	And you dance, jump, sing, speak
E tira da garganta	And get out that shout
Aquele grito que entala	stuck in your throat
E vamos nós, abre alas	And so we go, make way

A nossa voz ninguém cala	No one will silence our voice
Fazendo enredo sem medo	Writing themes without fear
No peito e na mente	In our hearts in our minds
Andando para a frente	Moving ahead
o carnaval é da gente (é do povo)	Carnival is ours (the people's)
o carnaval é do velho (é do novo)	Carnival is the old guy's (the young guy's)
Eu sou Unidos da Carioca	I am Carioca United
Da gema do ovo	Real deal [of the egg yolk]
Desafiando o mal	Challenging evil
Pulando esse muro	Jumping over that wall
Iluminando o escuro	Lighting up the dark
e o futuro	and the future
do nosso carnaval	of our Carnival

▓▓ FOUR ▓▓

Tropicália, Counterculture, and the Diasporic Imagination in Brazil

Christopher Dunn

Since the 1920s, popular music has been celebrated as a privileged vehicle for the production and representation of regional and national identities in Brazil, a tendency that is particularly marked in the case of urban samba. Although the development of modern samba in Rio de Janeiro was mediated by foreign music, it retained an aura of rootedness and authenticity as a cultural practice associated with the urban *povo* [masses], especially the Afro-Brazilian working class.[1] As in other parts of the Americas, music associated with socially marginalized communities would acquire emblematic status for various modernizing projects espousing cultural nationalism and political populism.[2] Popular music would play a central role in the constitution and expression of a cultural patrimony, that ensemble of symbolic goods and practices which help to produce and maintain consensus, mitigating conflicts based on social, racial, ethnic, and regional differences.[3]

By the early 1960s, stylizations of urban samba and rural folk music also gave expression to anti-imperialist critiques and social activism on behalf of the poor. At this time, many left-wing activists believed that the masses were politically "alienated," but nevertheless had revolutionary potential that could be tapped by artists and intellectuals through political and cultural consciousness-raising.[4] They were preoccupied with cultural authenticity and sharply criticized the effects of mass-mediated cultural products from the United States. Nationalist concerns took on greater urgency after the military coup of April 1, 1964, which ousted the populist president João Goulart and installed a right-wing regime allied with the U.S. government and multinational capital interests.

Given the asymmetrical distribution of economic and cultural capital in the world, music that stylistically and discursively affirms local or national belonging may indeed promote solidarity and foment politically and socially progressive attitudes. However, a basic premise of this chapter is that these musical practices are not *by definition* more empowering or efficacious than those informed by exogenous or transnational cultures. As Ingrid Monson has noted, "local traditions may or may not be experienced as liberating from the perspective of the people born within them."[5] Likewise, appropriations of exogenous forms may serve as a marker of class distinction and smug cosmopolitanism, but can also serve to critique reified or prescriptive traditions and identities that artists and audiences may regard as culturally and politically confining.

The post-coup 1960s was a period of crisis for progressive forces in Brazil that provoked a critical rethinking of nationally defined cultural imperatives that were articulated in several fields of artistic production, particularly in popular music. In 1967–1968 two young singer-songwriters from Bahia, Caetano Veloso and Gilberto Gil, led an ephemeral, but high-impact movement known as Tropicália that appropriated local and foreign musical styles and relativized prevailing notions of authenticity in popular music. At the time, musicians identified with a post-bossa nova category known as MPB [Música Popular Brasileira] promoted the politics of cultural authenticity and rejected the international rock movement and its Brazilian surrogates, the Jovem Guarda [Young guard]. Tropicália radically altered the field of Brazilian popular music, creating new conditions for the emergence of eclectic and hybridized experiments in popular music. The Tropicalist movement would also come to be regarded as something of an inaugural moment for a broad range of artistic practices and behavioral styles identified as "countercultural" during the period of military rule.

While critics have recognized the influence of the Tropicalist experience on other MPB artists, pop iconoclasts, and Brazilian rock of the 1970s and 1980s, they have been less attentive to the relationship between Tropicália and Brazilian music informed by cultural practices of the African diaspora and its attendant discourses of racial pride and social critique. After the advent of recording technologies, the musical complexes of the Black Atlantic circulated widely in the twentieth century, generating a transnational diasporic imagination based on comparable, albeit distinct, histories of slavery, colonialism, and racial oppression.[6] In his landmark study *The Black Atlantic* (1993), Paul Gilroy emphasizes the role of popular music in the genesis and development of a black "counterculture of modernity" that is positioned simultaneously within and against the Enlightenment legacy of the West. Gilroy underscores the "syncretic complexity of black expressive cultures" that defy "purist" or "essentialist" notions of racial and cultural "authenticity." His project highlights the dialogic and multidirectional flow of information in the Afro-Atlantic world, yet remains confined to a North Atlantic and Anglophone context.[7] He also pays scant attention to how expressive cultures of the Black Atlantic intersected and dialogued with other countercultural practices of urban youth that emerged in the 1960s and 1970s. The recent history of Brazilian popular music suggests that these connections have been vital to the remapping of personal and collective identities and the reformulation of what is taken to be "authentic" in national culture.

Within their generational and cultural milieu, Gil and Veloso stand out as artists who have engaged intensively with Afro-diasporic culture in order to advance critical perspectives on Brazilian modernity and its attendant discourses of cultural nationalism and authenticity. This chapter examines their roles as cultural mediators positioned at the intersection of countercultural and Afro-diasporic movements in Brazil beginning with Tropicália in the late 1960s.

The Universal Sound

The Third Festival of Brazilian Popular Music, aired by TV Record in São Paulo, marked the beginning of a new phase of internationalization in Brazilian popular music. At this event, Caetano Veloso and Gilberto Gil introduced what they called the *som universal* [universal sound], a synthesis of the tradition of

Brazilian song and the latest developments in international pop. It was the first time that electric instruments were used at a Brazilian music festival.[8] At the time, the use of electric instruments and rock arrangements was often regarded as a capitulation to U.S. cultural imperialism. Gil's "Domingo no parque" [Sunday in the park] was the most innovative musical performance of the 1967 festival.[9] He appeared onstage with the psychedelic avant-rock band from São Paulo, Os Mutantes, and a percussionist who beat out twangy, staccato notes on the *berimbau*, a one-string bowed instrument that sets the rhythm for *capoeira*, an Afro-Brazilian dance/martial art from Bahia. In terms of style and performance, Gil's song made a critical intervention in debates surrounding cultural authenticity in Brazilian popular music. If rock enthusiasts were energized by the electric performance of Os Mutantes, the MPB nationalists could at least find consolation in the rootsy touch provided by the *berimbau*.

Gil and Veloso were devotees of João Gilberto, the primary innovator of bossa nova in the late 1950s, and identified with the legacy of Brazilian popular song. Yet they had also grown impatient with post-bossa nova musicians who sought to define aesthetic priorities according to the imperatives of a nationalist and populist cultural project that would put pressure on the military regime. For sectors of the MPB camp, folksy and defiantly unplugged protest music based on rural musical forms best expressed the hopes for future redemption of the *povo*.[10] In contrast, Gil and Veloso began to engage with the musical innovations of the Beatles, Jimi Hendrix, and James Brown, together with Afro-Brazilian and Spanish American musical forms. Veloso recalled their position in Sartrean terms: "By using electric guitars in melodic compositions with elements of Argentine tango and African things from Bahia, we assumed a posture of 'being-in-the-world'—we rejected the role of the Third World country living in the shadow of more developed countries."[11] For his part, Gil claims that he "identified with the whole liberationist attitude of America, the New Left, American university life, new experimental literature and theater, the Black Power experience in the United States, drug experimentation . . . with the iconoclastic attitude of internationalist youth."[12] It is worth noting that Gil found inspiration in a broad range of cultural and political movements and phenomena that were not necessarily allied in the United States.

Gil and Veloso were joined in São Paulo by several colleagues from the Bahian artistic scene, including the vocalist Gal Costa, singer-songwriter Tom Zé, and poets José Carlos Capinan and Torquato Neto. They developed productive artistic relationships with key figures of the literary and musical vanguards of São Paulo. Concrete poet and theorist Augusto de Campos wrote enthusiastic reviews of their work in the local press and later introduced them to the work of modernist iconoclast Oswald de Andrade, whose poetics of *antropofagia* [cultural cannibalism] directly inspired Tropicalist appropriations of exogenous styles.[13] Meanwhile, the Bahians began work with several composers of the experimental Música Nova movement, most notably with Rogério Duprat, who had introduced Gil to Os Mutantes and wrote the arrangements for "Domingo no parque."

By early 1968, the so-called *grupo baiano* [Bahian group] and its counterparts from São Paulo had begun to elaborate a cultural project which was dubbed *tropicalismo* or *Tropicália* in the mainstream press.[14] As a cultural movement, Tropicália defies any compact definition, and as a specifically musical phenomenon it resists classification in terms of style or rhythm. On one level, it may be understood as a certain cultural sensibility related to the political and existential crises of left-wing urban artists, intellectuals, and students in Brazil during the late 1960s. It is worth briefly examining this context. The military coup had been regarded as a terrible aberration which would inevitably falter under the pressure of mass mobilization.[15] After the coup, a viable opposition movement failed to materialize, but a lively oppositional cultural scene developed in Rio de Janeiro and São Paulo. However, under the repressive conditions of military rule, artists and activists remained largely isolated from a working-class constituency.[16]

In March 1967, hard-line forces within the military maneuvered their more moderate counterparts out of power and the redemptive hopes for a democratic civilian restoration seemed increasingly remote. Instead of elaborating a cultural project based explicitly on political protest, the Tropicalists focused on the dilemmas and aporias of Brazilian modernity. The literary and cultural critic Roberto Schwarz provided the first in-depth analysis of the movement, arguing that the Tropicalists proposed an ambiguous national allegory which juxtaposed archaic, underdeveloped emblems of Brazil with the "white light of ultra-modernity."[17] For Schwarz, the Tropicalist allegory was ultimately founded on the privileged status of artists who could satirize the failings of Brazilian modernity from a position of cosmopolitan irony.[18] Subsequent scholarship has elaborated on this allegorical reading of Tropicália, even while disputing Schwarz's contention that Tropicalist representational strategies were absurdist and politically innocuous. Celso Favaretto, for example, argued that the Tropicalist allegory derives its critical effect precisely from its refusal to resolve historical contradictions, thereby producing an indeterminate and discontinuous image of Brazilian modernity.[19] These disparate fragments could then be activated in order to expose that which was concealed or effaced by official culture.

Tropicália Otherwise

The 1960s saw international articulations of new individual and collective subjectivities based on race, ethnicity, gender, and sexual orientation. Frederic Jameson relates the emergence of these new "subjects of history" to "something like a crisis in the more universal category that had hitherto seemed to subsume all the varieties of social resistance, namely the classical conception of social class."[20] In the Brazilian context, Tropicália was an early response to the crisis described by Jameson.[21] Silviano Santiago, for example, related Tropicália to a larger critique of the Brazilian left and its inability to comprehend "signs of alterity" that resist dialectical resolution.[22] Elsewhere he argued that the Tropicalists sought to "insert into a universal context those values that were marginalized during the process of the construction of Brazilian culture."[23] More recently, Liv Sovik has detected in Tropicália a specifically postmodern sensibility that evokes the quotidian life of "internal Others"— social, racial, and sexual subalterns—without exalting them as the source of cultural authenticity and revolutionary transformation.[24] The Tropicalists did not consciously inaugurate a "cultural politics of difference" in Brazil, but they did propose a discourse of alterity and marginality that encouraged more explicit expressions of new subjectivities in popular culture in the following decade.[25]

In the final months of 1968, Gilberto Gil began to articulate publicly an affinity for international black music. During performances, he often wore a stylized African tunic or a Black Panther-style leather jacket, and grew a beard and an afro. At the eliminatory round of the Third International Festival of Song (FIC III) he performed "Questão de ordem" [Question of order], a song clearly inspired by Jimi Hendrix that satirized political orthodoxies of the regime and the opposition. The jury disqualified him, and even journalists sympathetic to the Tropicalist project criticized him.[26] Weeks later, Gil and Caetano Veloso staged an alternative event at the Sucata nightclub in Rio during the final rounds of the

FIC III, which featured international pop artists. During one of the Sucata shows, Gil was joined onstage by Jimmy Cliff, who was representing Jamaica in the FIC III. They performed "Batmacumba," a song featured on the group's concept album, *Tropicália ou panis et circencis* (1968), which combined rock guitar riffs and Afro-Brazilian percussion.[27] This was a significant diasporic moment that prefigured Gil's exploration of reggae music in the 1970s and Cliff's involvement with the Brazilian music scene, which continues to date. In 1980, Gilberto Gil and Jimmy Cliff performed together throughout the country, stimulating further the expansion of reggae culture in Brazil.

Mutual influence also is evident in the recordings of the Tropicalists and singer-songwriter Jorge Ben, who had been experimenting with fusions of samba, R&B, and Jovem Guarda-style rock for several years. In late 1968, Jorge Ben made regular appearances on the Tropicalist television program "Divino maravilhoso." Veloso has affirmed that "Jorge Ben was not only the first great black composer since bossa nova, . . . but more importantly, he was also the first to make [his blackness] a stylistic determinant."[28] On his eponymous album of 1969, for example, Ben mixes English and Portuguese in a song for a local bandit: "Take it easy my brother Charles / Take it easy meu irmão de cor [my brother of color]." Gil and Ben later recorded *Gil e Jorge* (1975), an acoustic jam session that foregrounded their explorations of Afro-Brazilian culture. Although not typically recognized as a participant in the Tropicalist movement per se, Jorge Ben was one of the primary musical interlocutors of the Bahian group during and after the movement. Together with Gil, he articulated the specifically Afro-Brazilian and Afro-diasporic cultural dimensions of Tropicalist and post-Tropicalist musics.

Although the Tropicalists were criticized most severely by left-wing nationalists, they eventually provoked suspicions among military authorities who were disturbed by their anarchic and carnivalesque public "happenings." In late December 1968, Veloso and Gil were detained by agents of the military police, jailed for two months, placed under house arrest, and eventually exiled to London in July 1969. During the period of house arrest in Salvador, Gil recorded an album heavily marked by soul and R&B that also featured an exultant samba, "Aquele abraço," in which he sends an "embrace" to the Brazilian people, especially the city of Rio de Janeiro. It was a farewell to the city and to the nation on the eve of his departure. The song, later included on Gil's third solo album (1969), was enormously popular and stayed at the top of the charts for several months.

Soon after arriving in London, he was awarded the prestigious Golfinho de Ouro [Golden Dolphin] for "Aquele abraço." The award was offered each year by the Museu da Imagem e do Som [Sound and Image Museum] in Rio de Janeiro, an institution that had previously been very critical of Gil and the Tropicalists for deviating from Brazilian musical traditions. Gil rejected the award and wrote a scathing rebuke that was published in the alternative newspaper *O pasquim* in 1969. What starts off as a diatribe against the museum for its folkloric conception of popular music develops into a more profound critique of paternalism and racism in Brazilian culture:

> I have no reason not to refuse an award given for a samba which [the museum] supposes was made to defend the "purity" of Brazilian popular music. . . . Let it be clear . . . that "Aquele abraço" doesn't mean that I am "regenerated," that I've become a "good negro samba player" [*bom crioulo puxador de samba*] which they want from all blacks who really "know their place."[29]

Given the history of samba and state power since the 1930s, Gil's repudiation of the stereotypical black musician who is supposed to play samba amounts to a brazen critique of dominant cultural paradigms. His rejection of "purity" is especially prescient in its questioning of the limits imposed on black artists in the name of racial or cultural authenticity, an issue taken up years later by African and Afro-diasporic musicians around the world.[30]

While in exile, Gil and Veloso circulated in the musical milieu of "swinging London," taking opportunity to see live performances of top rock acts including Jimi Hendrix, the Rolling Stones, and John Lennon and the Plastic Ono Band.[31] They also performed on occasion and even shared the stage with Sérgio Mendes at the Royal Festival Hall in 1970. For this event, Caetano Veloso was billed as "Brazil's Leading Contemporary Folk/Rock Artist," a description that was ironic given his critique of folkish acoustic music in Brazil. One critic from *The Guardian* reported that he enjoyed their "sensual calypso," but remarked that the Bahians still had not become "acclimated to European tastes."[32] Gil and Veloso looked upon these kinds of misunderstandings with a measure of humor and irony. The poster for their Royal Festival Hall concert announced: "Our guitar playing is bad, our technique is primitive, our English is awful. But we are very interesting people."

Gilberto Gil immersed himself in the vibrant countercultural scene of London, where he recorded his fourth album (1971), featuring new compositions in

Poster for Royal Festival Hall concert of Gil and Veloso, 1970. Courtesy of Abril Imagens.

English. Working together with lyricist Jorge Mautner, he began to articulate themes of exile and redemption in songs such as "Babylon," which suggests an identification with the liberationist discourse of Jamaican reggae. Caetano Veloso, for his part, became the first Brazilian artist to make an explicit reference to this emerging Caribbean musical culture in London in the song "Nine out of Ten" on the LP *Transa* (1972): "I walk down Portobello Road to the sound of reggae / I'm alive." Although the work of both artists still evidenced greater affinities with Anglo-American rock, their condition as political exiles interacting with Caribbean immigrants instigated new diasporic perspectives that would become more explicit later on in the decade. Of particular salience was their embrace of reggae, which they introduced to Brazil upon their return.

Contracultura

Veloso and Gil returned to Brazil definitively in 1972, during the most repressive phase of military rule. The armed opposition had for the most part been liquidated and many political activists were either in jail or in exile. The lively and highly contested cultural terrain of the late 1960s had given way to a context of political disillusionment and social malaise combined with new countercultural perspectives on personal liberation through psychotherapy, drug experimentation, macrobiotics, and non-Western religions. This new sensibility, often referred to as *desbunde* [drop out] or *curtição* [trip out], found expression in alternative journals, underground films, and new experiments in popular music inspired by Tropicália. Of all the Tropicalists, Gil was the most identified with this counterculture—he followed a macrobiotic diet, espoused tenets of Buddhism, and experimented with drugs.

According to Heloísa Buarque de Hollanda, the urban countercultural milieu of the early 1970s tended to identify less with the *povo* or "revolutionary proletariat" and more with racial and sexual minorities and other groups regarded as "marginalized."[33] These communities seemed to offer symbolic refuge to hippies and other countercultural adherents who felt alienated from the patriotic discourse of the "economic miracle" touted by the military regime. In the early 1970s, many of them gravitated to Bahia, which they regarded as a privileged site of telluric and ludic pleasure away from the fast-paced life of Rio and São Paulo. Veloso remembers that "Salvador—with its electric and liberated carnival, with its deserted beaches and beach villages, with its colonial architecture and its Afro-Brazilian religions—became the preferred city of the *desbundados* [dropouts]."[34] Another observer noted a reciprocal exchange of discourses, practices, and styles between the largely middle-class counterculture and working-class black youth in Bahia during this time.[35] There was a resurgence of pop songs celebrating Afro-Brazilian culture, particularly the Candomblé religion, a thematic current developed by Dorival Caymmi beginning in the late 1930s.[36] Countercultural allegiance to Afro-Brazilian religion and culture was most notably dramatized in 1976, when Gil, Veloso, Gal Costa, and Maria Bethânia embarked on a national tour to promote *Doces bárbaros* [Sweet barbarians], a concept album that featured several songs about Candomblé deities, the *orixás*. The title track articulates insurgent designs to be carried out by the "sword of Ogun," the "blessing of Olorun," and the "lightning bolts of Iansã."

Under pressure from moderate sectors of civil society, the military regime initiated a period of decompression [*distensão*] in the mid- to late 1970s. New possibilities and imperatives came into focus with the emergence of independent social and political movements representing blacks, women, and urban labor. This period also marked the resurfacing of public controversy among various sectors of the left-wing opposition. Many of these debates concerning the role of the intellectual, the social and political efficacy of art, cultural imperialism, and the relationship among cultural producers, media industries, and the state had already been rehearsed in the 1960s. The touchstone for the most heated polemics was an interview given in August 1978 by filmmaker Carlos Diegues, who invoked the specter of "ideological patrols" to denounce his critics of the orthodox left. Several mainstream and alternative newspapers and magazines immediately seized upon the trope and began soliciting opinions from public intellectuals and artists. Two university professors compiled a collection of their own interviews relating to the polemic. Several people interviewed had recently returned from abroad following the passage of an amnesty bill for political exiles in August 1979. Many were skeptical of revolutionary projects and critical of ideological positions that had predominated in the 1960s. Fernando Gabeira, a former urban guerrilla involved in the kidnapping of the American ambassador in 1969, stated: "In the 1960s I criticized my position as a petit-bourgeois intellectual; now in the 1970s, I'm advancing this self-criticism, analyzing my position as a *macho latino*, as a white guy, and as an intellectual."[37] The Tropicalist movement was a key point of reference for these emerging critiques. Gil and Veloso found themselves again engaged in heated polemics with artists and critics who doubted the oppositional value of their political and aesthetic positions.

Blackitude Brasileira

The 1970s saw the proliferation of commodified forms of African-American popular culture throughout the Third World, with especially strong resonance in postcolonial African and Caribbean nations. In several different contexts, soul music, blaxploitation films, and African-American sports luminaries had an impact on emerging Pan-African and diasporic youth cultures, generating "contingent modernities" that were often at odds with state-sanctioned culture.[38] Manthia Diawara describes the significance of African-American cultural and political icons for his cohort while growing up in Bamako, the capital of Mali, in the mid-1960s:

> For me and for many of my friends, to be liberated was to be exposed to more rhythm & blues, to be up on the latest news about Muhammad Ali, George Jackson, Angela Davis, Malcolm X, and Martin Luther King Jr. These American

heroes were becoming an alternative source of cultural capital for African youth. They enabled us to subvert the hegemony of *francité* after independence.[39]

Postcolonial Malians found in African-American culture and politics a symbolic repertoire to critique French universalism and paternalism. In a similar fashion, young Afro-Brazilians were beginning to appropriate these cultural products and icons to challenge the nationalist ethos of *brasilidade* [Brazilianness], which tended to obfuscate racial discrimination and inequality by exalting the nation's *mestiço* identity. In other words, cultural processes related to a transnational, diasporic hybridity would function as a critique of an established notion of hybridity (e.g., *mestiçagem*) associated with national identity. African-American popular culture, with its emphasis on racial pride and social protest, served as a symbolic marker for delineating black specificity in Brazil, a society that tended to blur these distinctions.

In the mid-1970s, a cultural movement dubbed "Black Rio" or "Black Soul" emerged in the working-class neighborhoods of Rio de Janeiro's northern zone. Inspired directly by the musical, visual, and sartorial styles of African-American soul and funk cultures, the movement was quickly reproduced in other Brazilian capitals such as São Paulo, Belo Horizonte, and Salvador. The Black Rio movement revolved primarily around dance parties that attracted thousands of youths in platform shoes, bell-bottom slacks, and afro hairstyles. Recordings of pre-disco funk from the United States dominated the scene, yet local funk-samba fusion bands, like Banda Black Rio, also produced innovative records.[40] A new generation of Afro-Brazilian singer-songwriters began to record songs influenced by soul, R&B, and blues.

The Black Rio movement was criticized in the Brazilian press from several angles. Conservative critics allied with the military regime, such as Gilberto Freyre, charged that soul music was an insidious importation of African-American cultural and political discourses that were irrelevant to Brazil's "racial democracy."[41] Some Afro-Brazilian activists, including samba musicians, criticized the movement for its lack of cultural authenticity.[42] One black professional denounced it as a cynical marketing scheme based on racial agitation: "I feel that there is a move towards racial radicalization in Brazil. I think this is a dangerous game designed to stimulate racism as a marketing strategy for the sale of consumer products specifically for blacks."[43] Leftists critiqued Black Rio on the grounds that it was mere entertainment, produced and commodified by multi-

national capital, which diverted attention from class politics. The soul movement was ultimately ambiguous: if on the one hand it was a highly commodified
product complicit with global capital, it also advanced a self-conscious diasporic
identity among young Afro-Brazilians. Black Rio faded in the early 1980s, but
bailes funk [funk dances] continued to proliferate in predominantly black working-class zones of major Brazilian cities. In the 1990s, a Brazilian rap movement
also emerged, giving voice to more aggressive critiques of racial discrimination
and social marginality.

In Salvador, Bahia, where Afro-Brazilians constitute about 85 percent of the
population, the Black Soul movement had particular repercussions, contributing to a local phenomenon known as *blackitude baiana*.[44] Between 1974 and
1980, new Carnival organizations, like Ilê Aiyê, Malê Debalê, Olodum, and
Muzenza were formed to disseminate aesthetic and political values based on racial affirmation. These developments were inspired as much by local cultural
practices, like Candomblé and samba, as by transnational phenomena such as
Pan-Africanism, Third Worldism, anticolonial liberation movements (particularly in Lusophone Africa), Black Power, soul, funk, and later reggae and rap
music. By the mid-1980s, new forms of Afro-Bahian music, characterized by new
hybrid rhythms such as *samba-reggae*, began to circulate nationally. Almost from
the beginning, the new Afro-Bahian music was transnational and diasporic in
terms of musical and discursive values.

Gil and Veloso lent their considerable cultural capital to these new Afro-Brazilian cultural movements, both in published interviews and recorded songs.
Countering the denunciations of Brazilian soul in the national press, Veloso supported the movement in terms of identity politics: "I like seeing Brazilian blacks
identify with American blacks. I adore Black Rio. I think the blacks are affirming
themselves more as blacks than as Brazilians and this is important."[45] Lélia Gonzales, one of the founding leaders of the Movimento Negro Unificado [MNU—
Unified Black Movement], claimed that Gil gave a "big boost" to the black
movement by performing at MNU-sponsored events when other artists refused
to participate for fear of being associated with a movement perceived as radical
and divisive.[46] While other MPB artists and critics criticized these affirmative
Afro-Brazilian cultural movements, often on the grounds that they were not au-
thentically Brazilian, the Tropicalists embraced them as an expression of diasporic modernity and as a vital component to the general critique of authoritari-
anism in Brazil.

Reinventing Brazil

In 1977, Gil and Veloso traveled to Nigeria to represent Brazil at the Second International Festival of Black Art and Culture (FESTAC), which featured global luminaries of black music such as Stevie Wonder and Miriam Makeba. At this event, they also had contact with the Nigerian musician Fela Kuti, the leading proponent of Pan-African and diasporic Afrobeat.[47] Brazil's official participation in this international cultural event was fraught with its own ambiguities and contradictions. The Brazilian government was developing extensive diplomatic and commercial relations with postcolonial Africa (especially the recently independent Lusophone nations) even as it ruled a nation marked by pronounced racial inequality and maintained close ties with the apartheid regime of South Africa. On one level, participation in FESTAC served the interests of the Brazilian government, which was eager to capitalize on historical and cultural connections with West Africa.[48] Yet it would also give impetus to the Afro-diasporic turn in Brazilian popular music.

Gil and Veloso subsequently recorded albums inspired by their experiences in West Africa and by the new Afro-Brazilian cultural movements. Veloso's album *Bicho* (1977) features a song based on Nigerian *juju* music, "Two naira fifty kobo" (a typical cab fare in Lagos at that time), which invokes a divine force that "speaks Tupi, speaks Yoruba" and affirms the cultural affinities between Brazil and Nigeria. *Bicho* also included several upbeat disco-inflected songs like "Odara," a Yoruba term commonly used by Candomblé practitioners to signify "good" or "positive." Veloso promoted the album with a series of performances with Banda Black Rio in which he actively encouraged audiences to dance, which is unusual for MPB concerts. In response to the so-called ideological patrol of the traditional left, Veloso slyly advanced the notion of an "*odara* patrol" to stigmatize the Eurocentrism of his critics on the Left and the Right.[49] Such use of the term *odara* owed much to a romantic countercultural imagination that often associated black culture with corporal liberation, collective exaltation, and freedom from instrumental rationality.[50] Nevertheless, these songs also located Afro-Brazilian culture at the very center of Brazilian modernity, instead of assigning it a premodern role as the bearer of cultural purity.

In the same year Gil recorded *Refavela*, a brilliant and far-reaching reflection on Africa and Afro-Brazilians within a contemporary diasporic perspective. It was the second in a series of albums with the prefix *re* in the title, suggesting a period of reinvention and regeneration for the artist and for the nation as it entered a period of gradual political opening. The title song, for example, celebrates the *favela* [shantytown] as the locus of black creativity and social activism while invoking emergent cultural movements such as Black Rio. The lyrics suggest that the Black Rio movement had the potential to revitalize poor Afro-Brazilian communities of the *favela* by linking them symbolically with Africans and Afro-descendants around the world. One stanza, for example, describes the "paradoxical" relationship between the local and the transnational in diasporic culture:

> A refavela / Revela a escola / De samba paradoxal
> Brasileirinho / Pelo sotaque / Mas de língua internacional
>
> [The refavela / Reveals the paradoxical / samba school
> Quite Brazilian / In its accent / But international in its language]

Charles Perrone detects in this song connections to the cosmopolitanism of the Tropicalist project: "The 'paradoxical samba' that Gil composes and defends is the logical extension of that Tropicalist position to the specific sector of black Brazilians."[51] On the same album, Gil recorded "Ilé Ayê," a funky pop version of "Que bloco é esse? [What's that group?] (P. Camafeu), a 1975 Carnival hit and a defiant affirmation of the "black world" in the face of racial prejudice:

> Branco se você soubesse o valor que preto tem,
> tu tomava um banho de piche e ficava preto também
>
> [White guy, if you understood the value of blacks,
> you would bathe in tar and become black too]

Other compositions such as "Babá Alapalá" and "Balafon" underscore the historic and contemporary cultural connections between West Africa and Brazil, especially Bahia. English versions of these two songs were later recorded on the album *Nightingale* (1979), Gil's first attempt to break into the U.S. pop market, targeting primarily an African-American audience.

Refavela provoked controversy and dissent in the popular press, revealing that these kinds of gestures of racial affirmation posed some difficulties for sectors of the Brazilian critical establishment. Writing for *Jornal do Brasil*, music critic Tárik de Souza dubbed Gil's effort "rebobagem" [restupidity], and interpreted the album as an imitation of soul music with "confused lyrics."[52] He seemed particularly incensed that Gil would "reduce to mere soul" Tom Jobim's canonical bossa nova composition "Samba do avião" ("Song of the Jet"). Other critics ridiculed Gil's new personal aesthetic when he began wearing braids with cowry shells and West African dashikis. As Gonzales once remarked, Gilberto Gil "is a guy who disturbs" precisely because he intervenes on the symbolic level.[53]

The greatest hit of Gil's career came in 1979 with the song "Não chore mais," a Portuguese version of Bob Marley's reggae ballad "No Woman, No Cry." His version coincided with the beginning of political opening and was associated with a popular movement calling for amnesty for political exiles. According to Gil, the song sought to associate Jamaican Rastafaris and Brazilian hippies who were persecuted for smoking marijuana.[54] But it is also a ballad of mourning for the victims of authoritarian rule and a song of hope urging Brazilians to focus on the future:

> Amigos presos /Amigos sumindo assim / Pra nunca mais /
> Tais recordações / Retratos do mal em si / Melhor é deixar pra trás

> [Friends arrested / Friends just disappearing / Forever/ These memories /
> Portraits of evil incarnate / Better to leave it all behind]

At the end of the song, the tempo speeds up to a danceable beat as Gil intones "*tudo, tudo, tudo vai dar pé*," an almost literal translation of Bob Marley's "everything is gonna be all right." The overall effect of the song is to situate democratic aspirations in Brazil within the context of Third World and Afro-diasporic struggles.

Tropicalist Reprise

During the 1990s, Tropicália reemerged as a key point of reference for new musical and cultural movements and the subject of several public commemorations, most notably during Carnival. In 1994, as the famous samba school Mangueira of Rio de Janeiro paid tribute to the "sweet barbarians" (Gil, Veloso, Gal Costa, and Maria Bethânia), the *bloco afro* Olodum from Salvador celebrated Tropicália and its legacy as its Carnival theme. Combining social critique with pop appeal, Olodum had gained national and international fame in the late eighties and early nineties with its percussive fusions of samba, reggae, and other Afro-Caribbean rhythms. Reveling in cosmopolitan hybridity, the group proclaimed in one of its Tropicalist theme songs (featured on the album *O movimento*) that "Olodum is hippie/ Olodum is pop/ Olodum is reggae/ Olodum is rock/ Olodum has flipped out." Another song from the same album contemplated the technological modernization of two famous Candomblé temples typically associated with premodern African tradition: "parabolic antennas in Gantuá/ computers in Opô Afonjá/ Tropicalists poets of light." In Olodum's reading of Tropicália, Afro-Bahian culture is represented as cosmopolitan and ultramodern, not as a timeless reservoir of tradition. The 1998 Carnival of Salvador, Bahia, was entirely dedicated to Tropicália, which occasioned the recording of new versions of Tropicalist classics by contemporary Bahian pop bands playing *axé music*.[55]

Traces of Tropicália are also evident in *mangue beat* from Recife, a musical movement that combines local forms such as *baião*, *embolada*, and *maracatu* with elements of heavy metal, rap, funk, and reggae. The leading band of the *mangue* movement, Chico Science & Nação Zumbi, issued a playful manifesto in the liner notes of its first recording that suggested affinities with Tropicália, seventies counterculture, and Afro-diasporic music: "Mangueboys and manguegirls are individuals interested in comics, interactive TV, hip-hop, street music, John Coltrane, non-virtual sex, ethnic conflict, and all advances in applied chemistry related to the alteration and expansion of consciousness." The band's second album, *Afrociberdélia*, included sampled riffs of Tropicalist recordings, vocal tracks by Gilberto Gil, and a drum 'n' bass-inspired version of Jorge Mautner's "Maracatu atômico," a post-Tropicalist song that had been recorded by Gil in the 1970s.

Gil and Veloso also produced a rereading of the Tropicalist experience on their collective album, *Tropicália 2*, from 1993. The album references artistic projects and key figures related to the Tropicalist moment—Cinema Novo, concrete poetry, Tom Zé, and Jimi Hendrix—and also engages such recent musical phenomena in Brazil and abroad as *samba-reggae* of the Bahian *blocos afro* and rap music. Although the album was commemorative and celebratory, the two Bahians did not shy away from social and political critique. On the feature track, "Haiti," Veloso describes witnessing police violence against poor black youth at an Olodum festival in Pelourinho, the historic center of Salvador:

> Não importa nada: nem o traço do sobrado
> Nem a lente do Fantástico, nem o disco do Paul Simon
> Ninguém, ninguém é cidadão
>
> [Nothing matters: Not even the outline of the villa
> Not even the lens of Fantástico, not even Paul Simon's record
> Nobody, nobody is a citizen]

By referencing the presence of the film crew from a popular nationally televised program and celebrated collaborations with Paul Simon, Veloso underlines the global prestige and popularity of Olodum. Yet the scene reminds Veloso of Haiti in the early 1990s under a repressive military regime: "O Haiti é aqui, O Haiti não é aqui" [Haiti is here, Haiti is not here]. "Haiti" is a slow rap, punctuated occasionally by citations of drums playing in Olodum's *samba-reggae* style. Diasporic musical forms and textual references function as a critique of the local context.[56]

George Lipsitz identifies Afro-diasporic music with an emergent postcolonial sensibility that evidences a certain measure of skepticism regarding the primacy of nation-states in addressing historically constituted social and political dilemmas.[57] Anti-imperialist calls for "national liberation" have ceded to a multiplicity of discourses that foreground the contradictions and conflicts of the national project itself. Of course, the national context remains important since the flows of economic and cultural transnationalism do little to undermine the forbidding obstacles of borders and visas for most people, especially the citizens of poor nations. Yet the global circulation of material and symbolic goods may have a considerable impact on local and national debates.

In some ways, Tropicália was akin to a postcolonial critique in that it recognized the peripheral position of Brazil in the world economy, but also challenged static notions of national culture. The vehicle of this critique often involved the cultural products originating from, or mediated by, the United States and Europe, which provoked charges of political alienation and inauthenticity. One prominent historian of popular music, for example, suggested that there was an organic link between the international orientation of Tropicália and the economic program of the military regime with its heavy emphasis on multinational capital investment. In his estimation, the Tropicalists "served as a vanguard for the government of 1964 in the realm of popular music."[58] Among other limitations, this homology does not encompass the ways in which Tropicália foregrounded the glaring social contradictions and the repressive mechanisms of modernization under military rule. This critique also flattens out international popular music into a simple tool of neocolonial domination, ignoring how it may also serve as a conduit for countercultural, anti-racist, and anti-imperialist discourses.

In the case of Brazil, creative appropriations of transnational aesthetics and discourses have contributed to a broader critique of prescriptive ideologies of

Gilberto Gil performs in New York, 1995. Photo © by Jack Vartoogian.

national identity. Tropicália and the subsequent work of Veloso and Gil inaugurated this critique in the realm of popular music, responding to and inspiring new expressions of Brazilian modernity inscribed within global countercultural and Afro-diasporic dynamics.

Notes

1. See Hermano Vianna, *The Mystery of Samba: Popular Music and National Identity in Brazil* (Chapel Hill: University of North Carolina Press, 1998).

2. For a detailed discussion of musical nationalism among modernist intellectuals, see José Miguel Wisnik, "Nacionalismo musical" in Wisnik and Enio Squeff, *O nacional e o popular na cultura brasileira: música* (São Paulo: Brasiliense, 1983), 131–152.

3. Néstor Gárcia-Canclini, *Hybrid Cultures: Strategies for Entering and Leaving Modernity*, trans. Christopher L. Chiappari and Sylvia L. López (Minneapolis: University of Minnesota Press, 1995), 108; originally published in Spanish in 1990.

4. Renato Ortiz, *Cultura brasileira e identidade nacional* (São Paulo: Brasiliense, 1985), 72–73.

5. Ingrid Monson, "Riffs, Repetition, and Theories of Globalization," *Ethnomusicology* vol. 43, no. 1 (Winter 1999), 54.

6. Paul Gilroy, *The Black Atlantic: Modernity and Double Consciousness* (Cambridge, Mass.: Harvard University Press, 1993), 80–81.

7. J. Lorand Matory has demonstrated the dialogic nature of Afro-Atlantic culture particularly as it relates to Latin America. He argues that early forms of diasporic nationalism, based primarily on transatlantic ethnic and religious affiliations, developed through the comings and goings of Afro-Latin (primarily Brazilian and Cuban) returnees to West African port cities such as Lagos and Porto Novo in the nineteenth and early twentieth centuries. See "The English Professors of Brazil: On the Diasporic Roots of the Yorùbá Nation," *Comparative Studies in Society and History* vol. 41, no. 1 (January 1999), 72–103; and "Jeje: repensando nações e transnacionalismo," *Mana* vol. 5, no. 1 (1999), 57–80. For a broader exposition of this argument that encompasses both the Northern and Southern Hemispheres, see his essay "Afro-Atlantic Culture: On the Live Dialogue Between Africa and the Americas," in *Africana: The Encyclopedia of the African and African American Experience*, ed. Kwame Anthony Appiah and Henry Louis Gates Jr. (New York: Basic Civitas, 1999), 36–44.

8. Carlos Calado, *Tropicália: a história de uma revolução musical* (São Paulo: Editora 34, 1997), 131.

9. "Domingo no parque" was later included on his second album, *Gilberto Gil* (1968). Veloso's festival entry, "Alegria, alegria" [Joy, joy] was featured on his first solo album, *Caetano Veloso* (1968).

10. Walnice Nogueira Galvão, "MMPB: uma análise ideológica," in *Saco de gatos* (São Paulo: Livraria Duas Cidades, 1976), 93–119.

11. Christopher Dunn, "The Tropicalista Rebellion: A Conversation with Caetano Veloso," in *Transition: An International Review* 70, vol. 6, no. 2 (1996), 121.

12. Personal interview with Gilberto Gil in Rio de Janeiro, May 23, 1995.

13. See Augusto de Campos et al., *Balanço da bossa e outras bossas* (São Paulo: Editora Perspectiva, 1974).

14. For a more complete account of the movement, see my book *Brutality Garden: Tropicália and the Emergence of a Brazilian Counterculture*, forthcoming from the University of North Carolina Press.

15. Heloísa Buarque de Hollanda, *Impressões de viagem: CPC, vanguarda e desbunde: 1960/70*, 3rd ed. (Rio de Janeiro: Rocco, 1992), 35.

16. Roberto Schwarz, "Culture and Politics in Brazil, 1964–1969," in *Misplaced Ideas: Essays on Brazilian Culture*, ed. John Gledson (New York: Verso, 1992), 127.

17. Ibid, 140.

18. Ibid, 143.

19. Celso Favaretto, *Tropicália: alegoria, alegria*, 2nd ed. (São Paulo: Ateliê Editora, 1996), 110–111. Favaretto works explicitly with the concept of allegory developed by Walter Benjamin in *The Origin of German Tragic Drama*.

20. Frederic Jameson, "Periodizing the 60s," in *The 60s without Apology*, ed. Sonya Sayres et al. (Minneapolis: University of Minnesota Press, 1988), 181.

21. In a 1979 interview, Caetano Veloso noted that the contradictions of the traditional Left were already apparent to him while he attended the University of Bahia in the early 1960s. He affirmed that he identified with the Left, yet always felt "a bit put off by the disdain for things like sex, religion, race, male-female relations . . . " among his more politically active colleagues. See Carlos Alberto M. Pereira and Heloise Buarque de Hollanda, *Patrulhas Ideológicas: Arte e Engajamento em Debate* (São Paolo: Brasiliense, 1980), 108.

22. Silviano Santiago, "Fazendo perguntas com um martelo," preface to Gilberto Vasconcellos, *Música popular brasileira: de olho na fresta* (Rio de Janeiro: Graal, 1977), 12.

23. Silviano Santiago, "Os abutres," in *Uma literatura nos trópicos* (São Paulo: Perspectiva, 1978), 134.

24. Liv Sovik, "Ponha seu capacete: Uma viagem à Tropicália pós-moderna," *Revista da Bahia* vol. 32, no. 26 (May 1998), 60–67.

25. See Cornel West, "The New Cultural Politics of Difference," in *Out There: Marginalization and Contemporary Cultures*, ed. Russell Ferguson et al. (Cambridge, Mass.: MIT Press, 1990), 19–36.

26. A leading cultural commentator of the time wrote, "Gil has slipped into a more African current, more identified with modern international black music, but he isn't understood by the public, nor by me . . . Now, with his crazy howling, even while seeking liberty and disorder, he does not offend anyone, he does not enchant anyone, he does not move anyone, he does not overturn anything . . . He only irritates . . . " Nelson Motta, "Para onde vai Gilberto Gil?" *Ultima hora-Rio*, October 14, 1968.

27. See brief note, "Bastidores," *Ultima hora-Rio*, October 14, 1968.

28. Caetano Veloso, *Verdade tropical* (São Paulo: Companhia das Letras, 1997), 197.

29. Gilberto Gil, *Gilberto Gil: Expresso 2222*, ed. Antonio Risério (Salvador: Corrupio, 1982), 44.

30. See the discussion of "purity" and "authenticity" in relation to contemporary African artists Youssou N'Dour and Angélique Kidjo in Timothy Taylor, *Global Pop: World Music, World Markets* (New York: Routledge, 1997), 125–145.

31. Calado, *Tropicália*, 272.

32. Quoted in "As duas invasões da música brasileira," *Veja*, March 11, 1970.

33. Buarque de Hollanda, 66.

34. Veloso, 469.

35. Antonio Risério, *Carnaval ijexá* (Salvador: Corrupio, 1981), 23.

36. Reginaldo Prandi, "The Expansion of Black Religion in White Society: Brazilian Popular Music and the Legitimacy of Candomblé," paper read at the Twentieth International Congress of the Latin American Studies Association, Guadalajara, Mexico, April 19, 1997.

37. Pereira and Buarque de Hollanda, 187.

38. May Joseph introduces this term while discussing the circulation of African-American cultural products in Tanzania during the 1970s, which were not entirely in step with Julius Nyrere's experiments in African socialism. See "Soul, Transnationalism, and Imaginings of Revolution: Ujamma and the Politics of Enjoyment," in *Soul: Black Power, Politics and Pleasure*, ed. Monique Guillory and Richard C. Green (New York: New York University Press, 1998).

39. Manthia Diawara, "The Song of the Griot," *Transition: An International Review* 75 (1998), 21.

40. The British label Universal Sound released a compilation of this work as *The Best of Banda Black Rio* in 1996.

41. See Michael J. Turner, "Brown into Black: Changing Racial Attitudes of Afro-Brazilian University Students," in *Race, Class and Power in Brazil*, ed. Pierre-Michel Fontaine (Los Angeles: Center for Afro-American Studies, UCLA, 1985), 79; and Michael G. Hanchard, *Orpheus and Power: The Movimento Negro of Rio de Janeiro and São Paulo, 1945–1988* (Princeton: Princeton University Press, 1994), 115.

42. The Black Rio movement coincided with the emergence of the alternative samba school Quilombo, which sought to reclaim samba as a vehicle for social protest and black pride. Composers affiliated with the school, such as Nei Lopes, were highly critical of the soul phenomenon.

43. Cited in Ana Maria Bahiana, *Nada será como antes-MPB nos anos 70* (Rio de Janeiro: Civilização Brasileira, 1980), 216.

44. Risério, 23.

45. Ibid, 31.

46. Pereira and Buarque de Hollanda, 210.

47. George Lipsitz notes that Fela Kuti had become radicalized politically after

living and working in Los Angeles for nearly a year in 1969–1970. See *Dangerous Crossroads: Popular Music, Postmodernism and the Poetics of Place* (New York: Verso, 1994), 39–40.

48. Anani Dzidzienyo, "The African Connection and the Afro-Brazilian Condition," in *Race, Class and Power in Brazil*, 135–153. Dzidzienyo notes that vocal critics of Brazilian race relations, such as Abdias do Nascimento, were excluded from the Brazilian delegation, which primarily featured artists, scholars, and Candomblé religious leaders who celebrated the cultural links between Brazil and Nigeria.

49. Veloso denounced his Rio- and São Paulo-based antagonists as "racists" who resent Bahians and northeasterners and compared them to the white South African minority. Interview with Reynivaldo Brito, "Caetano desabafa: sou da patrulha odara. E daí?" *A Tarde*, March 2, 1979.

50. Lélia Gonzales noted the irony of countercultural notions about Candomblé, a religion that maintains strict hierarchies that necessitate the ritualized display of respect and deference to superiors: "If you go to a Candomblé, where in order to talk to a priestess you have to kneel on the ground, kiss her hand, and ask for permission, are you going to talk about democracy?" Pereira and Buarque de Hollanda, 212.

51. Charles A. Perrone, *Masters of Contemporary Brazilian Song: MPB 1965–1985* (Austin: University of Texas Press, 1989), 124.

52. Reprinted in Tárik de Souza, *Rostos e gostos da música popular brasileira* (Porto Alegre: L & PM Editores), 228.

53. Pereira and Buarque de Hollanda, 209.

54. Gilberto Gil, *Gilberto Gil: todas as letras*, ed. Carlos Rennó (São Paulo: Companhia das Letras, 1996), 204.

55. *Axé music* refers to a type of radio-friendly pop music based largely on the rhythms of the *blocos afro*. Renditions of "Batmacumba" by Ilê Aiyê, "Domingo no parque" by Margareth Menezes, and "Alegria, alegria" by Daniela Mercury appeared on *Tropicália: 30 anos* (Natasha 289 122, 1997).

56. As Barbara Browning has noted in reference to this song, "Haiti is here—you could be in Port-au-Prince—but also in L.A., in Kingston, in Havana, in Lagos." See *Infectious Rhythm: Metaphors of Contagion and the Spread of African Culture* (New York: Routledge, 1998), 4.

57. Lipsitz, 28–29.

58. José Ramos Tinhorão, *Pequena história da música popular: da modinha à lambada* (São Paulo: Art Editora, 1991), 267.

Discography

Banda Black Rio. *The Best of Banda Black Rio*. Universal Sound US 3, 1996.

Ben, Jorge. *Jorge Ben*. (1969) Polygram 518 119–2, 1993.

Chico Science & Nação Zumbi. *Da lama ao caos.* Sony 81594, 1995.

———. *Afrociberdélia.* Sony 850.278, 1996.

Gil, Gilberto. *Gilberto Gil.* (1968) Polygram M-518 121–2, 1993.

———. "Questão de Ordem." Phillips 441 427 PT, 1968.

———. *Gilberto Gil.* (1969) Polygram M 518 122–2, 1993.

———. *Gilberto Gil.* (1971) Polygram M 518 123–2, 1993.

———. *Refavela.* (1977) WEA M994642–2, 1994.

———. *Realce.* (1979) WEA Tropical Storm WH 53068, n/d.

———. *Nightingale.* Elektra/Asylum 6E-167, 1979.

Gil, Gilberto, and Jorge Ben. *Gil e Jorge.* (1975) Polygram 846 402–2, 1993.

Gil, Gilberto, Caetano Veloso, et. al. *Tropicália ou panis et circencis.* (1968) Phillips 512 089–2, 1993.

———. *Doces bárbaros.* (1976) Polygram 838 565–2 and 842 920–2, 1989.

Gil, Gilberto, and Caetano Veloso. *Tropicália 2.* Polygram 528178–2, 1993.

Olodum. *O movimento.* Warner Music 107800521, 1993.

Various. *Tropicália: 30 anos.* Natasha 289.122, 1997.

Veloso, Caetano. *Caetano Veloso.* (1968) Polygram 838 557–2, 1990.

———. *Transa.* (1972) Polygram 838 511–2, 1989.

———. *Bicho.* (1977) Polygram 838 562–2, 1989.

I sing in Spanish to feel what it's like to
be in someone else's skin. Or, as my
manager says, to expand market share.
—Caetano Veloso, during the 1997
Fina Estampa concert tour

✖✖✖ FIVE ✖✖✖

Globalizing Caetano Veloso
Globalization as Seen through a Brazilian Pop Prism

Liv Sovik

In 1967 when he won fame as spokesman of what became known as Tropicália,
Caetano Veloso proved to have a feeling for what was begging to be said, for giving shape to the concerns of a generation. At the time, he caused scandal with
his disregard for both the Left-populist canons of the União Nacional dos Estu-
dantes [National Student Union] and, with less gusto and out of admiration for the
"violence" of rock, those of the chamber-music variety of bossa nova. Since then,
he has been quoted time and again, whether on personal idiosyncrasies ("close
up no one is normal"),[1] irresistible attractions ("only the dead don't follow a *trio
elétrico*"),[2] or Senator Antônio Carlos Magalhães ("the Caymmi of evil").[3] The
epigraph, part of the script from Veloso's concert Fina Estampa of largely
Hispano-American music, was met with laughter and applause by his audience
in Salvador in 1997. An examination of what the phrase expresses will be used to

understand something of contemporary Brazilian attitudes toward globalization and to throw some light on theoretical discourse about it, looking at the poles Veloso proposes: cultural production as an expression of high aesthetic purpose, on the one hand, and as product for sale on the other.

Thirty years have passed since Tropicália (or *tropicalismo*, Tropicalism) caused scandal, and Veloso's authorized version of it has apparently been fully incorporated into the culture of the Establishment. In 1996 when *Globo repórter*, the weekly prime-time news feature program, chose the theme of Brazilian national identity, it rolled out the old chestnut of racial diversity without conflict. It was Veloso who opened the program, saying that he and his whole family are mulatto. Veloso assumed the role of favorite son of Dona Canô (also interviewed as emblematic mother of the Brazilian race) and of Bahia, "the most mestizo of states" in "Brazil, country of all races," as the program script had it.

That *tropicalista* discourse is now more subject to borrowing by the heirs of Getúlio Vargas and Gilberto Freyre than it seems to question the current status quo has, in general, passed without comment in the Brazilian press. What has changed over the last thirty years that makes an iconoclastic discourse on national identity an element of official consensus? Part of the answer may lie in changes in the pop poet's own attitudes. He no longer evokes Carmen Miranda, for example, and often assumes the discourse and dress of a respectable fifty-year-old father of three. Now, too, he is more powerful. There is a common feeling, at least among Bahians, that he is part of the *"máfia do dendê"* [palm-oil mafia], a political-cultural network centered in Bahia that works for its own benefit. That mafia may or may not exist, but Veloso is formidable in his own right and the press's recent circumspection may be owing to fear of Veloso's sharp tongue. He sees nothing wrong with polemics and notes that they sell newspapers and magazines. Besides engaging in a long-term play of animosity with a New York-based culture critic, the late Paulo Francis, he called columnist Carlos Heitor Cony "incredibly ignorant" for saying in 1972 that bossa nova musician João Gilberto, Veloso's idol, thought he was Greta Garbo; and he said concrete poet Décio Pignatari was weak for having suggested that Gilberto Gil and Caetano Veloso were unduly silent during the campaign for direct elections in 1984.[4]

If Veloso appeared to enjoy immunity from criticism for a while, renewed discussion arose over the meaning of *tropicalismo* in contemporary Brazil with the publication of Veloso's memoirs of Tropicália, *Verdade tropical*.[5] The title of the *Folha de São Paulo* Sunday cultural supplement *Mais* of November 2, the day

Veloso reads from his book *Verdade tropical* during "Livro Vivo" show, Rio de Janeiro, 1998. Photo by Cristina Granato.

after the book was released, is symptomatic of the critics' approach: "Tropicalismo: do cárcere ao poder," from prison to power. Seemingly contented in the eye of the storm, Veloso claims he has not changed substantially over these thirty years: "The most important point is that what led me to *tropicalismo* has brought me this far," he writes (497).

What has changed, then? Another way of explaining Tropicália's altered meaning and relative acceptance as a discourse of the status quo is by cultural change, as understood by Raymond Williams. What *tropicalismo* expressed in the 1960s was a structure of feeling, something "at the very edge of semantic availability."[6] In Williams's terms, the form of subjectivity it expressed in the 1960s can now be articulated and made explicit. The "social experience *in solution*" (133) of the 1960s has now precipitated. Precisely how are *tropicalista* forms and discourses suitable to the current period? An answer to this question, asked in historical and theoretical context, may provide some clues to current Brazilian sensibility about globalization.

Tropicália addressed the twin disruptions of the abrupt end of the democratic regime and the institution of consumer culture, now part of the past. The terms of the discussion in which it took shape were defined by the opposition of political-cultural values to market values and procedures, Brazilian populist nationalism to foreign influence and domination.[7] The argument about the relationship of these poles was common ground for discourses by the partisans of protest music and the *tropicalistas*. The former were opposed to *iê-iê-iê* (Brazilian 1960s rock, influenced by the likes of the Beach Boys and the early Beatles), and to the military regime; they were against the commercialization of culture and for a cultural action linked to the masses as they were defined by the Centro Popular de Cultura [Popular Center of Culture], linked to the student movement. For these people, U.S. imperialism was present in the "invasion" of rock, as well as in the power politics of generals and governments.

A simplified version of these opinions can be found in Sérgio Ricardo's memoirs of the period, *Quem quebrou meu violão*. He condemns television as "the direct enemy of culture itself," identifies the artist with the interests of the people and the culture industry with the worst of U.S. interventionism:

> Everything came out of the Pentagon of culture in the First World, with dates, publicity, places and times all prearranged. The gentlemen in soft-soled shoes, the middlemen of that world, pressed buttons and that was it. . . . Like Pilate, the gentlemen in soft-soled shoes did not feel responsible for anything, alleging that their only objective was business.[8]

A further illustration of how the culture industry and political issues were intermingled is found in an interview of Edu Lobo: "Before, I thought it was a kind of prostitution to appear on a TV program that I didn't have any affinities with; I thought it was a concession, that I was selling out. Now I don't. Now I think it's important to be on all the programs."[9]

Artists reflected on their relationship to the audience and the people, while from the fans' side consumption of cultural products was equated with political action. Telé Cardim, leader of a *torcida* [rooting section, or organized fan group] describes the scene: "I was a protester. I went to the hall like a lot of people there, a lot of university students, to protest against the regime through the Brazilian popular music movement at the festivals. I took firecrackers with me and when I didn't like a song, I popped them off on the stage."[10] These *torcidas* identified their political action with their own force as a market and, together with other, less active fans, made the careers of singers such as Carlos Lyra, Edu Lobo, Chico Buarque, Geraldo Vandré.

e of musical repertory and style and relationship to the student

ssional audience at the time, there was an implicit and explicit

..al issue of the relationship of pop music to the people of Brazil

influence of U.S. culture, a discussion now carried out under the heading of globalization. Tropicália cannot be seen as simple acceptance of the foreign influence and specifically of *iê-iê-iê*. Its view of foreign influence was much more subtle, as is evident in the initial passages of Veloso's book, where he reflects on rock fans now and in the 1950s:

> A young talented Brazilian who loved rock and wanted to develop his own rock style at the end of the 1950s faced not only the ultramelodic Brazilian musical tradition, of Luso-African foundations and Italian whims—and the Catholic atomosphere of our imagination—but the difficulty of defining himself socially as outcast or elite. (44)

Veloso's interpretation of receptivity to U.S. cultural influence focuses on the symbolic value of fan behavior, rather than the political-cultural actors (the artist, the people, television, imperialist forces) present in the imaginary of the protest singers. For him, cultural nationalism did not take the shape of searching for the folk roots of MPB [Música Popular Brasileira], as it did for Edu Lobo, or singing the ills of life under drought in the rural northeast, as it did for João do Vale. Rather, he valued Brazilian cultural heritage as it appeared in an urban, media-dominated environment, paying special attention to the bossa nova and João Gilberto, rock and Roberto Carlos, and at the same time showed no anguish over influence. Neither pariah nor the subject of privilege, rock is proposed as a fact of cultural life that is tributary to the force and vitality of more homegrown culture.

Tropicalismo expressed, then, a structure of feeling that makes an issue of culture's relationship to politics. It answered a desire to recognize something positive in the new mass-mediated cultural environment. It reinterpreted the experience of frustration of a generation bred on nationalist populism whose political rights had been abruptly restricted, a generation surprised, at the same time, by new mechanisms that commercialize and *comercializam*, vulgarize and sell culture. *Tropicalismo* brought acceptance of a situation of in-betweenness, as the epigraph reminds us. It propounded a popular music neither rock nor bossa nova, neither right-wing nor left, neither explicitly interested in being purely Brazilian nor anything but that. Veloso can say that then, as now, he is not entirely dedicated to either feeling what it is like to be in someone else's skin or to seeking market share (as he regularly implied that Elis Regina's camp was).

One wonders what this in-betweenness may have to do with the postcolonial interstices discussed by Homi Bhabha. On one level, Tropicália can be seen as an illustration of the dynamics of Bhabha: "articulation of difference from a minority perspective [that] seeks to authorize cultural hybridities that emerge in moments of historical transformation."[11] Echoes of the collective LP *Tropicália* can be heard, particularly of the kitsch of "Coração materno," where a pristine voice sings a melodrama to a string accompaniment, as Bhabha continues:

> This process [of restaging the past] estranges any immediate access to an originary
> identity or a "received" tradition. The borderline engagements of cultural
> difference may as often be consensual as conflictual; they may confound our
> definitions of tradition and modernity; realign the customary boundaries between
> the private and the public, high and low; and challenge the normative expecta-
> tions of development and progress. (2)

Speaking of the Bahians who migrated from the northeast to the "marvelous south," one could borrow Bhabha's words when he affirms that "the truest eye may now belong to the migrant's double vision" (5). But, as has been explained, the current tone and meaning of what Veloso, at least, represents do not meet the aspirations Bhabha has for the uncanny, unhomely hybridity—aspirations to contestatory truth, innovation, and political importance.

Perhaps Bhabha has overestimated the role of the interstices in the resistance to "normative expectations of development and progress." Or else what was once emergent, a structure of feeling, is now hegemonic, ideologically tied. Veloso's view of cultural politics, in the second case, is respectable as never before because the industrial production of culture is taken for granted, even in its global scale and its U.S.-American tone. Veloso's sharp criticism of the militant Left is now conventional wisdom. The scandal caused by Tropicalism is no longer possible because certain differences that it juxtaposed in a single discourse are no longer chasms: between MPB and rock, for example, or between unkempt appearance and the discourse of tradition. More recent songs by Veloso, like "Fora da ordem" and "Haiti,"[12] further close gaps between poles; they are what would have been identified with the more poetic end of protest music in the 1960s. In this sense, the potential critique of Bhabha, here, is that Tropicália recalls that the interstices too can become official culture. Certainly they have been in Brazil for a long time, as the in-betweenness of a mixed-race country has been a flagship of nationality.

Taking another tack, one could perhaps use Roland Barthes's concept of the alibi[13] to explain the meaning of Veloso's statement as he opposes identification with the Other to the rationale of marketing: both clauses are equally present, while each covers for the other. Veloso may have said what he said simply to defuse the ever-present accusations of some older fans that he has sold out. But if, as posited above, *tropicalista* discourse has been accepted by the Establishment or even become hegemonic, what hegemony is this? To take another view of how Veloso's voice addresses the political issues of cultural values versus the market, the focus should pass from discussion of the first term, "being in someone else's skin," dear to the postcolonialists, to the second, more traditional field of debate over power and hegemony: the global market for cultural goods.

In Brazil as elsewhere, the theme of globalization has until recently been discussed mainly in terms of economic production and the international division of labor. Among noted exceptions to this economic focus in Brazil are the works of Milton Santos,[14] who deals with the effects on territory of instantaneous, global perception of events, and Octávio Ianni, who speaks of world citizenship and a worldwide civil society.[15] Perhaps the work that comes closest to combining issues of the culture industry and the globalization of culture, however, is by Renato Ortiz. His *Mundialização e cultura* (1994) launched the concept of *internacional-popular*, with its echoes of the *nacional-popular* that dominated the discussions of cultural politics and policies in the 1960s and 1970s. Ortiz identifies culture and industry very closely. Globalized production is seen as a sign of cultural change: "There are a number of signs of deterritorialization of culture. A Mazda sports car is designed in California, financed by Tokyo, the prototype is made in Worthing . . ."[16] This production system leads to "an international-popular culture whose fulcrum is the consumer market" (111).

According to Ortiz, this culture is American because its dynamics of production and consumption first took root in the United States. Cultural goods, from Marlboro ads to Charlie Chaplin movies, are then reterritorialized as they are consumed in different places. Their Americanness is neutralized as they are moved away from their original status as emblematic of U.S. nationality and from the discourse of national identity based on having two cars in every garage. Being immediately recognizable, images of Disneyland, Hollywood, and Coca-Cola become "an international-popular memory" composed of "worldwide cul-

tural references" (126). These cultural reference points establish "a collusion between people. 'Youth' is a good example of this. T-shirts, rock-and-roll, electric
guitars . . . are shared all over the planet by a certain age group" (129). This collusion contributes to the maintenance of a world order, according to Ortiz's
critique.

At first glance, Ortiz's view and Veloso's acceptance of rock as part of
humanity's heritage seem to coincide. However, there are differences of stance
and standpoint. Ortiz's introductory statement puts his position as follows: I
made an effort to deterritorialize myself and even my writing. So I do not speak
as a Brazilian or Latin American, though I know it is impossible and undesirable
to liberate myself completely from my condition. I speak as a "world citizen" (9).
Veloso embraces rock not as the basis of a shared humanity but of a cross-fertil-
ized Brazilian culture. He is interested in "how to propound original solutions to
the problems of man and the world, based on our own ways of being" (87). And:
"I myself could say that I do not experience what interests me in my own work
from the perspective of the 'American century' but from that of going beyond it"
(500). And again: "Responsibility for the fate of tropical man, a hidden dynamo
. . . —that is the intimate motivation of what was called *tropicalismo* in Brazilian
pop" (501).

Both Ortiz and Veloso see and accept the importance of American industrialized cultural imports to contemporary Brazilian culture. For Ortiz they are universally recognizable images, intimately related to a capitalist order, to which
everyone is subject as world citizen. His is a homogenized, even idyllic, view of
worldwide consumer culture. Brazil and its culture are always onstage with
Veloso. In his ability to absorb globalization into nationality rather than allowing
the opposite to happen, he is heir to traditional Brazilian identity discourse since
antropofagismo [cultural cannibalism], where the foreign Other is swallowed by
a Brazilian cannibal self.[17] The position taken by Veloso within this tradition,
with its tensions and fusions between self and Other, is on the side of fusion, of
self-affirmation and not internal conflict.

In Veloso's statement, a kind of inside-out cannibalistic self (feeling what it's
like to be in someone else's skin) is active within the rules of *capitalismo
selvagem* [savage capitalism], placing the highest value on expanding market
share. Veloso's statement accepts the rules of the market as the setting for mass
cultural production. By taking for granted the economics of pop and pointing
out the difference between political and artistic values, *tropicalismo* opened the

door, in the 1960s, to market-driven cultural diversity, the mark of today's cultural production. With the either-or, neither-nor structure noted by Barthes, it elides presuppositions and transcends the conflicts it poses, in this case the conflict between economic and artistic interests.

Under the aegis of globalization, differences between countries' interests are understood in economic terms, not political ones. Whether or not Veloso has changed over time, he was always interested in aesthetic issues with political facets, discarding approaches that focus first on political dynamics and then their cultural dimensions. The flurry of laughter and applause greeting Veloso's remark are caused, then, by the shock of reconciliation in paradox of an established polarity, between artistic experimentation with cultural traditions and commercial interests. Though diametrically opposed in everyday and more theoretical criticism, these poles are reconciled in cultural production and consumption. At the same time, the audience hears one more affirmation of something the *tropicalistas* have said from the beginning; and they hear it from an authority, someone recognized as one of the greatest producers of Brazilian musical culture, someone who knows the foreign Other and the market. He says, in sum, that foreign influence carried on the tides of globalization may be a puzzle for Brazilian popular musicians and their audiences, but given the vitality and market potential of MPB, in Brazil and abroad, it is not a problem.

Notes

1. From "Vaca profana," a song written for Gal Costa and first recorded by her on *Profana* (RCA 7432121524, 1984).

2. The line is from "Atrás do trio elétrico," one of Veloso's Carnival tunes recorded on *Muitos carnavais* (Philips 838 563, 1977). *Trio elétrico* is an ensemble that plays atop a truck equipped with sound amplification equipment; the top of the truck forms a stage for performers. Participants in the Carnival of Bahia—and increasingly other places— follow the many trucks with their favorite *trios* through the streets.

3. Dorival Caymmi, author of such songs as "O que é que a baiana tem?" sung by Carmen Miranda, is the bard of a now classical vision of Bahian folk culture. Magalhães is a national political figure and the head of Bahia's very effective political machine, whose cultural policy is to promote Bahia as a fountainhead of Brazilian culture and to sponsor, and even control, practically all mass emerging cultural phenomena; his barrel-chested physique, striped shirts, and white hair recall Caymmi.

4. See Heber Fonseca, *Caetano: esse cara* (Rio de Janeiro: Revan, 1994), 93ff.

5. Caetano Veloso, *Verdade tropical* (São Paulo: Companhia das Letras, 1997). Subsequent citations in text.

6. Raymond Williams, *Marxism and Literature* (Oxford: Oxford University Press, 1977), 134. Subsequently cited in text.

7. These reflections on how 1960s *tropicalista* identity discourse addressed both the domestic and the foreign Other—and even gender identity—are based on my dissertation, "Vaca profana: teoria pós-moderna e tropicália," Universidade de São Paulo, 1994.

8. Sérgio Ricardo, *Quem quebrou meu violão* (Rio de Janeiro: Record, 1992), 61, 62. The title means "who broke my guitar" and refers to an incident at a festival when the author broke his instrument and hurled it into the audience after a loud and unruly public made it extremely difficult for him to perform.

9. Christina Autran, "Edu Lobo—um môço e seu violão," *Manchete* yr. 15, no. 814, November 25, 1967.

10. In José Saffiotti Filho et al., *Tropicália 20 anos* (São Paulo: SESC, 1987), 78.

11. Homi K. Bhabha, *The Location of Culture* (London: Routledge, 1994), 2; next citations in text.

12. "Fora da ordem" [Out of order], *Circuladô* (Polygram 510–639, 1991). The song describes the violence and decay of the Brazilian urban scene, with allusions to buildings in ruins before they are completed, drugs and guns. Its chorus says: "Something is out of order, the new world order." "Haiti," the first track on Caetano and Gil's *Tropicália 2* (Philips 518.178, 1993), critiques racial politics in Bahia as it narrates a scene of police violence observed in Salvador's Pelourinho district: "*O Haiti é aqui*" [is here], it affirms.

13. Roland Barthes, *Mythologies* (St. Albans, England: Paladin, 1973), 123ff.

14. See Milton Santos, *A natureza do espaço: técnica e tempo, razão e emoção* (São Paulo: Hucitec, 1996); and *Técnica, espaço, tempo: globalização e meio técnico-científico informacional* (São Paulo: Hucitec, 1994).

15. See Octávio Ianni, *A era do globalismo* (Rio de Janeiro: Civilização Brasileira, 1996); and *A sociedade global* (Rio de Janeiro: Civilização Brasileira, 1992).

16. Renato Ortiz, *Mundialização e cultura* (São Paulo: Brasiliense, 1994), 108. Subsequently in text.

17. See Augusto de Campos et al., *Balanço da bossa* (São Paulo: Perspectiva, 1968), especially his essays "Boa palavra sobre a música popular" and "A explosão de 'Alegria, alegria,'" Celso Favaretto develops these ideas in *Tropicália: alegoria alegria* (São Paulo: Kairós, 1979). Christopher Dunn, *Brutality Garden: Tropicália and the Emergence of a Brazilian Counterculture* (Chapel Hill: University of North Carolina Press, in press) discusses them in the context of the tradition of reflection about Brazilian cultural identity.

SIX

Cannibals, Mutants, and Hipsters
The Tropicalist Revival

John J. Harvey

1928

While provincialism prevailed in Latin American literature and arts under the umbrellas of regionalism, nationalism, indigenism, and social realism, Brazilian poet Oswald de Andrade had a different plan for his fellow artists: cannibalism. As writers, painters, and musicians from other Latin American nations launched manifestos and journals debating whether to dedicate themselves to local themes or remain open to foreign influences, Oswald urged Brazilian artists who found themselves on the global periphery to consume, digest, and regurgitate anew everything they could to make the entire universe their aesthetic patrimony. In the "Manifesto antropófago" ("Cannibalist Manifesto," 1928) Oswald urged artists to essay all themes and to incorporate an international repertoire of styles, assimilating them in the local vernacular in a practice of cultural devourment. "Only cannibalism unites us," wrote Andrade, "socially, economically, philosophically."[1]

In his reworking of the famous Shakespearean conundrum as "Tupi or not Tupi," Oswald referenced indigenous coastal peoples of Brazil notorious among European colonizers for eating human flesh. For the native Tupinambá, the physical and spiritual worlds were intermingled and it was possible to "eat" what came from both worlds. In the Tupinambá practice of anthropophagy, people were killed in revenge for the death of an ancestor, but at the same time their death meant the birth of another self in the cannibal, who scarified himself and assumed a new name after the human sacrifice.[2] With the figure of the cannibal as a metaphorical anchor for his manifesto, Oswald de Andrade made a multivalenced critical statement. By recalling the exaggerated, baroquely fabricated colonial representations of some New World inhabitants as savages or cannibals, Oswald played with the still prevalent notion of Brazilians as "underdeveloped" or as existing in a cultural time lag in relation to the more "advanced" countries of Western Europe and the United States. Also, though the Shakespeare quote is from *Hamlet*, certainly Oswald must have thought of *The Tempest* with its story of Caliban, the colonial native who dominates his master's language in order to blaspheme him. Oswald cannibalized the most hallowed words of the most revered icon of Occidental letters, relocating them within a Brazilian context in order to question the reductive logic within which they operated. Oswald de Andrade's cultural cannibal would consume and digest it all, appropriating many styles with voracious irreverence.

1968

Os Mutantes [The mutants] take the stage for the eliminatory rounds of the International Festival of Song. Clad in surreal plastic outfits, the group settles in: Rita Lee Jones on vocals and the Baptista brothers, Arnaldo and Sérgio, on bass and guitar. The crowd eyes the longhaired, strangely dressed, foreign-looking Os Mutantes with suspicion. Backing Caetano Veloso on "É proibido proibir" [It's forbidden to forbid], the band launches into an amplified barrage of distorted noise that immediately elicits a hostile response from the audience, which begins to boo and hurl tomatoes, grapes, and wads of paper at the performers. Os Mutantes increases the distorted guitar attack in a defiant mocking of the spectators. The band members turn their backs to the crowd and continue the sonic assault.

At a time when most popular music in Brazil was still "unplugged," Os Mutantes used Moogs, homemade electric guitars, amplifiers, effects pedals, experimental studio production technology, and John Cage-style avant-garde performances. While Roberto Carlos and his Jovem Guarda [Young guard] used amplified guitars to play music known as *iê-iê-iê*, the most popular mass-mediated Brazilian rock of the time, their translations of *With the Beatles* (1963) were mild compared to Os Mutantes' debut LP, which sounded more like *Sgt. Pepper's Lonely Hearts Club Band* (1967).

In the mid-1960s, particularly after the military coup in 1964, cultural struggles between the *engajados* and the *alienados* ("engaged" with national identity and "alienated" from it) became marked.[3] The acronym MPB, for Música Popular Brasileira [Brazilian popular music), originated in 1966 to denote folk-based material of protest songs performed at televised song festivals that had become quite important. The composers were often idealistic youth concerned with producing a truly "popular" art. The core singer-songwriters who are today considered the best of MPB emerged from the festival era: Chico Buarque de Hollanda, Milton Nascimento, Caetano Veloso, and Gilberto Gil (see Ulhoa). The commercial success of Jovem Guarda, on the other hand, was clearly related to a marketing strategy. In 1965, the São Paulo advertising firm of Magaldi Maia & Prosperi, recognizing the growing interest in so-called youth music, set out to channel admiration for idols and fads into market success. Prime TV time was purchased to present *iê-iê-iê* and hype related products.[4] Roberto Carlos, known as the "King," had actually begun his career in Rio de Janeiro as an unsuccessful bossa nova singer. It wasn't until CBS record producers approached him and suggested that he compose and sing music "for youth" (i.e., early 1960s rock 'n' roll) that he began to sell well. It was the 1966 hit "Quero que vá tudo pro inferno" [Let everything go to hell] that simultaneously established Roberto Carlos as a mass-media idol and broadened the distance between him and the MPB camp, whose protest ethic clashed with the seemingly apolitical attitude reflected in the title of his song.

Tensions between *engajados* and *alienados* were already high in 1968 when Os Mutantes pushed Jovem Guarda's approximation of Anglo-American rock 'n' roll to extremes. The group's debut must have seemed like a bold provocation to those who saw themselves as the guardians of an aesthetic patrimony. To the audience at the International Festival of Song, the name Os Mutantes, taken from a science-fiction novel by French writer Stefan Wul, must have seemed appropriate. The members of Os Mutantes were still in their teens when the vanguard composer Rogério Duprat introduced them to Gilberto Gil, founding member of the movement of *tropicalismo*. Gil spoke of the trio to Caetano Veloso, who had not yet become one of Brazil's best known artists. Having already released its eponymous album under the direction of Rogério Duprat, Os Mutantes was enlisted to back the collaborative album *Tropicália: ou panis et circencis* (1968), which became a musical manifesto of the multimedia arts movement of *tropicalismo*. The Tropicalists challenged the dualism of *engajado/alienado*. To bridge the gap between "national" and "international," the Tropicalists used such procedures as playing electric instruments together with traditional Afro-Brazilian instruments (e.g., *berimbau*). Their musical and performative styles fused rock elements with popular Brazilian forms such as the *samba-de-roda, baião, marcha*, and *frevo*, as well as rhythms associated with folkloric dances such as the *bumba-meu-boi* and *maracatu*. Inspired by the critical revision of Brazilian modernism undertaken by the concrete poets, the Tropicalists incorporated Oswald de Andrade's idea of cultural cannibalism in order to create hybrid arts that challenged the restrictive political and aesthetic dualisms of the time. Os Mutantes, blending the critical posture of MPB with the mass-media savvy of Jovem Guarda, soon drew the attention of the Tropicalists.

Os Mutantes' LPs are diverse in style. After its first LP in 1968, the group released another eponymous album in the Tropicalist vein in 1969. Os Mutantes went on to release A *divina comédia ou ando meio desligado* [The divine comedy or I'm kinda out of it] (1970), and two other albums before Rita Lee left the band to pursue a solo career. From the very first track of *Os Mutantes* (1968), "Ou panis et circenses," the image of the circus, or, more specific to Brazil, the Carnival, is a dominant motif and functions as a kind of controlling metaphor for the significance of the band's music. Besides the inextricable links between the production of popular music and the yearly pre-Lenten celebration in Brazil, the Carnival is, ostensibly, polyphonic. It is a time when a multitude of voices, identities, and bodies usually unacknowledged or even proscribed by official discourse appear, albeit briefly, in public. Carnival costumes parody and confuse gender, social class, and race, crossing prohibited boundaries and borders.[5]

Like Oswald de Andrade, who perceived the ideological danger in the reduction of the world to this or that, one or the other, local or foreign, "to be or not to be," Os Mutantes rejected the kind of aesthetic conservatism that posited the very notion of an "authentic" Brazilian music as opposed to an alienated, imported music. The band constantly supplemented and complicated narrow visions of tradition, patrimony, and nationalism in a musical style aptly described as "carnivalesque."

Objections to Brazilian rock in the 1960s were often expressed as a general aversion to electric instrumentation. At a moment in Brazil when the use of electric guitars was still limited, Sérgio Dias Baptista played a number of unusual, homemade electric guitars provided by Cláudio César, the third Baptista brother referred to as the "invisible Mutante." In his workshop, César fabricated guitars and equipment with built-in distortion, harmonic filters, and other sound effects that were not yet common in the United States, as well as amplifiers, a wah-wah pedal, and a guitar wired to a sewing machine. The adoption of technology was key to the Tropicalist movement, helping to destabilize facile alignments of "authentic" or "indigenous" with a notion of an edenic premodernity.

In an eclectic style that would later be referred to as "postmodern," Os Mutantes questioned the cultural hierarchies that privileged high culture over low or mass culture, chic over kitsch. Ulhoa writes: "MPB aesthetics emulate the Western art music canon, which means that MPB music is considered 'art' or erudite . . . MPB artists aim at the creative communication of emotion by means of an elaborate language understandable to persons of 'culture' and 'good taste'"(172). By fusing the self-consciousness of MPB with the commercial, mass aesthetic of Jovem Guarda, Os Mutantes proved that mass forms could be self-critical in a sophisticated register. The group accepted the inevitability of reification in mass-mediated popular music, critically underscoring the dynamics of the market in its music instead of claiming the kind of purity sought by some of the MPB crowd. Using bricolage, pastiche, and irony, Os Mutantes introduced critical alternatives to the austerity of the protest ethos. Thus its members were appropriate candidates for collaboration in *tropicalismo*. Charles A. Perrone writes of the Tropicalist movement:

> Caetano Veloso and his colleagues exercised a critical revision of Brazilian culture through song and expanded the horizons of popular music as a "legitimate" mode of artistic expression. They elaborated on the innovations of Bossa Nova and on the Jovem Guarda. In their experimental music, the Tropicalists applied literary concepts, particularly from the Oswaldian wellspring of irreverence, juxtaposition and iconoclasm.[6]

It was this kind of "irreverence" toward hegemonic valorizations of cultural production that drove the music of Os Mutantes. The band examined its own location in relation to European and North American culture industries as a primary theme, and it was precisely this kind of "juxtaposition" evident in members' reading of their own global cultural location which, I will argue, would later attract a young Anglo-American audience.

In the 1960s, Jovem Guarda produced "covers" (versions) of British and North American songs. Os Mutantes continued this practice, but the group made the implications of its position in relation to these foreign culture industries a central theme. Roberto Carlos had begun a dialogue with Brazilian musical history in his compositions. He incorporated elements of the Brazilian popular musical tradition known as *música romântica* [romantic music], which dates back to the nineteenth century *modinha* [sentimental song]. The samba also built on the *modinha*, and Roberto Carlos drew on both of these. Os Mutantes extended the kinds of reflections on local influence produced by Roberto Carlos in order to address an increasingly globalized mass-media market and the function of influence there within. This international awareness distinguished its songs from *iê-iê-iê* songs. Os Mutantes' songs reflected, in form and content, the concrete differences between Brazil and the First World that gave rise to different aesthetic responses. Caetano Veloso underlines the sense of contrast involved in their respective implementations of rock 'n' roll:

> For me, the use of the expression "garage rock" to define an anti-bourgeois, savage, countercultural rock style is still strange. I grew up without a car among people who neither had one, nor felt themselves entitled enough to dream of having one . . . an American would be truly surprised at how strange the notion of the garage as a cavern of subversion seemed to us, which says a lot about our economic differences, but even more about the elaborate shock absorbers that dampen the impact of mass cultural phenomenon arriving from the so-called "first world" in countries like Brazil.[7]

Os Mutantes took as a central theme the contrasts described by Veloso, underscoring the slippages in cross-cultural translation. Like bossa nova, which "mistranslated" West Coast cool jazz and played *desafinado* [out of tune] in relation to the norms and expectations for Brazilian sentimental crooners, it was the way in which Os Mutantes irreverently translated Anglo-American rock that would attract musicians of the North American pop vanguard to the group's music some thirty years later.

1998

In the North American independent-music scene of the 1990s, irony, pastiche, masquerade, sampling, plagiarism, and a variety of other cultural cannibalisms were widespread. Irrevocably reified, rock had ceased to function as a mouthpiece for United States youth countercultures. "The culture industry has nailed down the twenty-somethings," wrote Tom Frank, editor and publisher of the Chicago underground journal *The Baffler*, in 1993, continuing:

> Now we watch with interest as high-powered executives offer contracts to bands they have seen only once, college radio playlists become the objects of intense corporate scrutiny, and long-standing independent labels are swallowed whole in a colossal belch of dollars and receptions . . . Now we enjoy a revitalized MTV that has hastily abandoned its pop origins to push "alternative" bands around the clock, a 50-million-watt radio station in every city that calls out to us from what is cleverly called "the cutting edge of rock."[8]

Estranged by the crass commercialism of the new corporate "alternative" bands foisted upon young people in the wake of the Seattle "grunge" trend, countercultural musicians in the United States looked elsewhere for innovation. Bored with the "pre-digested and predictable versions of formulaic heavy guitar rock" (Frank) which the North American cultural industry began to churn out, bands sought new inspiration. Acts such as Beck and the Beastie Boys changed rock's parameters by creating music from samples of obscure, antique recordings from around the world, creating stylized compositions that referenced musical histories across a wide expanse of time and space. "In 1998, the rising stars of the underground were the jet set," wrote Douglas Wolk in the leading popular-culture publication *Spin* magazine, "acts who are not only international but internationalist—that is, intent on creating cross-cultural hybrids that pick up where Beck, the Beastie Boys, and the vinyl-junkie obsession with old, 'exotic' sounds left off."[9]

This conjuncture provided fertile ground for a U.S. reception of Tropicalism and Os Mutantes, with their questioning of cultural boundaries and trajectories. Bootlegged and exchanged, the early Os Mutantes albums began to circulate

Os Mutantes, ca. 1970. Courtesy of Arquivo Estadual de São Paulo.

among alternative musicians in the United States. All sorts of activity in the recording industry provides evidence of a significant consumption and awareness
of the music. In 1993, the late Kurt Cobain of the iconoclastic grunge band Nir-
vana returned from Brazil to the United States with Os Mutantes' records, and
he promoted them while touring. Cobain even left a note for Arnaldo Baptista
that read: "Arnaldo, the best of luck to you and remember to beware of the system. They'll chew you up and spit you out like the pit of a cherry."[10] Dusty
Groove, an Internet-vendor record store in Chicago specializing in rare and imported records, began to sell Os Mutantes' rereleases in the United States. *Spin*
magazine declared that "the first few albums by the group Os Mutantes . . . have
become cult items in the US" (quoted by Wolk). Both *Spin* and the *New York
Times Magazine* ran feature-length editorials on the Tropicalist revival.[11] David
Byrne's Luaka Bop record label, which had already released six compilations in a
Brazil Classics series, announced that it would release a double-CD compilation
of Os Mutantes, featuring the band's greatest hits album, *Everything Is Possible!*
and the never-before-released English-language album *Technicolor*. A box set
called *Tropicália: 30 anos* was produced in Brazil for U.S. release; it included the
debut LP of Os Mutantes, Gal Costa, Gilberto Gil, and Caetano Veloso, as well

as *Tropicália: ou panis et circensis.* This box set introduced the key Tropicalist players to many more in the independent rock underground in the United States. Rumors about Os Mutantes' influence on central figures in the independent rock scene began to circulate. Aquarius Records, an independent record store in San Francisco, imported the first two Os Mutantes records and advertised them on its Web site in terms that emphasized the warm reception of the band by pop vanguardists in the United States:

> We could drop a lot of names in trying to convince you of this music's greatness (like how Beck finally persuaded David Byrne to release a compilation next year [1999], how Kurt Cobain wanted Mutantes to re-form so they could open for Nirvana in Brazil, and how Tim Gane picked up copies in Brazil because someone kept telling them that Stereolab sounded like Os Mutantes), but that's secondary info and all you really need is to hear the songs. You'll die, it's so good! Probably Windy's [Aquarius proprietor] favorite band of ALL TIME. If you buy one record all year, get one of these.[12]

As for Grammy-award winner Beck, he named his 1998 album *Mutations* and the radio single from the LP, which employed a Tropicalist style collage of lyrics and sounded like Jorge Ben's Tropicalist work, was aptly titled "Tropicália." In the summer of 2000, Mac McCaughan of the fuzz guitar group Superchunk released *De Mel, De Melão* under the moniker of his side-project, Portastatic. While Beck's references to Tropicália were relatively oblique, McCaughan's record was a straight tribute album featuring covers of Caetano Veloso's Tropicalist-era classics "Baby" and "Não Identificado," Gilberto Gil's "Lamento Sertanejo" from the 1975 album *Refazenda*, as well as a cover of "I Fell in Love One Day" from Os Mutantes member Arnaldo Baptista's 1982 solo album *Singin' Alone.*

Nineteen ninety-eight became known to many in the North American independent music industry as the "year of the remix." Inspired by the innovations of electronic artists and turntablists, rock musicians exchanged their work and "remixed" it, creating new versions and interpretations of each others' songs through the use of sampling technology. John McEntire of Chicago's Tortoise, Sasha Frere-Jones of Ui, DJ Amon Tobin, and other countercultural musicians highly respected in the U.S. underground went to work on a "remix album" of Tom Zé's 1998 *Fabrication Defect / Com defeito de fabricação*, which inspired the pairing of the artist with Tortoise for a U.S. tour (and a later one in Brazil too). While the record industry tried to regulate the dissemination of new music created with such technologies, Tom Zé, one of the founding musicians of the Tropicalist movement, included a manifesto in his album organized around a concept of plagiarism:

> Someone from the Third World, an android, is producing works which would fit in the traditions of the First World. This android is adding defects which come from illiterate people to that so-called superior culture. In other words, this person is adding new significations . . . without the android, without "fabrication defects," culture as a whole would be less rich with significations.

Like Os Mutantes, who underscored mutations that occur in the translation of Anglo-American rock into a Brazilian vernacular, Tom Zé suggested that it was precisely the excesses and "defects" that occur in the translation of artistic influences which make works of art interesting. This made him a perfect candidate for the slicing board of the remix studio and attracted more North American pop vanguardists to the Tropicalist movement.[13]

Tom Zé performs with Tortoise in Chicago during a 1999 U.S. tour. Photo by Christopher Dunn.

Meanwhile, the newly formed record label Omplatten, an imprint of New York City's Other Music, a record store specializing in obscure records, licensed the rights to the first three Os Mutantes records for release in the United States. The records won critical praise. In a *New York Times* article, Ben Ratliff wrote: "It's a double score of beauty and irony that even Beck hasn't topped. This is as modern as pop gets. This music sounds current: it can be appreciated with the same ears that understand the collage mentality of Pet Sounds, De La Soul, the Beastie Boys or Beck. We knew something like this must have existed but had no idea it would be so perfect."[14]

What had led the pioneers of the North American alternative music scene to discover Os Mutantes? The ironic use of primitive and awkward analog technology had become popular among North American independent rock fans. The saccharine electronic Moog honks, provided by the Arnaldo brothers, and the irony with which they are often deployed, as in the almost churchly baroque drama of their song "Meu refrigerador não funciona" [My refrigerator doesn't work], certainly helped to bridge the language barrier, assuring them a warm reception by fans of bands such as Stereolab, which had become famous for its obsession with the Moog. In the United States, electronic music had begun to threaten the dominance of the standard bass/drum/guitar configuration, and 1990s rock musicians sought new sounds. Os Mutantes' playful, vanguardist use of unorthodox sounds—as in "Le Premier Bonheur du Jour," where spray bursts from an aerosol can fill out the rhythm section—was well received. Such practices alone, however, do not account for the band's revival in the United States. To understand more fully the significance of the recent popularity of Os Mutantes among North American countercultural musicians, we must return to Oswald de Andrade's idea of cultural cannibalism.

In the dependency-theory models of cultural transmission prevalent during the height of Os Mutantes' career, an economically, technologically, and culturally superior core, usually represented by Western Europe or North America, transmitted ideologies and products to the less advanced countries of Latin America, which uncritically consumed them. Such models posited a one-way cultural flow, from center to periphery, and assumed a homogeneous reception. Though this model explicitly addressed economic structure, uneven development, and resultant sociopolitical restraints, it reflected a logic in relation to culture industries that profoundly affected the artists of the time.

Acknowledging the prevalence of such an outlook, Os Mutantes played with the Third World time-lag stereotype. The band emphasized the strangest and tackiest aspects of late-1960s psychedelic pop in its awkward translations of Anglo-American counterculture. To the current U.S. pop vanguard, who sought innovation through the incorporation of an international repertoire of sounds and for whom parody, collage, and wink-nudge retro stylings had become almost commonplace by 1998, the discovery of the thirty-year-old, defunct Os Mutantes seemed, ironically, "as modern as pop gets," as Ratliff (1998) suggests.

Mainstream rock music in the United States showed a sharp decline in record sales in 1998, failing to produce the kind of superstars who have traditionally fueled the industry. According to a key industry source, although record sales as a whole increased 12 percent during 1998, the rock category saw a "major decline."[15] However, while commercial rock stagnated in 1998, independent rock bands and labels flourished. The figure of the rock star began to fade as the rock market splintered into subgenres: indie, emo, math, post, and so on. A new figure arose: the hipster. If the rock star favored excess and bombast, the hipster favored subtle irony. While the rock star measured success in sexual conquests, level of drug consumption, and number of seats filled in the stadium, the hipster measured it in degree of knowledge of historical rock obscurity. The hipster favored the basement to the stadium, college radio to commercial FM, ill-fitting thrift clothes to tight leather bodysuits. The hipster was a more globally aware, historical cultural miner who dealt in countercultural capital. For the hipster, rock 'n' roll was bankrupt as a genre. Facing what he perceived as the exhaustion and reification of many rock styles, the hipster embarked on an excavation of international rock history. The hipster tried to innovate what he perceived as a stagnant rock scene through a self-conscious international infusion.

Alternative rock bands such as Yo La Tengo, from the United States, and Stereolab, from England, brought to their recordings an encyclopedic knowledge of international pop and pop history, jumping genres and geographical frontiers with postmodern abandon, inflecting a formidable array of styles with their own chronologically and geographically located sensibilities. Yo La Tengo's voluminous discography consists almost entirely of cannibalisms of obscure North American bands. Stereolab mined Sun Ra, Krautrock, French Pop and, later, Tropicalist records, redeploying these styles in a musical extrapolation on Andy Warhol's soup cans.

It was precisely the kind of aesthetic strategies that drove Os Mutantes that guided the works of bands such as Yo La Tengo and Stereolab. Os Mutantes foregrounded the very act of cannibalism, essaying the politics of influence in its music. In the above-cited "Meu refrigerador não funciona" [my refrigerator doesn't work] Os Mutantes delivers with these words a tribute to the celebrated vocalist Janis Joplin, whose interlocutor departs only briefly from a parodic, exaggerated American accent to proclaim the only Portuguese lyrics in the song in a choked breakdown reminiscent of the hash-pipe poetics of Jim Morrison. Rita Lee played Nico to the Mutantes' Velvet Underground, signifying on the comparison with the mysterious multilingual blonde diva of the ultimate North American underground band by creating excessive imitations of the American and British accents of the psychedelic chanteuses of the 1960s, as in "Quem tem medo de brincar de amor" [Who's scared to play love] from Os Mutantes' *A divina comedia*. It was this type of approach, where one felt most acutely the tax of Third World cultural importation, that had captivated young North American audiences in 1998. For, like Oswald's "mistranslation" of "to be or not to be," North American bands involved in a similarly self-conscious reflection on creativity and influence perceived that Os Mutantes' clumsy handling of American musical motifs was quite deliberate.

Os Mutantes' cultural strategies presaged the ways in which postmodernist thinking would deconstruct dualistic and reductive arguments regarding the relationship between contemporary subjects and their mass-mediated environments.[16] As politics and aesthetics entered the realm of the postmodern, Louis Althusser's idea of "interpellation," a process in which subjects were inescapably produced through the ideologies of the State Apparatus, or Theodor Adorno's idea of "the culture industry" as such an apparatus, or Herbert Marcuse's idea of "homogenization" as the result of the imposition of the culture industry and its hegemonic apparati on interpellated subjects, would be less emphasized in favor of critical schemata that acknowledged different economies of reception and a politics of the quotidian. Whereas Adorno and Marcuse were more compatible with the dualism of *engajado/alienado*, postmodernism's theories better described the kind of work the Tropicalist movement was producing.

Iain Chambers writes in *Migrancy, Culture, and Identity*:

> Opposed to the abstractions of an ideological critique of mass culture—invariably presented as a homogeneous totality, without contradictions or room for subtle, subaltern or alternative voices—are the details and differences that are historically revealed in how people go about using and inhabiting this culture, invariably

domesticating and directing it in ways unforeseen by the producers of the "culture industry."[17]

Os Mutantes' repetitions and receptions of American pop dialogue with notions of "homogenization" and "the culture industry" in a more complex way than was allowed by traditional Marxism. Os Mutantes' central strategy was, as Chambers suggests, to "inhabit" and "domesticate" foreign cultural products in such a way as to question the band's relationship to such products and the industries that produced them. David Byrne, a songwriter whose breadth of projects has been fueled by an interest in international musics, comments: "For a long time, people outside the US were feeling like the flow of culture was one way— that it came from the great god of Coca-Cola and Disneyland. At one point, the balance started to shift. In some places, people have realized that they themselves are hybrids of both the global culture and that of their own country" (quoted by Wolk).

In "Baby" (1968), Caetano Veloso's ode to the commodity fetish, the voice tells his girlfriend that she needs to learn English and to know about diners, swimming pools, and margarine. With this song, Os Mutantes and the Tropicalist artists acknowledged the politics of reification, underscoring the ways in which they were indeed the kinds of hybrids that Byrne describes. They managed to express this in their music, however, without the nostalgia that weighed upon MPB songs of the period.

A useful discussion of the figure of the hybrid in Latin America is found in the work of Néstor García Canclini.[18] He points out that, in the encounter with international mass-media products and ideologies, "peripheral" consumers do not uncritically or homogeneously receive these messages, but rather interpret and appropriate such artifacts in the vocabulary of their own cultural capital, "reconverting" these international artifacts to their greater advantage. This is related to what Oswald de Andrade called "cannibalism." It was the most important weapon in Os Mutantes' cultural arsenal. As the name suggests, it wasn't the group's faithful translation of American pop for a Brazilian audience, but rather its "mutations" of the music that made it special. This formed a common ground that attracted Beck, the United States' principal pop mutator, to Os Mutantes' revival. The band's list of mutations is long. Its members reconfigured French pop, American psychedelic rock, *moda-de-viola* music of Brazil, bossa nova, the Beatles, Brazilian Carnival music, and mod rock. To accommodate the melange of sounds and sound effects such as television news themes, cannon fire, and crowd noise, Os Mutantes spent nearly two months in the studio recording its debut album under the direction of Rogério Duprat. A generation ago, Os Mutantes absorbed a global repertoire of influences only recently made convenient in the 1990s by advances in international mass media and the rise of the electronic music movement. In a process similar to that described by García Canclini, the motifs were cannibalized, mutated, defected, and signified upon so that they were almost emptied of content until redeployed in the mix and impregnated with a new meaning belonging wholly to the group. This put Os Mutantes in a category all its own: "This is free sound. It's mutant, and it can't be stopped," said Os Mutantes collaborator Caetano Veloso during the landmark 1968 performance.

Os Mutantes' complicated relationship to influence and tradition, as well as its subsequent adoption by an Anglo-American musical vanguard involved in a similar reflection on influence and innovation, reminds us of the Borgesian conundrum raised in "Kafka and His Precursors": "In the critics' vocabulary, the word 'precursor' is indispensable, but it should be cleansed of all connotation of polemics or rivalry. The fact is that every writer creates his own precursors. His work modifies our conception of the past, as it will modify the future."[19]

Did Os Mutantes and the Tropicalists invoke postmodernity in pop music or did a musical postmodernity in the United States and Europe, characterized by the exhaustion of many styles and motifs, create them as a necessary precursor? Is the revival of Os Mutantes and the Tropicalists by Anglo-American hipsters an instance of the First World avant garde mining the Third World for inspiration in the same fashion as the primitivism so characteristic of European modernism, or does the adoption of a group whose very cultural strategies question such cultural relationships signify a more sophisticated relationship to otherness among a postmodern Anglo-American counterculture? Perhaps the very tactics employed by Os Mutantes thirty years ago will complicate the domestication of this group within an Anglo-American rock and countercultural tradition in a way that suggests the durability of its aesthetic interventions.

Notes

1. For an annotated version in the original, see Jorge Schwartz, *Vanguardas latino-americanas: polémicas, manifestos e textos críticos* (São Paulo: EDUSP-Iluminuras-FADESP, 1995), 142–147. For an annotated translation and bibliographical references, see Leslie Bary, *Latin American Literary Review* vol. 19, no. 38 (1991), 35–47; and for interpretation, "The Tropical Modernist as Literary Cannibal: Cultural Identity in Oswald de Andrade," *Chasqui* vol. 20, no. 2 (1991), 10–19.

2. Martha Ulhoa Carvalho, "Tupi or Not Tupi: MPB: Popular Music and Identity in Brazil," in *The Brazilian Puzzle*, ed. David J. Hess and Roberto DaMatta (New York: Columbia University Press, 1995), 159–179. Subsequent citations in text as Ulhoa.

3. Christopher J. Dunn, *The Relics of Brazil*. Dissertation, Brown University, 1996.

4. Charles A. Perrone, "Changing of the Guard: Questions and Contrasts of Brazilian Rock Phenomena," *Studies in Latin American Popular Culture* 9 (1990), 66.

5. The most influential account of this function is Mikhail Bahktin, *Rabelais and His World* (Bloomington: Indiana University Press, 1984). See especially the introductory chapter.

6. Charles A. Perrone, "Pau-Brasil, *Antropofagia, Tropicalismo*: The Modernist Legacy of Oswald de Andrade in Brazilian Poetry and Song of the 1960s–1980s," in *One Hundred Years of Invention: Oswald de Andrade and the Modern Tradition in Latin American Literature*, ed. K. David Jackson (Austin: Abaporu Press, 1992), 134.

7. Caetano Veloso, *Verdade tropical* (São Paulo: Companhia das Letras, 1997), 44.

8. Thomas Frank, "Alternative to What?," *The Baffler* 5 (1993), 5–14, 119–128. Subsequent citations in text by name.

9. Douglas Wolk, "Esperanto A Go-Go: The Global Pop Underground," *Spin* vol. 15, no.1 (January 1999), 68. Subsequent citations in text.

10. Carlos Calado, *A divina comédia dos Mutantes* (São Paulo: 34 Letras, 1996), 332.

11. Gerald Marzorati, "Tropicália, Agora!," *The New York Times Magazine*, April 25, 1999, 48–51; and Ben Ratliff, "The Fresh Prince of Brazil," *Spin* vol. 15, no. 6 (June 1999), 106–112.

12. http://aquarius.bianca.com.

13. Sean Lennon, the son of the Beatles' John Lennon, was one of the musicians who remixed the album of Tom Zé, who commented: "I listened to [Sean Lennon's] remix without any intention of understanding it, because when an old man understands a child, one of them is struck by lightning."

14. Ben Ratliff, "Tropicália: From Brazil, the Echoes of a Modernist Revolt," *The New York Times*, May 17, 1998. Next citation in text by date.

15. *The Gavin Report* 2248 (March 26, 1999), 5.

16. For a discussion of theories of the postmodern in relation to the strategies of the Tropicalists, see Rebecca Liv Sovik, *Vaca profana: teoria pós-moderna e tropicália*. Dissertation, Universidade de São Paulo, 1994.

17. Iain Chambers, *Migrancy, Culture, Identity* (New York: Routledge, 1994), 97.

18. Néstor García Canclini, *Hybrid Cultures: Strategies for Entering and Leaving Modernity* (Minneapolis: University of Minnesota Press, 1995).

19. Jorge Luis Borges, "Kafka and His Precursors," *Labyrinths* (New York: New Directions, 1964), 201.

Discography

The Beatles. *With the Beatles.* Parlophone, 1963.

——. *Sgt. Pepper's Lonely Hearts Club Band.* Parlophone, 1967.

Beck. *Odelay.* Geffen, 1996.

——. *Mutations.* Geffen, 1998.

Os Mutantes. *Os Mutantes.* Polydor, 1968.

——. *Mutantes.* Polydor, 1969.

——. *A divina comédia ou ando meio desligado.* Polydor, 1970.

Portastatic. *De mel de melão.* Merge, 2000.

Stereolab. *Transient Random Noise Bursts with Announcements.* Duophonic, 1993.

——. *Emperor Tomato Ketchup.* Duophonic, 1996.

Tom Zé. *Fabrication Defect / Com defeito de fabricacão.* Luaka Bop, 1998.

Various artists. *Tropicália ou panis et circenses.* Phillips, 1968.

Various artists. *Postmodern Platos (Tom Zé Remixed).* Luaka Bop, 1998.

Yo La Tengo. *New Wave Hot Dogs / President Yo La Tengo.* City Slang, 1987/1989.

——. *This Is Yo La Tengo.* City Slang, 1991.

——. *Painful.* City Slang, 1993.

SEVEN

Defeated Rallies, Mournful Anthems, and the Origins of Brazilian Heavy Metal

Idelber Avelar

The concept behind this book has allowed me to explain to myself why my own musical preferences as a teenager back in Brazil (British postpunk: Echo and the Bunnymen, Joy Division, Durutti Column, Siouxie and the Banshees, Bauhaus) maintained a surprising dialogue, and were not that socially incompatible, with the death / thrash metal (Slayer, Venom, Metallica, Sepultura) favored by my younger brothers and friends. It has allowed me to understand why that particular phenomenon is an important chapter of contemporary Brazilian popular music related to the trajectory of MPB [Música Popular Brasileira] in the 1970s and 1980s. The ease with which punks, headbangers, goths, and other "tribes" dialogued and collaborated with each other in Brazil owes something to a common rejection of the stardom of MPB, and to a perception that the canonical forms of Brazilian popular music had been co-opted by the remarkable entertainment industry developed during the 1970s. Our relationship with Brazilian music was highly problematic indeed, and this was true not only of us goths, but of our punk and headbanging friends as well. For us "Brazilian music" meant the MPB stars on TV, impeccably dressed, moving their lips to the recordings of their songs played on Friday nights or Sunday afternoons on one of those Globo-network variety shows. That institutionalization reached a high point, I would contend, with the role of popular music in the campaign for free and direct presidential elections (1984) and, after the defeat of said campaign, in the rise of the first postdictatorial civil government, the center-right coalition led by Tancredo Neves and José Sarney.

There is a story yet to be told about the role of dominant forms of Brazilian popular music in the consolidation and legitimization of the opposition bloc that would succeed the military regime in 1985. Not having been freely elected, but led by a congressional alliance with sectors of the regime into a victory in the electoral college, the Tancredo-Sarney ticket enjoyed considerable legitimacy, derived from the massive campaign for direct elections that they joined belatedly—that campaign was launched by the Workers' Party—and subsequently abandoned to negotiate a consensual formula with the military regime. The campaign for *diretas já* counted on conspicuous support from artists in all fields—filmmakers, writers, actors—but it was undoubtedly the voices of the major figures of MPB that resonated the loudest and came to be most directly associated with a cultural contingent that supported the struggle for free elections. It was also, however, a certain sector of MPB that came to take on a burden for having been linked with a regime—Sarney's, after Tancredo's death—that was not able to maintain the popular legitimacy generated by *diretas já* for longer than a few months, due to its staunchly reactionary composition.

Not, of course, that MPB was ever a vital part of the election of the center-right bloc that succeeded the military. If anything, music played a lateral role in gathering support for a coalition that, after the defeat of the direct-election amendment in Congress, would have been able to impose itself anyway, such was its strength within the Brazilian élites. Symbolically, however, the presence of some MPB stars in the Tancredo-Sarney rallies changed the perception of them held by a portion of the music public until that moment. This change became more pronounced after Tancredo's death and the rise to the presidential palace (March 1985) of a man who had been allied with military power throughout his political career, José Sarney.

The liberal-conservative betrayal of the campaign for direct and free elections after its defeat in Congress, and Sarney's subsequent assumption of power, were supported by several MPB stars, most notably, in my memory at least, by Milton Nascimento. He cocomposed (with Wagner Tiso) the song "Coração de estudante" [Heart of a student], which would become the musical stamp of the center-right coalition. To be true to Milton, it had first been the anthem animating the campaign for free elections, and was later appropriated by the so-called New Republic. If you saw the liberal-conservative leadership of that alliance holding hands at rallies singing "Coração de estudante" with Milton Nascimento, you know why goths, punks, headbangers, Workers' Party activists, feminists, black-movement militants, anarchists, environmentalists, and several other tribes were united in hating it. If you did not, let me jump straight to the conclusion: the crowning of "Coração de estudante" as the hymn of Tancredo and Sarney's campaign epitomized, in the minds of several musical tribes linked with the internationalization of Brazilian popular music in the 1980s, the capitulation of MPB to the status quo, its metamorphosis into the mouthpiece of the respectable and decent Brazil of the New Republic.

The fact is important because Milton's music had been closely associated with an oppositional imaginary during the military dictatorship. His career had largely coincided with the rise and fall of the military regime (his first album is from 1967), and he had translated like no other the ephemeral hopes and lasting disillusionment proper to the Brazilian popular and middle classes during the "long night" of the 1960s and 1970s. Embedded, as Charles Perrone has pointed out, "in the folk roots and historical heritage of Minas Gerais," Milton's music evoked nostalgia and melancholy but also offered a powerful message of political protest and dissent.[1] The unique combination of jazz, European classical music, traditional Minas Gerais toadas, folk rhythms, and religious chants; the legacy of Brazilian art music, Spanish-American genres, and avant-garde forms; the rich textures of his melodies; the mesmerizing alternation of haunting contraltos and chilling sopranos; the evocative and intensely poetic lyrics (signed by Milton himself or by his songwriting partners Ronaldo Bastos, Fernando Brant, Lô Borges, Beto Guedes, or Márcio Borges, members of the collective called the Clube da Esquina [Corner Club]; all of these factors made of Milton's music an inescapable reference in the Brazilian cultural landscape of the 1970s.

By 1985 Milton was a firmly established name, internationally recognized not only for his contributions to the Brazilian songbook but also for his connections with "world music" and his several invited collaborations with luminaries of American jazz. In Brazil his name had always been political in a more direct or less mediated sense than those of Caetano or Gil, and he had been popular in his roots in a more recognizable way than had Chico Buarque. Perhaps coherent with the less mediated character of his relationship with the political field, his wager on the Sarney regime in 1985 ended up being more naively formulated and more enthusiastic than those of Caetano, Gil, Chico, or any other prominent MPB figure (Chico Buarque in fact having been very critical and skeptical early on in the Sarney regime). As a consequence, Milton would later suffer the greatest loss of political and cultural capital following the failure of Sarney's regime, its constant leanings to the Right, and its betrayal of the popular legitimacy inherited from the campaign for free elections. Meanwhile, Belo Horizonte—the city most closely associated with the imaginary latent in Milton's songs—was becoming the capital of Brazilian heavy metal, a genre that emerged precisely by spitting on the New Republic, whose forging had been symbolically supported by Milton's art.

These various developments in the cultural and political fields do not maintain a cause-effect relationship with each other, but are certainly related in more ways than their simple chronological coexistence. The hopeful imaginary not only of Milton's anthem to the New Republic, but also of much of his earlier (musically and lyrically much richer) production, had to decline if the imaginary of *mineiro* heavy metal was to establish its voice, or at least make enough room to become socially audible. Heavy metal indeed came to manifest the hidden unconscious, the negation, so to speak, of the Clube da Esquina. Milton's collective had drawn the musical horizon of the state of Minas Gerais for two decades and therefore represented recent tradition's most solid foothold. Heavy metal was claiming legitimacy through a strategy of radical negation, one directed both at tradition and at everything that is part of present actuality, the totality of what is. Milton was the musical embodiment of both the past and the present, precisely the two major targets of the headbanging negation.

At an unconscious level (that is a level never theorized by the heavy-metal movement as such), Milton was the negative condition of possibility for heavy metal. His music had both refracted and produced a certain iconography of Minas Gerais's oxcarts, baroque churches, and steep unpaved paths being swept away by modernization and preserved in the elegiac homage music would pay to them:

Acabaram com o beco
mais ninguém vai morar
cheio de lembranças vem o povo
do fundo escuro beco
nessa clara praça se dissolver
"Beco do Mota" (Nascimento-Brant, 1969)

[They did away with the alley
no one lives there any longer
folks full of memories come
out of the deep dark alley to
dissolve in this here clear square]

Eh! minha cidade, portão de ouro,
aldeia morta, solidão
aldeia morta, cadeado, coração
e eu reconquistado, vou caminhando,
caminhando e morrer
"Os povos" (Nascimento-M.Borges, 1972)

[Oh my town, golden gate,
dead village, solitude
dead village, padlock, heart
and I, reconquered, keep on
walking, walking and to die]

It was primarily the idyllic imaginary of a peaceful, premodern, melancholy yet hopeful Minas Gerais mourned by the Clube da Esquina that heavy metal came to contest. One of Milton's most memorable scenes depicted the son of a rural family taking leave of the interior and returning with a diploma and the *sinhá mocinha* [missy] to be introduced to the parents (see "Morro velho" [Nascimento] 1967). Such images helped create a songbook and a poetic reserve of rituals of emigration, abandonment, and departure. Heavy metal had to negate that imaginary, for it never experienced that attachment to Minas Gerais, cultivating instead an enraged cosmopolitanism that canceled out those mournful rituals of departure. In that particular case, it was the very backbone of Minas Gerais's popular and artistic symbology that was being negated.

The symbolic antagonism between Clube da Esquina and heavy metal becomes clearer with a few historical clarifications. What is meant here by heavy metal bears little resemblance to the less strident and perhaps more musically varied forms sometimes also alluded to with that label and epitomized in the 1970s by such groups as Led Zeppelin, Black Sabbath, and Deep Purple. These acts indeed had some following in Brazil during the 1970s and 1980s, but it would be difficult to argue that much major Brazilian popular music, including pop and rock genres, owed much to them, certainly not as intensely as, say, Bahian rocker Raul Seixas did to Elvis Presley or Os Mutantes did to the Beatles. The death metal that would become remarkably popular in the 1980s and 1990s among the working- and lower-middle classes in Belo Horizonte—with concurrent presence in São Paulo, Porto Alegre, and other metropolises—was propelled by bands such as Slayer, Venom, and Metallica, and produced a rather different effect, proper to the movement's do-it-yourself ethic: it generated countless bands among its following. Of those, Sepultura is simply the one that eventually achieved international recognition and sales measured in millions, the tip of an iceberg that included dozens of bands within half a dozen neighborhoods. Some additional names are important to mention, if for nothing else than to stake out the very vocabulary that differentiates them from the Clube da Esquina: Overdose, Witchhammer, Destroyer, Butcher.

The resemanticization of a certain Catholic iconography of Minas Gerais is the major line of continuity between Milton and the metal bands that emerged against the horizon delimited by his gigantic artistic figure. Not that the two strategies bore any resemblance: while Milton reappropriated messages and symbols of charity, fraternity, and hope in a political, popular, and emancipatory sense (culminating in the albums *Sentinela* and *Missa dos quilombos*), heavy metal proposed no appropriation, but rather a strategy of radical negation, inversion, and voiding of the Catholic iconography so strong in Minas Gerais. On their second album, Sepultura shouted:

> . . . Christians, Today They Still Cry
> But The Bastards Adore Images
> Remembrances From The Past, From The Crucifixion
> Rotting Christ, Nailed To The Cross
> From The Semen Of The Mankind
> We'll Spread Our Seed
> And We'll Show To The Devoted
> The Truth, The Painful Truth
> ("Morbid Visions," *Morbid Visions*, 1986)

The imperative for death metal was the destruction of the signifier itself, not its preservation with a different meaning. Metal did not distinguish a truer and recuperable message in the *mineiro* religiosity; it decided instead to cancel it out through extensive use, decontextualization, and ultimately the voiding of its symbolic apparatus. Inverted crosses, satanic allusions, and eschatological obsession are part of a poetic strategy completely built around the negation of something Milton's music was famous for expressing: the hope that underneath the conservative, conventional, traditional, and religious universe of Minas Gerais resided some emancipatory, fraternal, and compassionate kernel politically and culturally available. Death metal was primarily a negation of that availability.

Death metal's relationship with Minas Gerais should be understood as an unconscious relation, naturally different from Milton's explicit project of symbolically remaking the state. In fact the proper names "Milton Nascimento" and "Belo Horizonte death metal" (or "Milton" and "Sepultura," if one prefers the synecdoche) describe opposite movements vis-à-vis the symbolic kernel of Minas Gerais's mythology. While the imaginary of Milton's music depicts a centripetal move toward the center, Belo Horizonte, which progressively but circularly runs away from the interior, death metal, on the contrary, arises out of an already urban, *belo-horizontina* crowd of impoverished middle-class youth who of necessity cannot but establish a centrifugal relation to Minas Gerais and its center. Milton mourns the ritual of migration from the interior to the capital by taking the standpoint of the peasant father who stays and later receives the returning son—or fantasizes he is doing it, which poetically there amounts to the same. In death metal, the movement and the operation are symmetrically opposed: they depart from an already disillusioned urban experience, and project out of that cage a migration that has been completely dissociated from mourning. Already in Milton's first album, the song "Três Pontas" gave a poetic indication of a pattern of returns to the interior associated with the possibility of storytelling:

todo mundo vem correndo para ver, rever	[all came running to see, again
gente que partiu pensando um dia em voltar	folks who left thinking of returning
enfim voltou no trem	and returned on the train
e voltou contando histórias	telling stories
de uma terra tão distante do mar	of a land so distant from the sea]
(Nascimento-Bastos, 1967).	

To do a truly just analysis of this masterful song we would have to show how the accumulation of percussive energy in the moments when Milton powerfully extends the monosyllables (e.g., "trem," "ver," "mar") allegorizes, in itself, the movement of memory that the lyrics depict, the condensation of mournful energy in a sound that is the explicit theme of the song. Be that as it may, in Milton the most intense musical moments tend to coincide with the mournful portrayal of memory in the lyrics. The inventive horizons opened by music are coextensive with the possibility of storytelling alluded to by the lyrics. There is a correlation, in other words, between the poetic reserve generated by the music and the mnemonic reserve that the lyrics mournfully attempt to depict.

On the other hand, the possibility of storytelling in death metal has been divorced from memory, since death metal depicts a world where apocalypse has already happened, or is imminent to the point of canceling out any possibility of memory:

> What Has Gone Through Me Will Never Return
> Future Won't Let Me Look Back
> ("Primitive Future," *Beneath the Remains*, 1989)

Death metal's futuristic-eschatological matrix is the inverted correlate of Milton's linking of memory and mourning. While he returns to the past in order to stage it as a present lamenting its own passing, Sepultura arises out of an unbearable present to project its own annihilation in a future understood as a final judgment. While Milton has been responsible for the musicalization of Minas Gerais's memory in the 1960s, 1970s, 1980s, and to a certain degree the 1990s, death metal has turned the 1980s and 1990s into a time of no memory, for the time of metal is always the temporality of the last day, a day by definition incapable of any memory and therefore purely present to itself. In Hegelian terms one could say that Milton composed the morning anthem while death metal produced the dusk-dwelling sound, the frequent encounters between Lucifer and a weakened God in the latter being nothing but an allegorization of the world's inability to recollect itself as memory, its inhabiting of an eschatological locus, its purely nightly existence:

> Beneath The Remains / Cities In Ruins
> Bodies Packed On Minefields / Neurotic Game Of Life And Death
> Now I Can Feel The End / Premonition About My Final Hour
> ("Beneath Remains," *Beneath Remains*,1989)

> The Terror Is Declared
> The Final Fight Started
> The Antichrist And Lucifer
> Fighting With Angels And God
> ("Warriors of Death," *Bestial Devastation*, 1985)

Only an academic moralist would pass judgment on the faulty English lyrics, but only someone immersed in the movement would be unable to see that the English errors themselves speak allegorical volumes about death metal: one of the most common lapses is the ungrammatical overuse of the definite pronoun (e.g., "To send souls to the hell"), coherent not only with the Portuguese language from which they translate, but also and most important with the radically immanentist vein of death metal, its tendency to singularize each thing so as to make it unfit for any metaphorization, its struggle against the generalist impulse in the English language. Death metal is, in that sense, also an explicit cry of revolt against transcendence, the very transcendence that Milton's music immortalized in its unique blend of international and Brazilian genres.

The canceling out of transcendence and memory in death metal is coherent with the movement's relationship with its surroundings. Particularly strong in neighborhoods of lower middle- or working-class composition (Santa Teresa, first home to Sepultura, or Sagrada Família), death metal relates to location only insofar as it is a location to be abandoned, a point from which to draw a line of flight. Its performative effect relies on the staging of an eschatological flight from its surroundings. Death metal counters the backwardness of a particular place with the dissolution of location as such in the apocalypse. Contrary to the abandoning and departures portrayed in Milton's music, there is no possibility of return, for one's particular location in time is always a suicidal location, a place in dissolution. As we will see, both moments—Milton's mournful rituals of migration and metal's memoryless apocalypse—hark back, through many mediations, to a contradiction in Brazilian capitalism, and especially to its particular manifestation in Minas Gerais's unique blend of tradition and modernization.

One of death metal's strongholds in Belo Horizonte through the 1980s and 1990s was the neighborhood known as Sagrada Família, home primarily to senior citizens, unemployed youth, and dogs. If you are familiar with Belo Horizonte, chances are you have at least heard of Sagrada Família—the name itself being quite ironic here. Situated a few minutes east of Belo Horizonte's highly modern downtown area, and bounded by the dynamic commercial cluster known as Floresta, Sagrada Família is the epitome of Belo Horizonte as the epitome of Brazilian capitalism. An island of traditionalism in the center of one of the most modern Brazilian cities, Sagrada Família is made up of old houses that have somehow survived the pressures of real-estate corporations, since they are inhabited by impoverished elderly who refuse to sell their property (since their only value is their location: they are property to be sold, destroyed, and re-placed). That refusal creates an economic impasse unexplainable by any ratio-nal theory model, namely the refusal to sell, the refusal to move to "better" places, the refusal to modernize when both your "self-interest" (at least as mea-sured by such theories) and every market tendency impel you to do so. These old folks stake out an experiential and mnemonic value in opposition to exchange value. These particular neighborhoods represent, then, a certain reserve of sheer memory value in a forward-looking and modernizing context.

The despair vis-à-vis temporality in death metal is strictly related to this par-ticular junction in the modernization of Brazilian metropolises, in which the only available opposition to market logic is the one built around cries for preser-vation and memory. This preservative relation to memory becomes unbearable for any headbanger, and negatively explains much of the apocalyptic temporality present in the music and performance of countless death-metal bands. Origi-nated primarily in a milieu fully exposed to modernization but excluded from its fruits, heavy metal experiences progress already from the point of view of its final failure. However, the movement's suicidal negation, its strong refusal to affirm, bars it from offering any other temporality alternative or subsequent to that final point. Time is halted and frozen into apocalypse because the only narrative available for organizing time has been that of progress, precisely the one upon whose ruins death metal puts up its tent. The irreconcilability between metal and its surroundings, then, is not only a spatial impasse: it is derived in fact from the impossibility of temporalizing that space, for the only available temporaliza-tion was based on an ideology explicitly negated, and denounced as a failure, by one's very surroundings. In that sense death metal takes to its ultimate limits—by allegorizing it as apocalypse—a particular temporal antinomy of Brazilian capi-talism.

Death metal depicts, then, a time in which the Benjaminian angel of history can no longer hope to return to the past and redeem piles of catastrophes, for it has drowned in them, suffocated by the past misery it once hoped to hold in its hands. Memory collapses into pure facticity, and cannot offer any experience of time other than the sheer presentness of the last day. The opposition with Milton could not be clearer here, as his music—with the elongated temporality of its melody and harmony—allegorized a certain extended time, the very stretched-out time depicted in the recollecting lyrics written by Brant, Bastos, or Milton himself:

Ponta de Areia, ponto final

[Sand Point, final point

da Bahia-Minas, estrada natural

Of the Bahia Minas line, natural road

que ligava Minas ao porto, ao mar

that linked Minas to the port, the sea

caminho de ferro, mandaram arrancar

railway they ordered torn up

. . . .

na praça vazia um grito um ai

in the empty square a cry of pain

casas esquecidas viúvas nos portais

forgotten houses widows on thresholds]

"Ponta de Areia" (Nascimento-Brant, 1975)

In "Ponta de Areia," a pinnacle of Milton's recording career and one of the richest melodies in the contemporary Brazilian songbook, the extended guitar, bass, sax, piano, and percussion lines—combined in highly dissonant fashion—are accompanied by one of the most powerful performances of Milton's falsetto soprano, which introduces the song before his contralto takes over and stretches all stressed vowels to their absolute limits. His voice takes a labyrinthine stroll along the stretched-out vowels, as if replicating the curves of the railroad mourned by the lyrics (an effect reinforced by reproductions of the train's whistling, carefully placed in dialogue with Nivaldo Ornelas's soprano sax). This coincidence between form and content is one of the keys to Milton's art, and it is invariably achieved through the staging of an extended, elongated, mournful temporality.

In contrast, the fast succession of repetitive movements in metal's distorted guitars emblematizes the annihilation of all extended temporalities and the apocalyptic canceling out of time which are proper to the movement. Since in death metal all time has coalesced on the last day, there is an undeniable coherence in metal's choice for crafting its music by taking repetition to its ultimate limits. The realm of sheer repetition can only come on Judgment Day. "To repeat until all differences are annihilated" is one of metal's mottos, a striking contrast with Milton, whose musico-lyrical art is premised on a careful use of repetition as a kind of modulator of differences. In fact, one of the major musical contrasts between death metal and neighboring genres, such as punk or other forms of metal, is the absence of any modulation, discontinuity, or alternation between the guitars and the rhythm section composed of bass and drums. The two replicate one another to exhaustion, again coherently with the annihilation of time depicted in the apocalyptic lyrics.

More than simply a "reflection" of the lack of alternatives for Brazilian working-class youth amidst a debt crisis, chronic unemployment, and hyperinflation, heavy metal represents an active, creative intervention in established mythologies of Brazilian cultural and political life. What is new, I would contend, about my argument here is the highlight on the convergence of two of those mythologies around 1985 (the civic mythology of Brazilian democracy and the Christianizing-redemptive mythology of Milton's music). It is important, then, to realize how such a convergence provided heavy metal with its primary, albeit unconscious, target of attack and negation in the mainstream. It's not by coincidence that the mid-1980s represent a major turning point for Brazilian heavy metal, with the consolidation of Cogumelo Discos (the first independent label for Sepultura, Overdose, and company) and a rise in sales and following that would soon catapult Sepultura toward international stardom. It was the New Republic's appropriation of the Christian kernel of Milton's music that initially allowed metal's inverted, negated Christianity to establish itself as an alternative mythology. The particular way in which the political field mediated between agents in the cultural field in this episode shows how comparisons in popular-music scholarship should not be limited to musicians who influence or dialogue with each other. In this strict regard, of course, there is little doubt that Brazilian heavy metal does not dialogue with or owe anything to Milton Nascimento's music. But it is clear to me that the mainstreaming of his artistic message opens up a national and regional space that heavy metal would subsequently occupy and implode.

Following that initial moment, metal would need to have it out with its own international mainstreaming. Much like any other heir to the negative thrust of the early-twentieth-century avant garde, death metal, punk, and other "tribal" pop genres invariably face dilemmas related to the potential contradiction between their growing popularization and their nihilistic messages. In this sense Sepultura is now facing, mutatis mutandis, the same crossroads faced by Milton in 1985, when his enthusiasm for the new liberal order (even if corrected and contradicted later by his disillusioned "Carta à República" [Letter to the republic]) came to emblematize the relative decline in the innovative energy of his music. In death metal the trap of institutionalization manifests itself in a particular way, namely the impossibility of maintaining the apocalyptic, radically negative discourse in a context of systematic growth in sales and popularity. In a search for affirmative forms of discourse, Sepultura would begin to highlight a certain Brazilianness, for example, through use of the national flag in international concerts, as well as attempt a dialogue with figures of Brazilian pop music, albeit from its "alternative" strand, as in their recent collaboration with Carlinhos Brown or their homage to Chico Science, among other things. Soulfly (founded by an original leader of Sepultura) with a 1999 version of Jorge Ben's "Ponta-de-lança africano (Umbabarauma)" also illustrates this shift from the nihilistic inversion of Christianity to the affirmative embrace of an alternative Brazilian tradition. It remains to be seen whether this shift spells heavy metal's definitive institutionalization as another genre in the supermarket of pop, the ultimate cancelation of its origins in negativity. Yet heavy metal's negative reversal of national and regional mythologies was initially made possible by the collapse of an immense artistic reserve—that of Milton Nascimento—into the symbolic reserve of Brazilian liberal democracy. Metal's response to that collapse was unique, and it was firmly rooted in the experiences of urban working- and lower-middle-class youth. This genuine and creative response undoubtedly accounts for the movement's irreducible moment of truth.

Note

1. Charles A. Perrone, *Masters of Contemporary Brazilian Song: MPB 1965–1985* (Austin: University of Texas Press, 1989), 133. See chapter 4, "Milton Nascimento: Sallies and Banners," and his discography of the period in the appendix.

EIGHT

The Localization of Global Funk
in Bahia and in Rio

Livio Sansone

An important phenomenon in the vast outskirts of global youth culture is the massive popularity of public funk dances in Rio de Janeiro and Salvador, Bahia, two largely black and *mestiço* cities of a nation that has been defined by many as "extreme West" and that evokes associations with many other countries.[1] The present study is moved both by a curiosity for the ways the locals reinterpret the global and by concern with two troublesome positions in the study of subcultures, styles, and new forms of ethnic identity among young black people in the modern city.

First, I disagree with the position that massification and homogenization of cultural forms among young people are processes that develop somewhat steadily, according to the same principles in different countries. This should be the case of the worldwide distribution and growth of reggae, funk, and hip-hop, and of the styles associated with these types of music. According to this view, the styles associated with these kinds of music are spreading worldwide from a center to the periphery, by equalizing youth's musical expressions and styles in a unique register, which is strongly inspired by that of the Anglo-Saxon capitals. Indeed, the relevance of the portrait drawn by mass media and the social sciences of the situation of young people and their music in parts of the English-speaking world reaches far beyond the geographic borders of those countries.[2] It ends up being a portrait that is distributed internationally by the media that brings about the globalization of Western urban culture. Such a portrait is becoming part and parcel of that global memory with which every new youth style or subculture, whether at the core or in the periphery of the circuit, has to come to terms.[3] In Brazil, the media, and the bulk of social scientists studying young people have been very curious about the possible emergence of youth styles according to the Anglo-Saxon pattern sketched above. This generates much more curiosity than the forms through which their local young people, starting from a different system of opportunities, reinterpret the symbols associated with global youth styles, for example, those of Rastas and punks. I imagine the same also occurs in many other countries of the Third World that are on the periphery of global youth culture. Yet one can adopt a perspective on the internationalization of youth culture that is neither ethnocentric nor based on linear evolutionism—a perspective that counters the view by which the only space for maneuver left to the "consuming" periphery is the manipulation of symbols and goods coming from faraway "providing" places.

The second position that concerns me consists of relating each youth gang, style, and subculture to a specific use of a single type of music. According to this tendency, a specific type of music is used basically as a marker of ethnic and stylistic difference—an ethnomusical difference that is often depicted as being relatively stable and accepted by the groups both inside and outside the ethnic line.[4] Altogether, the tendency is to link a particular musical genre to one group, one form of social identity, and one type of behavior. In the modern urban context, this kind of association reminds one of the traditional approach of many ethnomusicologists to less developed societies: to isolate one musical form and to associate it with a circumscribed group. This resulted in descriptions of ethnic identity and of musical creativity of the group in question that were most often more static than real.[5] According to this notion, musical forms are substantially "pure" forms that can endure the passing of time and of generations. In addition, it is suggested that by communicating with other musical forms of other groups, an observed form of music can produce fusions and crossovers. That is, musical creation is not seen, as such, as a process of fusion, quotation, and reflection. Within traditional ethnomusicology, and with respect to the music of New World blacks in particular, this notion of distinct music for distinct ethnic groups and ethnicities has had authentic champions, for example, John and Allan Lomax. Their oeuvre has been dedicated to showing the uniqueness of Afro-American forms.[6] The Lomaxes represent for ethnomusicology that which Melville Herskovits's notion of Africanism represents for anthropology: the pursuit of "original" and substantially pure traits related to African roots within contemporary (black) culture.[7] Recent research based on cities in northwestern Europe rather than on the United States has shown that youth styles, even those that are usually held as "black," are much more mixed than often assumed, that (black) ethnic symbols are not always deployed in opposition to nonblacks, and that these symbols can also be used to buttress one's own status, especially in the arena of leisure.[8]

A comparative focus on the consumption of funk music—one form of pop music that works as transponder (receiver and amplifier) of the process of globalization—can offer new perspectives for the study of the interplay of globalization and ethnicity, helping promote deserved careful review of most generalizations about youth culture within sociology and anthropology. These generalizations are based on the situation of the most advanced industrialized countries and apply only in part to Third World cities such as Salvador and Rio. The reception and transformation of youth and musical phenomena in these two cities show a more diversified situation than is often suggested in the study of globalization. Beyond a certain degree of globalization in the universe encompassing youth culture, the consumption of popular music, and the creation of black youth ethnicities, a series of local aspects are tenaciously maintained, which are determined by different structural contexts, cultural histories, and musical traditions. In other words, the worldwide hegemony of "Anglo-Saxon" youth culture is not unquestioned.

Brazilian funk is a youth cultural expression centered on the collective consumption of music. It is particularly well developed in Rio, Belo Horizonte, and Salvador. The *funkeiros* [funk aficionados] meet at funk dances and, in Rio, assemble on the beach in large and highly visible crowds. In Brazil the term *funk* started to be used in the 1970s to refer to modern black pop music from the United States (e.g., James Brown and the Jackson Five). In the 1990s, this term was used to refer to a variety of electronic musics that, at least in the opinion of most Brazilians, are associated with contemporary U.S.-based black pop music (e.g., acid, house, hip-hop, electronic funk, modern soul). Brazil is a huge and diversified country, and the meaning of the term *funk music* varies accordingly. In São Paulo and in the south, funk is basically hip-hop—whether imported or locally produced and sung in Portuguese. *Rapeiros*, lower-class mostly nonwhite rappers, emphasize lyrics rather than dance and like to dress in a style tailored to images of U.S. rap groups seen on TV and record sleeves and, to a lesser extent, at live concerts in Brazil. In Salvador, as seen below, funk is understood to mean any imported, electronically mixed dance music from the United States and Europe. In Rio and Belo Horizonte, the two cities with the largest funk scenes, the music is mainly Brazilian produced, usually a combination of two young working-class voices and a simple rhythm extracted from a cheap, preprogrammed beat box. The lyrics are sharp and cute descriptions of love (particularly in so-called funk melody tunes), violence, and social injustice. As far as violence and drugs are concerned, there are often two versions of the same song: a soft, official broadcast version and a "secret" version, with cruder lyrics, to be sung along with collectively at dances. Lyrics are never sexually explicit nor do they encourage sexual violence against women, a significant difference from much U.S. hip-hop. In terms of rhythm, the Brazilian-produced funk music is much simpler than most well-known U.S. or international hip-hop or modern (acid or electronic) funk. In its most popular forms, it is unsophisticated singing-shouting and—in this land of amazing percussive musical traditions!—combined with a very simple and repetitive background beat from a (cheap) electronic drum box. In fact, almost all music critics dismiss Brazilian funk as a poor lower-class urban version of any possible genre of electronic U.S. "black music." The leading dailies in Brazil like to report on the newest records in U.S. and British music, which normally sell very poorly in Brazil. Brazilian funk music is largely ignored by the press, except in the rare instances of healthy sales, such as with the record *Funk Brasil* (1994) and the releases of the duo MC Buchecha e MC Claudinho (1997), which sold about 1 million copies each. In fact, funk music has a sizeable share of the music industry in Brazil. Besides a series of record labels devoted exclusively to Brazilian funk, there are several radio and TV programs on funk. According to estimates in Rio de Janeiro alone, every weekend hundreds of thousands of young people attend about three hundred funk dances, which dot every region of this city of 12 million.[9] This pattern had its beginnings in the mid-1980s.

Funk in Rio de Janeiro

Much research corroborates the importance of funk music in the city of Rio and its grounding in community life, something that has even been called the "funk movement."[10] In Rio, funk reflects and at the same time redefines the divisions within lower-class communities and the frontier between "the community" and "the system." Funk, in particular funk dancing sessions, and the behavior of the *galeras de funkeiros* [the large, streetwise, almost gang-wise, peer groups of funk aficionados], have enjoyed attention from mass media, intellectuals, and a large part of public opinion in Rio.[11]

My investigation in 1995 in the Cantagalo *favela* (above Ipanema) does not represent an exception in this respect. As any other researcher in the field working in a lower-class area in Rio in the mid-1990s, I was immediately confronted with the omnipresence of funk music in the alleyways that form the main part of this self-built community. There, the dominant sound is the bass of the beat box, carried by radios or cassette recorders. The sound of samba is less present. There are other music tastes. Many speak of their preference for romantic music, for Roberto Carlos, for *pagode* and classic samba, or for the music of the ascendant folk-Pentecostal churches. Nonetheless, in this community it seemed that funk music had, as it were, saturated the soundscape, and that musical genres other than funk had a hard time finding their way into public spaces. Even though in my fieldwork I did not want to focus on funk aficionados—in fact I wanted to shed light on the lifestyle of less visible youth styles—I soon came to realize that if being a recognizable *funkeiro* is a circumscribed phenomenon, enjoying funk music is so common among young people that it does not characterize a subgroup or a style as such. From Friday through Sunday, the funk dance constitutes the core of public life on "the hill" (*morro*, as the inhabitants often define their community). This dance is an important opportunity to meet young people from "the asphalt" (as the inhabitants define those who live in neighborhoods with proper houses and paved streets) and from other neighborhoods, even though these interclass encounters are not as frequent as indicated by the statements of the organizers of the dance and of many local residents. In the discourse of the local residents, at least those who feel free to comment, the liminar function of the funk dance is celebrated if not exaggerated: the interclass and interracial mixing is put forward, whereas there is silence about "the movement" (the local cocaine ring) supposedly subsidizing the dance and/or using the dance to increase

Soul singer Tim Maia and band, 1979. Photo by and courtesy of
Maurício Valladares.

sales volume at the "smoke mouth" (public point of cocaine sales to locals and
outsiders). Alex, white DJ of the funk dance in Cantagalo, has lived on the asphalt for twenty-two years—of which "ten [were] spent in funk music." He says:

> The good thing about funk is that it is mixed. You see an amazing blonde women
> with a toothless black guy. Anything is possible. It's not like in discothèques, where
> you see 500 women, but none gives a damn about you because you don't have a
> brand-new car. Here you can be pitch black and, if you talk good, and the girl likes
> you, she goes with you. Most of the public in this dance comes from the asphalt.
> For those girls it is cool to come up the hill.

Cantagalo residents identify many subgroups among young people. In my
estimation, differences are many. One day, while inquiring whether there were
different groups of young people in the community, I heard the following categories: *funkeiros*, church groups (Catholic, Assembly of God, and God Is Love), a
theatre group, participants in the educational Surfavela project, soccer fanatics,
and finally visitors to Claudinho's sport academy. These groups are not differen-

tiated by an association with funk, because all of these groups like funk, including the Pentecostals, who love "religious funk." A growing number of bands relating to the Pentecostal circuit use funk rhythms and attire, often in combination with other sounds and looks. In truth, as Luciana says, "God and the world love funk." Funk is so popular that those who go to dances cannot be identified with only one of the above-mentioned subgroups. A majority of *funkeiros* attend classes or work ("you need money to go to the dances") and, from time to time, also enjoy other types of music. Only a minority "listens to funk music all the time." This group consists of about thirty young people in Cantagalo. For most of the others, funk is just another music that does not exclude other kinds of music. Nineteen-year-old Lúcia, for example, likes funk and does not miss a single dance, but also likes *pagode*, national pop music of the soft sort, and Bob Marley. She adds that, far from always being rough, funk dances can also be romantic: "The funk dance is nice for making out, when they put on the slow tunes." One of the few critical voices in the community is the group of young people who define themselves as "alternative." They are fond of MPB (mainstream Brazilian popular music), theater, and movie houses. They consider funk to be a "poor phenomenon," that is, unsophisticated.

Differences are much less defined in terms of leisure than in terms of outlooks on life and work. All young people, at least until approximately twenty years of age, go outside the community to enjoy the city during leisure hours. Most often, they leave and come back in groups. In terms of clothes and talking about them, hardly any subgroup can be identified. More than fashion itself, it is the way of walking, talking, and showing off that distinguishes a young "bandit" from the rest of his or her contemporaries. Almost everybody likes the beach (and beach life) and funk, with the partial exclusion of those who partake in the youth groups of the two local Pentecostal churches. Many bridges connect the hill to the asphalt: school, work, military service, the martial-arts academy, Carnival associations, surfing, beach life, and even the funk dance and the sale of marijuana and cocaine. Contacts are intense, though frequency and quality vary according to age, educational level, and physical attire. Attractive young men and women from the hill maintain the closest contacts with the playboys and *playboyas* (*favela* terms for attractive counterparts from the city proper). Few young people actually identify themselves as *funkeiros*. Still fewer identify with a specific *galera*. Only a small minority of those young people who identify themselves and are seen as "rebels" consider *funkeiro* a style associated with self-exclusion or opposition to the Establishment. In other words, we must remain wary of any a priori direct link between rage, revolt, violence, gangs, and funk.

Funk in Bahia

If the situation in Rio calls for a careful consideration of details, instead of easy generalizations, one must also take particular care when analyzing funk dances in Salvador. "Poor, black, and angry" proclaims the cover of an issue of the leading news magazine with extensive coverage of the funk phenomenon in Brazil, which, if already "out of place" in Rio, acquires absurd connotations in Salvador.[12] The Funk Feras [Beasts] and Funk Boys, two groups of dancers from the lower-class periphery neighborhood of Periperi in Salvador, soon came to realize that this special issue was not at all what they had expected. These young funk-dance aficionados had given serious and enthusiastic assistance to the *Veja* reporter: they hoped to be able to use the issue to promote their shows.

A few years after the soul music phenomenon in Rio, a similar movement started in Salvador, later to be developed and democratized by the *funkeiros*. Again, the mass media and modern music industry facilitated a symbolic and musical exchange with the African-American universe.[13] Rio played a key role in the soul and funk phenomena, both of which achieved importance outside the conventional, commercial channels for the promotion of music. In the case of samba and MPB, rather than the centrality of Rio, one can refer to a Rio–Salvador axis, with the latter delivering sounds and lyrics widely regarded as *de raíz* [roots] or even "hot" and "tropical."[14] For soul and funk lovers, Rio is definitely the center from which these sounds spread to other Brazilian urban centers.

> The exchange between Rio and Salvador already sheds light on the process of globalization of funk. Rio works like a center that is able to suggest standards and, at the same time, as a necessary yardstick for defining the sense of belonging of the group in Salvador.[15]

North American and black North American influences were already conspicuous in the musical cultures of black and *mestiço* youth in Salvador in the late 1970s. Soul, especially the look and style of James Brown, had a huge impact on behavior. The appellation *brau* (from Brown) denoted a lower-class young black man experimenting with the soul-brother style in Bahia. While having a disparaging connotation for middle-class kids, for lower-class black and *mestiço* youth *brau* was a term for a modern, sensual and black look. We do not know exactly how this symbology got to Salvador, whether directly from the United States or via Rio. In any case, it is clear that some symbols associated with U.S. blacks started to become part and parcel of the symbolic universe of most young people. Cultural attributes associated with U.S. blacks, including sound recordings, were manipulated and reinterpreted. The *blocos afro*, for example, Ilê Aiyê beginning in 1974, incorporated such symbols into their visual and verbal discourses as well, though in a less conspicuous fashion. This occurred in expressions relating both to negritude or blackness and to *baianidade* or Bahianness, a sweetened and ethnically nonconflictual form of blackness centered on a specific combination of happiness, cordiality toward all, and consumption.[16] That is, locals drew upon U.S. blacks in terms of assertiveness and manipulations of modernity alike. The slogans and symbols associated with Black Power were also an inspiration for the incipient black militancy movement. They were associated with possible combinations of being black and modern, conspicuously consuming garments and accessories attributed to U.S. blacks so as to differentiate oneself from the traditional Afro-Bahian look, without having to resort to a "white" look. In this context, the funk dance in the neighborhood of Periperi, Black Bahia, started to take place in the early 1980s, unnoticed by the Bahian mass media. From 1981 to 1996 the dance was held every Sunday except during Carnival.

A group of young Rio impresarios, the owners of a huge sound system, decided to set up a funk dance in Salvador, according to the model they had developed in Rio, São Paulo, and Belo Horizonte. The DJ was flown in weekly from Rio to animate the dance with new tunes. As usual, the authority of the DJ depended on his ability both to satisfy the taste of the public, which loves to identify with the tunes played, and to introduce innovations gradually. Little by little, Bahian DJs built up their own names and started to take the places of those from Rio. The supply channels for the records, however, still led to Rio. The only large venue available to host the first funk dance in Salvador was the Sport Club of Periperi, a huge hangar in the heart of this large urban periphery neighborhood. In fact, it is the major venue of the periphery of Salvador, and it hosts the performances of all major popular bands. Periperi represents the cultural core of the vast suburban area (home to an estimated 700,000 inhabitants in 1996). Any Sunday in Periperi offers an average of seven *pagodes* [samba dances], two *serestas* [serenades, or dances for seniors], countless informal drumming sessions on the local beach, auditions of the *bloco afro* Ara Ketu, and, last but not least,

the Black Bahia funk dance. Furthermore, the Estudio Periferia, the only recording studio available for bands not on the charts, is in Periperi. All of this is completely ignored by the media that cannot fathom a young Salvador that does not
fit the traditional patterns of Afro-Bahian blackness. Usually this is represented as
consisting of the interdependent parts of Afro-Brazilian religion, percussion,
and, more recently, an Afropop music known as *afro-reggae*, or as a *baianidade*
identity (the visible expressions of which are Carnival, beach, happiness, and the
pop music called *axé music*). In fact, the self-constructed lower-class suburbs of
Periperi and neighboring areas have never received much attention from the
Bahian mass media, which report almost nothing about the "suburbans," save
murders, traffic accidents, and the death toll from periodic landslides. In many
ways, one can say that Periperi is to the Bahian media what the suburban fringe
of the Baixada Fluminense is for the media in Rio. The main Bahian newspaper,
A Tarde, only started publishing small mentions of funk dances ten years after
their inception. Radios gave more coverage to Black Bahia, playing in particular
the softer tunes, called "funk melody" (Midlej e Silva 82). Radio coverage, nonetheless, vanished after 1991.

I visited Black Bahia from 1993 to 1995. The dance starts and finishes quite
early, lasting from 7 to 11 PM, to enable people to catch the last buses home and to
rest for Monday, a *dia de branco* [white man's day = work day]. Almost nobody
has a car. The overwhelming majority of the visitors live in the vast suburban
periphery around Periperi. A few come from neighborhoods as far away as Itapoã
(50 kilometers). On average there are 2,000 visitors. The vast majority are lower
class, black, and *mestiço*, between the ages of fifteen and twenty-five. Many are
students or are waiting for a (scarce) place in the free public schools. A minority
work, often in poorly paid clerical positions (e.g., as office boys, sales assistants,
and receptionists). The funk dance is visited by different groups. Girls are in the
majority on the dance floor and in the dance groups, though usually not in the
leadership. The appropriate funk look for girls is simpler and cheaper than for
boys: hot pants, minitop, and black clogs. There are a number of organized
dance groups whose members rehearse and dance together, for instance, the
Funk Feras, Funk Boys, and Cobras. These close-knit groups are not called
galeras as might have been the case in Rio. In Bahia the term *galera* has a more
collective meaning than in Rio: a multitude of people having fun together.
Among the organized dance groups there is rivalry, mostly of the symbolic sort,
ritualized in the dance steps and in dance-hall demeanor. It is hardly ever mani-

fested outside the club. The leaders of such groups tend to be older than the average participant in the dance. All the leaders are employed and insist on giving a positive image of themselves as "hardworking, straight" persons. One of the most influential leaders is a security officer of the most exclusive, and exclusionary, shopping center in Salvador. Even though it takes place in a poor neighborhood with a reputation for violence, the Black Bahia dance has a positive overall reputation. The name Black Bahia is not associated with violence, drugs, or marginality. In corroborating such an image, I never witnessed rows among *funkeiros* inside or in the neighborhood of the dance hall, and I was always surprised at how mannerly the visitors to the Black Bahia were. Courting takes place politely and calmly, without aggression or rudeness. Dance competitions took place according to strictly defined rules and never resulted in physical violence.

The emic (native) use of terms such as *funkeiro* or expressions such as "the funk-digging mob," as well as the conspicuous use of a funk look, becomes more frequent whenever one needs to establish a difference from others, such as the impresarios of the music venues that refuse to host a funk dance, alleging that samba dances bring in more money, or the visitors to samba dances in the same Sport Club Periperi, who are seen as potentially ousting funk from the club. As for samba, it is worth noting that the *funkeiros* also reserve a place for it in the program of their dance, the Love Beat, half an hour of slow dances in the midst of the evening. Those who have met through the more rapid funk dance steps may then dance closely and kiss. Skill or originality in funk dance steps increases one's chances in the courting market around the Black Bahia, as it does in samba and other dance arenas. The majority of the funk dancers also enjoy such other genres as *pagode*, but feel they are different from aficionados of the latter, less rude and prone to get involved in fights. In other words, they see themselves as more polite, well educated, and modern than the followers of *pagode*.

In the funk dance, besides a majority of *funkeiros*, there is a minority of *charme* aficionados (those who prefer the slower U.S. rhythm and soul, with its glamour and charm). The latter are dressed rather neatly if not "straight": neatly ironed zoot suits instead of oversized bermudas, caps and chains for young men (at least those participating in the organized dance groups), and evening gowns instead of miniskirts, hot pants, and bikini tops for girls. In Salvador *funkeiros* and *charmeiros* share circuits and spaces, as two variants of the same theme. Funk, funk melody, and charm can all be heard at the Black Bahia site, although funk more often than the others. Bahian *funkeiros* and *charme* aficionados consider *funkeiros* and *charme* aficionados in Rio more "exaggerated" and more aggressive, more interested in sticking to the appropriate funk look than in enjoying the dance as such. The Bahian counterpart, even though acknowledging that funk has strong roots in Rio, likes to think of itself as being "society" (by this English word the Bahians mean polite, upper class, and even snobbish).

Every Sunday the dance takes place according to the same pattern. Soon after the opening of the hall, the organized dance groups arrive. They arrange themselves on the edge of the dance floor, always in the same position. They form the core of the dance evening. Everybody watches them, comments on their dancing ability, and tries to imitate their newly invented steps. Only those who really know how to dance funk participate in these groups. No outsider dares joining one of these groups without previous contact and training. Nonetheless, there are a few informal groups for collective dancing, led by some experienced dancers who like to train beginners. Frequently these experienced dancers are ex-members of an organized dance group who hope to start an organized group of their own, as soon as they have enough good followers. These informal dance groups may bring together more than 100 dancers each. The vast majority of the visitors, however, do not take part in the formal or informal dance competitions taking place on the dance floor. They observe, try to imitate, and then enter the dance floor just to dance with one or two friends. Couples and flirters, in the main, do not participate in the organized dance groups; there is not enough time or tranquility for kissing, as one has to concentrate on the dance steps. The participants, in particular the members of organized dance groups, sing along with the song texts, almost always in English, either with onomatopoeic sounds imitating English words or by replacing the English words with Portuguese words having a similar sound. In the latter case, the substitutions the visitors find the funniest are those including swear words, usually addressed to rival dance groups. These include such epithets as "Funk Fera, vai tomar no cu" [up yours, Funk Fera].

At the Black Bahia nobody attempts to understand the lyrics in English and, in contrast to the funk dances in Rio, the DJ plays very few funk tunes sung in Portuguese, although these have become more frequent. The expectation of the audience is that the DJ will play U.S. funk. Material from Rio, which sells reasonably well around Rio, is poorly known and, in any case, held to be inferior and "less modern" than funk sung in English. Hip-hop from São Paulo has never really penetrated the Black Bahia, as it is considered too cerebral.

Funk and funk melody tunes follow each other. The dance finishes with the Love Beat, thirty-minute slows, melody, and *pagode*, during which the organized dance groups leave the dance floor to the couples and to the many who, until now, have just stared at those who "can dance for real."

What unites the *funkeiros*, the participants in the organized dance groups, those who are still trying to learn the right steps, and the occasional visitors, is the pleasure intrinsic in being at the dance hall and in dancing in large groups. Besides the organized dance groups, several larger groups are formed on occasion, under the leadership of one of the many recognized experienced dancers. More than 1,000 youngsters are attracted to the Black Bahia weekly just to watch *funkeiros*. When asked what they like most about the funk dance, visitors to the Black Bahia reply: first, the music and the dance; second, the chance to make friends or meet members of the opposite sex; and third, the distraction, excitement, emotion, environment, adrenaline, and style (Midlej e Silva 101–102).

Rio–Salvador Comparison

In many ways the funk dances of Periperi and Cantagalo are similar. In both situations, organizers and visitors emphasize that the dance is for all kinds of people, that there are many whites in the audience (though I personally observed only a small minority), and that the dance is a place of mixture and encounter among people of different class and color, a moment of social and racial democracy. Still, in the two cities the informants stress that there is a link between *raça* [race, being black] and funk, between dancing well and being black. In reality the funk dance is a place where black youngsters can feel at ease, where the black body and what many consider black demeanors are not penalized, but rather, at times, preferred. However, the funk dance is not the bulwark of any form of diacritical black identity whatsoever. In my interviews, all attempts to relate funk dance and the name Black Bahia with blackness were denied. In fact, informants could not understand why I insisted so much on considering funk an expression of black identity. Even if, in both cities, one perceives a growing pride in being black, this does not express itself according to the standards of (Brazilian) black militancy. Rather, it is articulated through experiments with look, body, and conspicuous consumption (of rounds of drinks, clothing, music, and transportation—taxis, mountain bikes, and motorbikes instead of the bus). Being mobile, able to leave one's own neighborhood during collective exploratory expeditions of the city, is for these young people a mark of freedom. In this sense, it is interesting that the country that inspires these young people, that makes them dream, is a mythical land stretching from the United States to Jamaica, a magic place inhabited by black people who can achieve, and not somewhere in Africa, to which Afro-Bahian culture had traditionally looked for inspiration.

In Rio and Salvador, there is a strong generational difference between the young people visiting the funk dance and their parents in terms of work ethos and consumption. There is a displacement of the center of gravity of the personality from the position of the individual in the production process (how you earn your money) to the consumption process (how much money you have to spend). In both situations, young people tend to see consumption as the way of achieving authentic civil rights, to be "real people." Generally, these citizens do not manage to satisfy dreams and expectations that have been created through the appeal of modern advertising and the workings of political democracy following an epoch of obscurantism and dictatorship. Although in the two cities the scales of preferences in life orientation of the majority of visitors to funk dances are similar, the points of departure are different. In Salvador the "right" kind of shoe is an Opanka plastic sandal that costs about $35. In Rio the shoe many *funkeiros* want at all costs is a Mizuno sneaker that costs about $100. The work ethos and life perspective of lower-class young people in the two cities are similar. For example, in both cities many girls are looking for alternatives to the condition of young-bride-soon-to-become-poor-mother. The development of international exchanges and the leisure industry seem to offer such alternatives as dancer, singer, fashion model, marriage to or support by a *gringo*, migration, and jobs involving travel. Many young men are also desperate for alternatives to bad jobs. In Rio, there are many more opportunities for a career in (drug-related) crime, albeit of short duration, or death by the age of twenty-five.[17] Some observers suggest that globalization is bringing about, among other things, the uniformization of work ethos and life perspectives among young people in different societies.[18]

Visitors to the funk dances in Periperi and Cantagalo also share a constant emphasis on individuality. While the media always portray the *funkeiros* as a group, the informants do not tend to see themselves as participants in one or another *galera*. All admit to having a peer group, but participating in a recognized *galera* is regarded as something conducive to trouble and as something bearing a stigma that, above all, makes one similar to the rest.

In the community I studied in Rio and in Salvador, no sociological types or stable youth subcultures form around the consumption of a single type of music, as we know them from the Anglo-Saxon literature.[19] Rather, there is a circumstantial use of music as divider and, occasionally, ethnic marker in particular moments. The informants show what one might call a cash-and-carry attitude toward musical genres and youth styles: they know how to move very well across different styles and genres. The real difference, as the following voice argues, is not between fashions, but between "bandits" and "straights":

> There are different styles of music. Charm is the most relaxed, funk is harsher; it gives more adrenaline. There is also melody to dance close. I don't like *pagode*, except for a few tunes by Raça Negra [a well-known São Paulo pop-samba group]. With charm you need dress shoes, neat trousers, and trimmed hair. Funk, instead, is liberal: imported cap of a famous U.S. baseball team. Style and label are important, and, besides, they are nice to wear . . . *Funkeiros* love imported clothes because they look better. National sneakers are for school or work. . . . Bandits have no style of their own, they dress in the *funkeiro* or *charme* aficionado style . . .(Pedro, better known as MC Porcão [big hog], sixteen years old, very black complexion).

In the case in question lifestyles are built around more complex mechanisms than musical taste, which tends to be eclectic rather than exclusive.

Informants in both Rio and Salvador show a certain relativity in self-definitions and self-representations in musical taste and with regard to color, position on the labor market, and religious life. I would say that the existence of most informants is characterized by relativism. A person who in the United States or Canada is simply "black" can be *negro* during Carnival and when playing or dancing samba, *escuro* [dark] for his workmates, *moreno* [of color] or *negão* [literally, big black man] with his drinking friends, *neguinho* [literally, little black man] for his girlfriend, *preto* [black] for the official statistics, and *pardo* [brown] on his birth certificate.[20] The same open response may be elicited by the questions "What color are you?"; "What type of music do you prefer?"; and "Are you unemployed?": "It depends." The type of music preferred changes, in the course of the same interview, in relation to the context: to court, a good *pagode*; to dance closely with your steady girl/boyfriend, *seresta*; on the street, reggae, *samba-reggae*, and *axé*; an occasional funk dance; and in bars a good *sambão* [informal percussion session, usually coupled with serious drinking].

The self-definition of employment status is also quite relative. Many, in the course of the same interview, manage to define themselves as student, worker, and unemployed! It depends on the situation, on the status they are putting forward, and on the most socially convenient answer in a particular moment. For example, to differentiate oneself from the category of "vagabond," one opts to define oneself as a "battler" (that is, a hardworking person). When speaking of the harsh economic crisis, the same person says he/she is "out of work," and whenever one wants to give the impression of struggling to improve one's living standard, one defines oneself as a student. This attitude recalls the "rule of the triangle" suggested by DaMatta.[21] Brazilians prefer triangular systems of classifications to oppositions. If one looks at Brazilian social relations through the lens of polar classification systems of, for example, color groups or sexual preferences, then Brazil is indeed "ambiguous," as Talcott Parsons, among others, had already suggested in 1957, not only of Brazil, but of the whole of Latin America.[22]

The situations in Rio and Salvador show important differences. In the latter, no link at all can be drawn between funk dances and cocaine rackets, if only because this sector of the criminal economy is rather undeveloped in comparison to the hot Rio situation. In Salvador there is no public selling point for cocaine and marijuana that the police cannot shut down if they so wish. If this does not occur, it has to do with policing policies, but not, as in Rio, with the fact that the police have lost the monopoly on violence or, at least, on the use of heavy weaponry in lower-class neighborhoods.

In Salvador, participating in the funk dances is one of the ways to partake in modernity, or to imagine a place of one's own within it, a version of modernity that can be combined with one's condition of young lower-class negro-*mestiço* and that can coexist with *negritude* or *baianidade*. Identification with funk is associated with the weekend; on weekdays little funk is to be heard at home, if only because few have sound equipment and records of their own. In Rio, on the contrary, at least as far as the media picture of *funkeiros* is concerned, for most youth, being *funkeiro* corresponds to having other projects and desires. According to these images, enjoying funk in a group relates not to the wish to participate (in modernity, in the city, in consumerism) but, rather, to a celebration of self-exclusion and of one's own marginality.

A difference between Periperi and Cantagalo exists in terms of musical culture. In Salvador, when one walks through the "invasions," as the shantytowns are called, and the lower-class neighborhoods, funk is not heard. I did not hear it either in the rum shops or the beach beer huts where the radio is always on. I

heard other kinds of music, such as *samba-reggae*, *axé*, "hard samba" ("hard" because of the percussion and pornographic lyrics), and *sambanejo* [a melange of
samba and country music]. Funk records from Rio, including the very famous
Rap Brasil, only reached Salvador in late 1995. They sold well for a couple of
weeks and then disappeared from the shelves. In Bahia, funk never managed to
hegemonize musical tastes among young people, and, even though it was held
in high regard by many young people, it always had to compete with other styles
of music and, in part, to integrate and accommodate them.

In Salvador the notion of *música negra* [black music] is widely used and
abused. Over the last two or three decades, musicians specializing in almost all
musical genres have been eager to stress their relationships with African rhythms.
In Rio, such concern with African roots is less present. The influence of foreign
music is strong in both cities, but in Salvador it concerns mostly reggae, merengue (that is, Spanish-Caribbean forms), and Afropop from different countries. In
Rio it is mostly disco dance, hip-hop, and techno pop. In Rio, black music, or
black presence within popular music, tends to be represented and to present itself as part of a discourse by which musical creativity and the quality of music are
a result of the interplay between *malandragem* [the street hustlers' inventive-
ness], *gafieiras* [traditional dance salons], sambas in the lower-class communities
and shantytowns, Carnival samba associations, nightclubs, and nonblack musicians or poets-composers. Funk has to position itself within this context, presenting itself as the youthful and first step in a tumultuous and noisy career through
music that after a few years will develop into a liking for charm music and, still a
few years later, samba (usually associated with enjoying other music genres too).
In Salvador, the leading discourse on black musical creativity maintains that it
results, above all, from the ability to be inspired by Candomblé (the Afro-Brazilian religious system), and that ideally such creativity, in its modern forms, should
express itself through *samba-reggae* and *axé music*. It goes without saying that the
two discourses create different contexts in terms of possible musical discoveries,
as well as the new forms that black culture and identity can take.

In musical terms, Salvador and Rio are historically interrelated. In this sense,
a mutual exchange continues. Rio has been central in the organization of the
Black Bahia; for many years both DJs and records came from Rio. The *charme*
dances that, less steadily than the funk dances, animated a number of Bahian
discothèques drew their inspiration from the Rio *charme* scene. In this sense, an
important difference is that in Salvador there has never been a large black

charme scene with considerable spending power, as there is in Rio. Perhaps one can see in the *charme* dance a modern version of what once was the *gafieira*—a popular and largely black institution that was almost absent in the history of Bahian leisure. In Salvador, dancing is usually seen as something for the young. In addition, dancing, particularly in the case of *samba-reggae* or "hard samba," can also be associated with the less respectable section of the lower class, with overly explicit sexual hints or even the base, "oversexed" behavior often associated with the poor. In other musical genres, such as *seresta*, dancing is associated with the older generation (over fifty). In the first case, the appropriate clothing is sportswear and beach wear; in the latter it is elegant suits and dresses. In Salvador "decent dancing"—dancing closely, in couples—is much less popular among people under fifty than in Rio. Even the actual dance steps are different. In Rio the dance posture is more inspired by self-control, sinuous movements, and virtuosity. In present-day Salvador a good dancer has to show it all. One's *jogo de cintura* [moves] are visible to all observers. Sexual innuendo and body contact are part and parcel of the history of samba, but nowadays these aspects are celebrated in Salvador more than anywhere else in Brazil. Perhaps this is the reason that in Bahia, among the intelligentsia and in the world of samba, there has never been that process of reciprocal seduction and inspiration that has characterized samba in Rio.[23]

One can see in the musical exchange between Bahia/roots/sensuality and Rio/modernity/*malandragem* the polarity between purity and manipulation that, more than just a dichotomy, forms an essential and creative part of any cultural form associated with black culture in different countries. Within black cultures there is always a tension between the expressions that are "purer"—closer to African roots—and those that are syncretic and manipulated, expressing the desire to be present, albeit as black people, in some of the dimensions of "white culture" as well as of modernity.[24]

In terms of the global flows of symbols and commodities at the foundation of international black culture, Rio and Salvador maintain peripheral positions. As for the centers of production and transmission of the majority of these symbols and commodities, the two Brazilian cities are on the receiving end, belonging to the huge backland of the Black Atlantic. The centers are situated in the dominant Anglophone world, in such cities as New York, London, and Los Angeles, although such other sites as Amsterdam, Paris, and Kingston have also taken important positions.[25] With regard to black global flows, Rio differs from Salvador.

Historically, Rio has had a more central position. This has to do with the size of the city, its proximity to the political and economical centers of Brazil, and the higher average income that facilitates less local lifestyles and patterns of consumption. Nonetheless, things have been changing as a result of the general increase in international exchange and travel. In this respect, even more important have been the developments in world music. These offer a subaltern and partial centrality to the "musics of the world," within which "black musics" are widely represented in part of the production of popular music in the First World.[26] In Salvador, thanks to the existence of a world-music industry and market, musicians, impresarios, and music producers maintain a growing number of direct contacts with the centers of production and marketing of music in the First World and, to a lesser extent, with other important centers of the Black Atlantic (above all Jamaica), without the intermediaries from Rio.

Tradition and Globalization

The cases of funk in Salvador and Rio run counter to the two tendencies in the study of black youth ethnicities outlined at the outset. There is a large degree of eclecticism in musical taste and in the use of music as ethnic marker; the periphery can take a reactive attitude, however subjugated, toward the stylistic dictates coming from the core of global flows. The complexity of local-global interplay is seen in the relationship between global youth culture and local musical traditions. The outcome of these encounters is not easy to foretell. Musical traditions—culture and habitus involved with music—are not waterproof. They are receptive to sounds, styles, and lyrics from other places. Some influences from outside come and modify local styles. Other influences leave a memory of themselves behind and disappear. Certain aspects of musical tradition remain tenaciously local. The musical traditions of Salvador and the surrounding region of the Recôncavo, and the high- and lowbrow discourses about Bahian music, constitute filters through which the influences from outside are perceived, reinterpreted, and, eventually, absorbed. The absorption of symbols, moreover, does not automatically imply assimilating the specific meanings that such symbols have in the context whence they come. The meaning of the term *funk* is not the same in Brazil as in the United States. In the 1970s, in addition, the meaning of the term *soul* was different in the two countries.[27] As seen above, there is even a difference in the understanding of what funk is between neighborhoods, as in the cases of Periperi and Cantagalo. In a similar fashion, in the Brazilian situations the term *black* means something political to the black militant and something else to the lower-class suburban black youngster, for whom the term, rather than being an ethnic or diacritic term, represents a mixture of a color indicator, international music, and modernity.

Within a particular context, the polemical character of funk, as well as of other types of black music, does not depend on any intrinsic quality of music or lyrics. What transforms a music held to be black music in the New World into an instrument of blackness, or into something that seduces nonblacks, is not the internal structure or logic of the music—for instance, the function of percussion or polyrhythmic character, as Allan Lomax and others have suggested—but rather the positions of this music and its consumption within the relations of power and pleasure between blacks and nonblacks. The notion of "black music" is a construction that reflects the local system of race relations, the demography and numbers of color, and local musical traditions. While the symbolic universe associated with international Anglophone black culture exerts a powerful and globalizing influence in Rio and Salvador, in such different contexts the significance of the term *black music* necessarily changes. The relationship between black music, culture, and identity is not static and, again, needs to be problematized.

This is not to say that there is not something unique about black music that cuts across borders. On the one hand, music plays an essential role all over the Black Atlantic in the construction of black identity, in both the traditional and modern versions of black culture. In my terminology, "black culture" in the singular is a basic taxonomic concept that refers to a number of common traits in the cultural production of black populations in different contexts. "Black cultures" in the plural refers, in turn, to the local or subgroup variants of the basic black culture. On the other hand, across time, Afro-American music developed not only as reminiscent of an African musical culture, but also in tune with highbrow and lowbrow (art and popular) European musics from different national or cultural traditions, drawing upon and reinterpreting instruments, dances, singing styles, and lyrics from Europe.[28] In this respect, the many versions of "black music," as well as musical production in general, can no longer be seen as separate from the process of internationalization and, later, globalization of Western urban culture and of the ways leisure time is spent in public.[29]

In the case of Rio and Salvador, of course, the strength of the "local" is also a function of the relative absence of the "global," or, rather, of its costly threshold that limits the accessibility of the "global" for the "locals" in question. Yet in this context, one of the reasons for the relatively weak penetration of the global is that local music taste still prefers local products. It is not simply as a result of protectionist cultural barriers, which are proposed from time to time but never effectively enforced, that so-called international music only controls a small portion of the sound-recording market in Brazil. On the contrary, international music—though heavily promoted by the multinational recording industry, radios, chain stores, and glossy periodicals (which target an upper-middle-class and higher readership)—rarely has a major success. Of the plethora of possible examples, I will give only three. The prestigious Rio daily *Jornal do Brasil* gave evidence of a stunning contrast: the two principal Top Ten charts based on weekly radio playlists always include five to six foreign titles, whereas the Top Ten charts based on sales in two of the main record outlets in Rio never mention more than two foreign albums. Moreover, the huge bootleg market, much of which is produced in the smugglers' paradise of Paraguay, centers almost entirely on local music, often of the rather popular sort. Further evidence of the dominant interest in local music is that recordings of Brazilian music are almost never to be found in cut-out bins, which have so many U.S. records. Ninety percent of the latter are in the muzak, soft-pop, and easy-listening categories. Interestingly, Latin singers, such as Julio Iglesias from Spain, Juan Luis Guerra from the Dominican Republic, and Laura Pausini from Italy, do better in the Brazilian market than do singers from the English-speaking world. The popularity of such Latin artists can be explained by the local preference for certain melodies and ways of singing that are quite similar throughout Spanish-, Italian-, and Portuguese-speaking countries. Latin tunes often make it in the Brazilian market with additional lyrics in Portuguese. On the other hand, Brazilian pop music—from the crooner Roberto Carlos to the percussion ensemble Timbalada—is often much more popular in Latin countries than in the English-speaking world. That is, the internationalization of (pop) music seems to occur more thoroughly within what one can call, to make a long story short, a cultural area or, in Anthony Smith's words, a "family of cultures."[30] Better to relate within a thing such as the "Latin world" than across different cultural and language areas and traditions.

Besides the resilience of territorialized musical traditions and tastes, different structural contexts contribute to the persistence of "localisms" within the global flows that relate to youth culture and black culture. While it is certainly true that today all youth styles are based on bricolage, it is also valid to say that this does

not work the same way in all situations. The lower- and lower-middle-class persons I interviewed for this study have few opportunities for the conspicuous and
aggressive consumption of the commodities most scholars regard as essential for
the creation of visible youth styles in First World cities (e.g., records, stylized or
label clothing, specialized magazines, home videos, scooters, cars, sound and
music equipment). These young people also have little disposable income for
their leisure public activities (for instance, discothèques, concerts, movies, fast
food). In other words, buying power and the share of income available for leisure
vary a lot amidst the young people of important cities of the Black Atlantic, such
as New York, London, Amsterdam, Rio, and Salvador. Imitating, subverting, or
creating a youth style is not the same in every place. For example, the stylistic
mosaic varies when one can buy and store music or can only enjoy it live, listening to the radio or playing drums with friends on the street. I will cite just one
case from elsewhere, based on my own research experience. In Amsterdam, the
creativity of young black people of Surinamese origin in terms of music and
youth styles has been based on an informational infrastructure consisting of
ghetto blasters, music videos, and TV channels specialized in (pop) music. Furthermore, the world stars of reggae and hip-hop music perform regularly in the
Netherlands. These opportunities and facilities are scarce in Rio and almost absent in Salvador. In Brazil, MTV is hard to get. In Salvador it started to broadcast
only in October 1996—more than ten years later than in New York, Amsterdam,
and London—and it is only received in the "noble" parts of the city where cable
TV is available. In Rio and Salvador, the familiarity with international stars of
reggae, soul, and hip-hop is often limited to major figures such as Bob Marley.
Amsterdam, London, Paris, and New York are important crossroads of the different strands and tendencies of international pop music. Rio and increasingly Salvador, in turn, represent important sources for the production of world music.
Examples are the compilations of David Byrne and the use of Bahian percussion
music by Paul Simon and Michael Jackson, whose video "They Don't Care
about Us," directed by Spike Lee, shows pictorial images of urban poverty in Rio
and Salvador as backdrop. This implies that the position and power of all these
cities in the global cultural exchange and, as a consequence, in the hierarchy of
the flows within the Black Atlantic, vary considerably.

The aim of this study has been to understand why in Rio and Salvador one
does not see those crystallized youth forms—such as the subculture in Britain
and the (ethnic) gang in the United States—that we have heard so much about

through ethnographies, journalistic accounts, and movies. In the two Brazilian cities, we have found types of behavior and styles that can be identified as youthful, but are not supported by strong buying power among the majority of young people nor by an articulated industry of youth consumption. The worldwide circulation of youth and music styles is growing fast. This exchange is particularly relevant when it comes to the musics of black youth. This, however, does not mean that these styles are based on similar cultural or structural conditions. The Black Atlantic youth subcultures and styles do not only develop according to one single pattern, usually inspired by what happens in the axis of London-New York-Los Angeles. We can have black youth subcultures and styles in countries where the relevance of race and ethnicity differs in the political arena, and we can have styles and subcultures with or without the possibility of a conspicuous consumption by young people. A punk is not the same thing in late-1970s London as in late-1990s São Paulo, and being Rasta today is not the same in Kingston, London, or Salvador. Sounds, and the symbols and dreams associated with them, globalize much more rapidly and ephemerally than do the fashion through which these sounds are collectively enjoyed and the concrete possibility of making these dreams come true in the periphery.

Notes

1. I am very grateful to all the participants in the S.A.M.B.A. research project of the Federal University of Bahia. This chapter would not have been possible without them. I owe a lot in particular to Suylan Midlej e Silva, who carried out a pioneering study on funk in Bahia. I am indebted to Micael Herschmann for his general advice on funk in Brazil. My work in Cantagalo (July and August 1995) included interviews with forty people aged fifteen to twenty-five. The research was made possible by a fellowship of the Rockefeller/UFRJ Race and Ethnicity Program, and was carried out in conjunction with Olívia Gomes da Cunha.

An earlier version of this chapter was published in Portuguese in *Abalando os anos 90—funk e hip-hop: globalização, violencia e estilo cultural*, ed. Micael Herschmann (Rio de Janeiro: Rocco, 1997), cited in note 9 below, and in English in FOOCAL (Netherlands), nos. 30–31 (1997), 139–158.

2. For a bird's-eye view, see Anne Campbell, Steven Munce, and John Galea, "American Gangs and British Subcultures: A Comparison," *International Journal of Offender Therapy and Comparative Criminology* vol. 26, no. 1 (1982), 76–90; and Michael Brake, *Comparative Youth Culture* (London: Routledge & Kegan, 1985), 1–28.

3. Jan Nederveen Pieterse, "Globalization As Hybridization," in *Global Modernities*, ed. Mike Featherstone et al. (London: Sage, 1995), 45–68.

4. Martin Stokes, ed., "Ethnicity, Identity and Music," introduction to *Ethnicity, Identity and Music: The Musical Construction of Place* (Oxford: Berg Publishers, 1995), 1–28.

5. Anthony Seeger, "Whoever We Are Today, We Can Sing You a Song about It," in *Music and Black Ethnicity. The Caribbean and South America*, ed. Gerard H. Béhague (Miami: North-South Center/Transaction Publishers, 1994), 5.

6. Allan Lomax, "The Homogeneity of African-Afro-American Musical Style," in *Afro-American Anthropology*, ed. Norman Whitten and John Szwed (New York: The Free Press, 1970), 181–202.

7. Melville Herskovits, *The Myth of the African Past* (New York: Harper, 1941); and "Drum and Drummers in Afro-Brazilian Cult Life," *The Musical Quarterly* vol. 30, no. 4 (1946), 477–492.

8. Roger Hewitt, *White Talk, Black Talk: Inter-racial Friendship and Communication Among Adolescents* (London: Cambridge University Press, 1986); Dick Hebdige, *Subculture—the Meaning of Style* (London: Methuen, 1978); *Cut 'n' Mix: Culture, Identity and Caribbean Music* (London: Routledge, 1987); Helena Wulff, *Twenty Girls: Growing Up, Ethnicity and Excitement in a South London Microculture* (Stockholm: Stockholm Studies in Social Anthropology, 1988); Livio Sansone, "The Making of Black Culture. From Creole to Black. The New Ethnicity of Lower-class Surinamese-Creole Young People in Amsterdam," *Critique of Anthropology* vol. 14, no. 2 (1994), 173–198; and Les Back, *New Ethnicities and Urban Culture* (London: UCL Press, 1996).

9. Hermano Vianna, *O mundo funk carioca* (Rio de Janeiro: Jorge Zahar Editor, 1988), cited below, and Herschmann.

10. Hermano Vianna., ed., *Galeras cariocas* (Rio de Janeiro: Editora UFRJ, 1997); George Yúdice, "The Funkification of Rio," in *Microphone Fiends: Youth Music and Youth Culture*, ed. Andrew Ross and Tricia Rose (London: Routledge, 1994); and Olívia Gomes da Cunha, "Novas faces da cidadania," *Cadernos de pesquisa* 4 (1996), 108–118.

11. Olívia Gomes da Cunha, "Cinco vezes favela—uma reflexão," in *Cidadania e violência*, ed. Gilberto Velho e Marco Alvito (Rio de Janeiro: Editora UFRJ, 1996), 188–217.

12. *Veja* no. 1322, January 12, 1994.

13. Antonio Risério, *Carnaval ijexá* (Salvador: Corrupio, 1981).

14. Arisvaldo Lima, "A diáspora afro-bahiana," *A tarde, Suplemento cultural*, August 6, 1994, 3.

15. Suylan Midlej e Silva, "O pertencimento na festa. Sociabilidade, identidade e comunicação mediática no baile funk 'Black Bahia' do Periperi." Master's thesis in mass communication, Universidade Federal da Bahia, 1996, 59; further references in text by author.

16. Osmundo Araújo Pinho, "Descentrando o Pelô: narrativas, territórios e desigualdades raciais no centro histórico de Salvador." Master's thesis in anthropology, Universidade Estadual de Campinas, 1996.

17. Alba Zaluar, *Condomínio do diabo* (Rio de Janeiro: Editora UFRJ, 1994).

18. For example, M. Sposito, "A sociabilidade juvenil na rua: novos conflitos e ação coletiva na cidade," *Revista USP* vol. 5, no. 12 (1993), 161–178.

19. Stuart Hall and Toni Jefferson, eds., *Resistance through Rituals* (London: Hutchinson, 1976); and Tricia Rose, *Rap Music and Black Culture in Contemporary America* (Hanover, N.H.: Wesleyan University Press, 1994).

20. Livio Sansone, "The New Blacks from Bahia: Local and Global in Afro-Bahia," *Identities* vol. 3, no. 4 (1997), 457–493; cited below.

21. Roberto DaMatta, "Para uma antropologia da tradição brasileira (ou: a virtude está no meio)," in *Conta de mentiroso. Sete ensaios de antropologia brasileira* (Rio de Janeiro: Rocco, 1993), 125–149.

22. Talcott Parsons, "The Problem of Polarization on the Axis of Color," in *Color and Race*, ed. J. H. Franklin (Boston: Beacon Hill Press, 1968).

23. Hermano Vianna, *O mistério do samba* (Rio de Janeiro: Editora UFRJ, 1995).

24. Sidney Mintz, foreword to *Afro-American Anthropology*, ed. Norman Whitten and John Szwed (New York: The Free Press, 1970), 1–16.; and Sidney Mintz and Richard Price, *An Anthropological Approach to the Afro-American Past: a Caribbean Perspective* (Philadelphia: Institute for the Study of Human Issues, 1976).

25. Sansone, "The New Blacks from Bahia," 457–493.

26. Denis-Constant Martin, "Who's Afraid of the Big Bad World Music?" [Qui a per des grandes méchants musiques du monde?] Desir de l'autre, processus hégémoniques et flux transnationaux mis en musique dans le monde contemporain," *Cahiers de musiques traditionelles* (Geneva) 9 (1996), 3–21.

27. Ulf Hannerz, "The Significance of Soul," in *Soul*, ed. Lee Rainwater (New Brunswick, N.J.: Transaction Books/Rutgers University, 1973), 15–30; and Hermano Vianna, *O mundo funk carioca*.

28. Denis-Constant Martin, "Filiation or Innovation? Some Hypotheses to Overcome the Dilemma of Afro-American Music's Origins," *Black Music Research Journal* vol. 11, no. 2 (1991), 19–38.

29. Paul Gilroy, *The Black Atlantic: Modernity and Double Consciousness* (London: Verso, 1993).

30. Anthony Smith, "Towards a Global Culture?" *Theory, Culture & Society* 7 (1990), 171–191.

Deus dos deuses, Olodum movimenta o mundo inteiro
e africaniza o dom que compõe a natureza

[God of gods, Olodum moves the whole world
and Africanizes the gift that creates nature]
— "Raça negra" [Black race] (Brito-Gibi), Olodum, 1986

NINE

World of Fantasy, Fantasy of the World
Geographic Space and Representation of Identity in the Carnival of Salvador, Bahia

Milton Araújo Moura

In the social life of Salvador, no event more clearly expresses the complexity of relationships in the city than its Carnival. This becomes even more evident when one considers its expansion in chronological and geographical terms. The musical and choreographic Carnival themes presented in Salvador in the last few decades have spread across the entire country, even reaching some international centers. They have also surpassed the conventional boundaries of Carnival, receiving attention in the Brazilian media throughout the year, intensifying in the summer. The culture of Carnival is today positioned as "the face of the city," in that both its actors and its audiences tend to perceive it in this way.

We might wonder how social practices associated with Carnival reflect the processes of globalization of the second half of the twentieth century, especially beginning in the 1970s. In the cultural sphere of Salvador, how are elements that integrate the city into global circuits of production and distribution of signs of beauty received? What kind of response do these media messages elicit? In order to locate some of the processes that define the Bahian Carnival, an overview of the historical context is necessary.

Between Integration and Marginality

Historians and economists tend to suggest that Salvador and the *Recôncavo*, the vast region surrounding All Saints Bay, remained considerably distanced from the dynamic processes of national and world economies from the late nineteenth century to the 1950s. The problems of an economy based on slave labor and run by planters, merchants, and slavers linked to the Africa-Brazil-Europe triangle became more pronounced at the beginning of the nineteenth century when the sugarcane trade experienced successive crises. This led to the complete concentration of political power in Rio de Janeiro, a process that began in 1763 with the transfer of the colonial capital there following the discovery of gold in Minas Gerais. At the beginning of the twentieth century, industrialization pushed other Brazilian cities to the forefront and the massive arrival of European and Asian immigrants culturally diversified these new urban centers. Though it remained the largest port in the country, Salvador was losing, slowly but surely, economic importance and political prestige on the national level.

The situation would only begin to change in 1953 with the arrival of the state oil industry and the creation of a working middle class. Nevertheless, industrialization only advanced in the 1970s with the arrival of a petrochemical complex that created a subsidiary web of supporting industries. This led to the rapid urbanization of the city, overwhelming its precarious infrastructure, modernizing local behaviors, and integrating the city into networks of mass-mediated information.

We might question, however, whether this period was "stagnant," as economists have claimed, given the sphere of social relations of the time. This becomes particularly relevant if we consider the ways in which, for centuries, Bahians have articulated different representations of collective identity or identities. Some elements suggest an intense socializing dynamic, integrating two large, heterogeneous ethnic groups in the production of a culture that presents fascinating challenges to scholars.

The Portuguese and their descendants maintained the greatest hegemony in the constitution of the city, assuring themselves primacy in economic, political, and religious posts since they conquered the territory once dominated by the Tupinambá Indians. Beginning in the sixteenth century, the Portuguese brought African slaves, who labored on sugar plantations and in networks of domestic and urban services. In the first two centuries of colonization, these slaves came mainly from Angola and Mozambique, in addition to some areas in West Africa, above all the Gold Coast. Beginning in the eighteenth century, the majority of slaves came from the Gulf of Benin. The Yoruba, a strongly urbanized ethnic group, accustomed to commerce and bringing with them a complex religious system, arrived en masse. In the first half of the nineteenth century, the Malês (Islamized West Africans) led urban slave revolts that affirmed a notable presence of the Yoruba in the social life of Bahia.[1] This most likely occurred around the same time that the syncretic Afro-Brazilian religion, Candomblé, was established as a "new tradition." Among the Afro-descendants, the cultural and religious customs of the Yoruba seem to have held hegemony in the process of integration, probably because of their large concentration and native urban experience.

The dynamic of integration of these two great historical subjects was both complex and unequal. On the one hand, they were people from other continents who brought with them elements of their native worlds in order to invent a new one. In a certain way, this was a process of globalization, as these subjects exchanged materials from their lands of origin and reprocessed them together with cultural matrixes.[2] Even while it experienced economic decline, the city of Salvador never ceased its cultural exchange with the world.

The entry of Salvador into a circuit of production and consumption of mass media also tended to reflect the combination of these two vectors. In the 1960s, the city produced acclaimed singers and songwriters whose success was due in large part to the re-elaboration of traditional elements. This is seen clearly in the work of Caetano Veloso and Gilberto Gil, the leaders of the late-1960s cultural movement known as Tropicália. A regional to national trajectory had already been made in the late 1930s by Dorival Caymmi, who became known for singing and recording what was called "traditional Bahian music" in Rio de Janeiro.[3] Bahia was portrayed, and still is, as laid-back and relaxed, oriented toward immediate and primary experience. The presence of Bahian icons was fundamental in the fabrication of Brazil presented by the media beginning in the 1920s, which became more pronounced during the Vargas dictatorship (1937–1945). Samba was erected as the "national music," and Bahia was frequently referenced as a sort of black mother of the country. The figure of the singer Carmen Miranda was emblematic in this process: Portuguese-born (evident in her accent), Miranda presented herself on Broadway with the traditional dress of Afro-Bahian market women and performed, by preference, songs imbued with a notion of territoriality.[4]

It was as if the imprint of Bahia had remained on the margins of "modernity," representing the permanence of tradition, of a past imagined as it might have occurred. This representation became an important ingredient in modern Brazilian music, which was always attentive to the international scene. Bahia came to function as an important "reserve of traditional identity" in the complex system of representations of contemporary Brazil. This representation was strongly characterized by its dimension of ethnicity, Bahia being associated with the notion of ethnic integration, emblematic of the ascension of Afro-descendants on the national scene.

In what follows, we will see how external factors introduced by the mass media were received in the Carnival of Salvador, which processed diverse references to mold identities in the public sphere.

The World on Parade

Many historians have noted elements of the fantastic and the "otherworldly" in the Bahian religious processions of previous centuries.[5] The etchings of European artists who passed through Salvador in the nineteenth century, above all Rugendas and Debret, testify to a vigorous mix of Portuguese and African religious elements in the processions, burials, and popular festivities of Bahia.

These were depictions of Bahian and Brazilian society before the political and religious elite, always in league with the police, began their crusade to "civilize" public performances. Starting in the second half of the nineteenth century, the processions became melancholic, well-behaved, and orderly, as Catholicism became more Romanized and the distance between the faithful masses and the official clergy increased. Coincidentally, in 1853 the *entrudo*, a Portuguese pre-Carnival festival known for its vulgar pranks, was outlawed. In 1897, just nine years after the abolition of slavery in Brazil, a Carnival organization known as the Embaixada Africana [African embassy] sent a "manifesto" to the police of Salvador. The text begins by requesting indemnity for the public lashings and for the deaths of the participants in the Malê Revolt of 1835. It goes on to announce "a musical band prepared by the honorable African community of this city to accompany the Embaixada." The participants would wear clothes from Algeria and present among the musicians would be the Ethiopian emperor, Menelik, whose leadership was fundamental in defeating Italian invaders the year before. The manifesto also announced the presence of Zulu warriors, armed with shields from their homelands and riding zebras, in addition to a great maestro brought from the center of Africa.[6] In sum, the document refers to various African groups that would parade proudly in a scene mirroring that of the elites, the white inhabitants of the city of Salvador who imitated the models of the carnivals of Nice and Venice. It is significant that this group would call itself an "embassy," for that gestures toward an allegoric confrontation of identities.

Animosity continued between the *entrudo* and the well-mannered, European-based Carnival of the elites. Descriptions of the instruments allow us to venture hypotheses regarding the rhythms, but we know very little about what street music actually sounded like at that time. We do know that the elite processions featured opera and the *marcha*, a popular musical genre at the turn of the century, which was similar to the repertoire of the ballroom clubs.

As Salvador modernized in the second half of the twentieth century, a few significant groups developed profiles that will help us understand the relationship between fantasy and representations of the world. In 1949, a group of stevedores, who constituted at that time the strongest labor union, formed the Filhos de Gandhi [Sons of Gandhi]. They were an *afoxé*, a Carnival group characterized by the use of the *ijexá* rhythm, very similar to the beat of Oxum [Oshun], the feminine deity of fresh water in the Yoruba pantheon. News of Indian independence was arriving with the figure of Mahatma Gandhi as a symbol of pacifism. A considerable number of Afro-Bahian Carnival revelers identified with the public profile of a nonwhite leader of international stature and assimilated a new ingredient in the elaboration of their public masquerade. The revelers were, however, aware of the political difficulties related to the militancy of the Left; an icon such as Gandhi was the antithesis of the Communist stigma. Although their outfits recalled those used by Gandhi, they were also similar to those used by some of the soldiers loyal to the British Crown. The appearance of the revelers associated them with the world of Gandhi without making the distinction as to whether they were specifically those of the pacifist leader or those of the loyalist troops.

Soon after, Orientalist images disseminated by films and magazines inspired the formation of the Mercadores de Bagdá [Merchants of Bagdhad]. The revelers of this group were not so much linked by the identification with a person but by the images of luxury, elegance, and distinction associated with the Orient. Many of the revelers worked for Petrobrás, thus marking the public emergence of a recently formed black middle class that wanted to celebrate its prosperity. They dressed as merchants and caliphs in satin, bright turbans, necklaces, bracelets, and feathers; some of them rode horses. Their organizer, Nelson Maleiro, played the part of a majestic *mestiço* maharaja riding on a Carnival float. Although they achieved magnificent effects combining woodwinds, percussion, and lights, the Mercadores de Bagdá were not concerned with musical genre. They indiscriminately used traditional sambas and the *marchinha* radio hits produced in Rio de Janeiro. Leading the procession were heralds playing bugles, a typical motif among the other groups of the time. Both the filhos de Gandhi and the Mercadores de Bagdá used images of camels and elephants, often present in Hollywood films about the Orient.

The resounding success of Hollywood westerns inspired the formation, in the late 1960s, of the *blocos de índio*, a new type of organization that energized the Carnival for more than ten years. To the youth of a city that was just beginning once again to grow, westerns and comic books presented nonwhite heroes who were proud of their costumes, war weapons, and horses, and bravely confronted cowboys and federal troops. Their music combined the *batucada*, a kind of highly accented samba, with current radio hits. The anthems of the groups exalted the power of the Indian, while calling for peace and fraternity, as these lyrics show: "The Apaches are on the war path and if it's war it's Carnival/ Fly, white dove of peace, and tell our brothers that the Apaches are now peaceful people." Although a few of the *blocos de índio* had names associated with the indigenous groups of Brazil, such as the Caciques do Garcia and Tupis, the iconography never referenced the Brazilian Indian, but rather the North American Indian.

The exaltation of force was very clear in the *blocos de índio*. The street presence of young blacks whooping like the Indians of the Westerns, strips of adhesive tape serving as facial markings, showing off with aggressive dances, some of them on horses, seemed like a provocation to the elite. The biggest and most famous group, the Apaches do Tororó, managed to bring together thousands of members and inspired an equal measure of adoration and fear in their audiences. During the Carnival of 1977 the police arrested and beat the Apaches in a display of strong repression that parodied the Westerns. The Apaches were subsequently limited to a thousand members and began to decline. It is likely, however, that the decline of these groups had more to do with a change in mass-media taste than with the police intervention. The Westerns had gone out of style, comic books had other heroes, and the black children and adolescents of Salvador already had, at the end of the 1970s, another model for the representation of blackness.

The big news of the Carnival of 1975 was emergence of Ilê Aiyê, which inaugurated a new type of Carnival organization, the *bloco afro*. Formed by black petrochemical workers, the group employed a variety of media input, reflecting the already strong influence of television which brought reports about the liberation of former Portuguese colonies in Africa and the success of African-American artists such as James Brown and the Jackson Five, as well as the mystical wave of Jamaican reggae. The iconography of Ilê Aiyê suggested a rustic, heroic Africa, abundant with military and religious chiefs appearing with pomp and circumstance. "Long live King Osei Tutu," went one song, "sing Ashanti, Liberdade, Curuzu." The lyrics named the great Ashanti chief of the nineteenth century for the leadership of the group hailing from the black neighborhood of Liberdade.

Bloco afro Ilê Aiyê performing during Carnival, 1998. Photo by Lázaro Roberto, Zumvi Arquivo Fotográfico, Salvador.

In the 1980s, other *blocos afro* emerged. Formed in 1979, Olodum became extremely popular in the mid-1980s, proposing a more diasporic notion of Africanity. Olodum represented the black diaspora in a manner similar to the critic Paul Gilroy, who imagined it as a transnational Atlantic civilization.[7] In 1986 the group caused a great sensation by celebrating socialist Cuba as its Carnival theme. Olodum broke onto the national scene in the following year when its principal theme song, "Faraó," proclaimed that Egypt, with all of its pharaohs and pyramids, its apexes and splendors, was black. A composition by Luciano Santos with a strong reggae influence, "Faráo" featured lyrics that associated Egyptian mythology with the emergence of Olodum in Maciel-Pelourinho, the historic center of Salvador, which was at the time still an impoverished ghetto. The song exhorted the Bahian public to "wake up Egyptian culture in Brazil / Instead of braided hair, we'll have the turbans of Tutankhamen." The world grew at once larger and closer while the notion of blackness became more diverse.

Other new Carnival creations appeared in the postwar period. The *trio elétrico*, a truck-top electric ensemble, was an invention of the 1950s. At first, the trios played instrumental music, until Caetano Veloso introduced lyrics to this up-tempo dance music in the late 1960s. Veloso's Carnival song, "Atrás do trio elétrico" [Behind the *trio elétrico*, 1969], allegorized happiness and portrayed the city as the site of pleasure and rendezvous. Groups using *trios elétricos* were eager to assimilate and perfect the use of technological innovations. The inventors, Dodô and Osmar, associated technical proficiency with artistic creation, having constructed their own electric guitars before rock music became a global genre with universal technologies. At the end of the 1970s, Moraes Moreira linked the *trio elétrico* with Afro-Bahian musical forms, above all the *ijexá* rhythm used by the *afoxés*. With his contribution, the repertoire of the *trios elétricos* came to include African motifs and icons. By this time, the *trios elétricos* had become motorized soundstages featuring bands playing diverse rhythms.

Beginning in 1983, the singer-songwriter Luís Caldas synthesized elements of salsa, rock, and samba, creating a choreographic fashion for each one. Around this time people began to talk about *axé music*. It is significant that this name, especially in Bahia, was composed of an English and a Yoruba word. *Axé music* was not the name of a genre or a style, but rather a mixed repertory ready to be consumed in Carnival and shows throughout Brazil, and later exported to North America and Europe. The most successful synthesis of local and global aesthetics in the Bahian Carnival was produced by Chiclete com Banana, a band

Caetano Veloso and *axé music* diva Daniela Mercury, ca. 1996. Photo by
Cristina Granato.

formed in the 1970s. Integrating elements of diverse origin, such as electric bass
and guitar, and African-derived percussion, the group exalted Salvador and its
permanent association with diversion and romance.

The music of Salvador is claiming its place in the realm of world music, in a
manner similar to that of reggae and Afropop artists. Olodum's successful collaborations with Paul Simon and Michael Jackson inspired other groups to develop international projects. Carlinhos Brown and his percussion troupe Timbalada, for example, have made notable forays into the international pop-music
world, positioning themselves, as did Dorival Caymmi in the 1930s, as represen-
tatives of the black Brazil whose origin is Bahia. The artistic re-elaboration of the
traditional has already become Brown's signature trait.

By the end of the 1990s, the production of texts with explicit ethnic identifications subsided in the contemporary Carnival of Salvador. We are experiencing a
movement of mass-mediated homogenization in which there is little difference
with regard to theme or repertoire between the *blocos afro* and the pop bands
playing on top of the *trio elétrico* trucks. While icons of past decades remain,
such as the Filhos de Gandhi and Ilê Aiyê, the organization of Carnival has be-

come a megaevent with each group functioning as a business. The growing professionalization of artistic activities and the Carnival infrastructure has led to the intermittent movement of artists from one organization to another, independent of origin, style, or political affiliation. Some groups, such as Olodum, have experienced publicity difficulties. Araketu, a group that originated as a *bloco afro*, was transformed into a pop band in the early 1990s. Any references to blackness only serve to lend the group a certain charm.

Groups such as Gerasamba and its spin-off É o Tchan developed a variety of samba known as *pagode baiano*, which became very popular in the 1990s. *Pagode* lyrics and choreography often associate being black and Bahian with sexual innuendo and sensual dancing. It is significant that the male dancers are black and the females white, one blond and the other brunette. Instead of explicitly referencing blackness, these groups celebrate the *negão* [big black guy], the *lourinha* [blondie], and the *moreninha* [little brunette]. The musical and choreographic repertoires of the *pagode* groups set the standard by which young people in Salvador display their sensuality in public. Their songs and dances are reproduced at all social levels, from the poorest barrios to the most sophisticated apartment buildings. *Axé music*, having incorporated *pagode* and other new developments, is still dominant in the mass-mediated Carnival.

For the youth of Salvador today, references to blackness have less to do with a notion of African origin than with the eroticism of black bodies. Sex tourism, which has increased in the last few years in Salvador, has provided a space for working out this dynamic. On the other hand, the ability with which young black men and women have negotiated this space has corresponded to an extraordinary growth in their self-esteem. It is significant that the cover of the Filhos de Gandhi's first commercial recording does not depict camels, elephants, or turbans, but rather the muscular torso of a young *mestiço*. This is the principal emblem of the public parades of most Carnival groups. The process of globalization of taste and aesthetic consumption in Salvador cannot be properly understood without taking into account the importance of erotic movement between black locals and white tourists.

Manipulating the *Mapa Mundi*

In the 1960s, when the Mercadores de Bagdá paraded by, people would say that their chief, Nelson Maleiro, looked like a Buddha: a *mestiço* Buddha, seated cross-legged on a pillow, among lances and shields decorated with Islamic military insignias. The scene illustrated the ease with which the characters of Carnival mixed and recomposed icons of the marvelous. In the same way, it is important not to lose sight of the fascination that foreign musical fashions have always inspired among artists and consumers. In the 1950s, when Spanish-Caribbean rhythms began to appear in the movies, local musicians frequently attended the films in order to learn the musical repertoire. They would also board foreign cruise ships docked in the bay to copy sheet music of rumbas, merengues, cha-cha-chas, and other musical forms.

Beginning with the "Faraó" boom, the rhythm with which Salvador appropriated the world map accelerated, following a logic different from that of conventional geography. Hundreds of artists began to compose songs with magical mixtures of countries, cities, characters, events, and dates. Could we say that these songs expressed a desire to manipulate the map, to invert it in our favor, to reconfigure it in such a way as to attend to our desires? The manipulation of diverse geographical spaces as something desirable and beautiful found its most propitious opportunity in the culture of Carnival.

The destiny of the majority of the inhabitants of Salvador was fundamentally linked to a terrible, forced displacement through the traffic of slaves from Africa to Brazil. These Afro-descendants were henceforth called upon to make sense of their diaspora. It is necessary to understand diaspora as a result not merely of a chronologically located migration but also of an existential condition of the majority of the population who experienced their place in this society based on the way in which their ancestors were integrated here. On the other hand, diaspora is also a collection of strategies that, in the past few centuries, Afro-descendants have continually employed in order to construct their existence in the world. The notion of place is fundamental in elaborating a text of identity.

Frederic Jameson affirms that the crisis of historicity "dictates a return, in a new way, to the question of temporal organization in general in the postmodern force field, and indeed, to the problem of the form that time, temporality, and the syntagmatic will be able to take in a culture increasingly dominated by space and spatial logic."[8] The author, like other thinkers who have reflected upon the contours of postmodernity, accents a fundamental disenchantment with history as the mark of our time and the gaze that organizes our notion of space. There is, however, an intimately complementary relation between conceptions of the world based on notions of space and those based on time. Underlying each of these efforts to represent the existence of the world we find, however, the notion of existence as a human drama. The idea of the journey appears more favorable to an understanding which, turning to the centrality of the experience of space, does not distance it from the centrality of the experience of time. The diverse musical movements of developing countries, far from apathetic, present themselves with a dramatic pulse, the same that accentuates the experience of pain.

Although it may still present it as a montage of fragments, artistic creation attempts to reorganize the world using a frame of reference, at least in the manner in which the fragments are chosen and arranged. Let us look at a document that will help us consider this reorganization of the world as a register of the diaspora. In 1828, after a slave rebellion in Santo Amaro, Bahia, the Consul Jacques Guinebaud commented: "The objective was very vague, as might have been expected from stupid blacks, several of whom believed they could return to their country by land. Others are incapable of extending their calculations beyond two primitive combinations: whip and flight."[9] Nearly two hundred years later, we can ask ourselves if our historical understanding continues to be too limited, like that of Consul Guinebaud, to decipher, in the mysterious lyrics of a song or a deposition, a text that makes sense. To return to Africa by land might refer to the organization of a *quilombo* [maroon community], that is, the reorganization of African social precepts in a foreign land; an attempt to reinvent the diaspora starting with displacement. This was what the religious leaders of the Yoruba learned to do, recomposing elements of the former version of their mythic text as they reorganized their social practices related to it, creating a New World version of the text.

Stuart Hall discusses identity as something transient, referring frequently to his life as that of a "diasporic intellectual." For Hall, the very content of identity is flexible, situational, and dependent on "very specific histories and cultural repertoires of enunciation."[10] We are now faced with the problem of authenticity with regard to Carnival music of black inspiration. What would constitute the blackness of this music and how would we identify it? Let us return to Hall: "first, I ask you to note how, within the black repertoire, style—which mainstream cultural critics often believe to be the mere husk, the wrapping, the sugar-coating on the pill—has become itself the subject of what is going on. Second, mark how, displaced from a logocentric world—where the direct mastery of cultural modes meant the mastery of writing, and hence, both of the criticism of writing (logocentric criticism) and the deconstruction of writing—the people of the black diaspora have, in opposition to all of that, found the deep form, the deep structure of their cultural life in music. Third, think of how these cultures have used the body—as if it was, and it often was, the only cultural capital we had. We have worked on ourselves as the canvases of representation" (402).

The problem would still remain, however, of the diverse, at times conflicting, formulations of identities. We could ask ourselves, then, if the array of Carnival performances is simply that, an array of Carnival performances, or if each production is an immense and dramatic search for identification, in which the reference to place and to the world occupies a special place. We all need to be from somewhere, and, for the displaced, *to be* from somewhere in such a new, complex, contradictory, and unequal society, it is necessary *to come* from somewhere. As the mediums of the Afro-Brazilian religion Umbanda, sing: "I am from Aruanda, I have come to visit you/ Eat a full plate/ And have a drink." Even the gods of the diaspora need to announce where they came from. The image of the ship that Paul Gilroy uses to describe the civilization of the Black Atlantic is appropriate for understanding identity, music, and gods as transient: "Ships immediately focus attention on the middle passage, on the various projects for redemptive return to an African homeland, on the circulation of ideas and activists as well as the movement of key cultural and political artifacts: tracts, books, gramophone records, and choirs" (4). From this perspective, the mixture of geographic references, rhythms, and themes of the music of the Bahian Carnival can be read as an expression of a consciousness that perceives the multiplicity of the world and seeks to locate itself, to elaborate its identity, within this multiplicity.

The World and the City

The very geographic location of Salvador figures in its relation with the world. The city spreads across the margins of a bay protected from winds and surf, garrisoned with fortifications and slopes that make access difficult. It has always been more of an administrative, political, military, and religious seat, as well as an important commercial marketplace, than a central producer of goods. On the one hand, it was always open to ships from allied nations, which, from the time of independence, brought all kinds of products to the city. On the other hand, the quantity of fortresses in the bay, now tourist attractions, testify to the care with which it was protected from invaders. Attempts to conquer the city were numerous, and almost always unsuccessful.

However, if the colonial founders of the city knew how to protect it from invaders, they had to negotiate space and power with the Africans they had brought over to work. The black population occupied the interstices, borders, and even the central areas of the capital. The music of the Africans was feared, their musical instruments inventoried in the same category as weapons in the police records. The political administration of music was a condition of governability, as various mandates from that time show clearly in their dispatches.[11]

Today, the music and dance of black performers in the city, above all those forms associated with Carnival, are omnipresent. The entrance of Salvador into the mass-media circuit and the process of globalization have favored the expansion of the musical and choreographic practices of the Afro-Bahians, thus opening a space for the legitimization of their presence in the cultural scene of Bahian society.

This occupation of spaces is problematic, however, as the very scene of Carnival shows. Afro-Bahian music is now played on top of the *trio elétrico* trucks and is consumed by all. Meanwhile, the individual Afro-Bahian does not have access to the groups that play this music, for lack of sufficient material resources. Within two meters of each other are two distinct groups, attracting and repelling each other. On one side is the large, dark-skinned majority of the population of Salvador, anxious to occupy the spaces of Carnival. On the other is the light-skinned minority composed of local elite and middle-class revelers and the tourists from Brazil and abroad. It is not difficult to imagine how tense this unequal existence is and how such tension might be released. The largest Carnival groups employ between 400 and 800 security guards. On the other hand, everyone is there, close and far away, year after year.

During Carnival, the polarization of the repertoire corresponds to the social structure of the city. On the main roads, *axé music* reigns, performed by the largest groups with the most popular artists who are admired and consumed by the general population. In the cross streets, alleys, parking lots, and public plazas, reggae, *pagode*, and *brega* [lowbrow pop] music is heard. The audiences of these two types of environments are not, however, completely fixed. The same person might pass several times, in the same day, between different musical areas and even between different worlds in the same city. What is experienced on one street corner could be an ocean away from what is experienced in a nearby parking lot.

Leftist intellectuals have leveled severe criticisms of this process, arguing that these cultural movements matter little since the industrialization and modernization of Bahia did not produce a historical subject capable of altering the scenario of poverty and marginalization of the majority of the population.[12] Seen from another angle, the scenario could be perceived more optimistically: blackness functions today as the official emblem of local beauty. Young Afro-Bahians have experienced a noteworthy increase in self-esteem. A contradiction emerges when we note that the popularity of Afro-Bahian music is intimately linked with the legitimization of the traditional conservative political elites, especially during election time.

What remains omnipresent in this brief history is the experience of the journey. Today, the tense attraction between light-skinned and dark-skinned men and women occupies the center of the parade. In the era of globalization, the choreography of different worlds that constitutes Salvador's Carnival has become, in a city that never specialized in the production of goods, its principal product. The artists of Carnival are eager to integrate themselves into global circuits of success and to achieve this they will have to participate in this journey.

Notes

1. João José Reis, *Rebelião escrava no Brasil: a história do Levante dos Malês (1835)* (São Paulo: Brasiliense, 1986).

2. Pierre Verger, *Fluxo e refluxo do tráfico de escravos entre o Golfo do Benin e a Bahia de Todos os Santos dos séculos XVII a XIX* (São Paulo: Corrupio, 1997).

3. Antonio Risério, *Caymmi: uma utopia de lugar* (São Paulo: Perspectiva, 1993).

4. The importance of the samba in the fabrication of a national image of Brazil through the radio is discussed by Hermano Vianna, *O mistério do samba* (Rio de Janeiro: Jorge Zahar/Editora UFRJ, 1995).

5. João da Silva Campos, *Procissões tradicionais da Bahia*, 1941, 165, quoted by Pierre Verger, *Procissões e carnaval no Brasil*. Ensaios/Pesquisas [Occasional Papers] no. 5, Centro de Estudos Afro-orientais UFBA, 1980, 6–7.

6. Raphael Vieira Filho, "A africanização do carnaval de Salvador, Bahia—a recriação do espaço carnavalesco (1876–1930)." Master's thesis, PUC-São Paulo, 1995, 105–107.

7. Paul Gilroy, *The Black Atlantic: Modernity and Double Consciousness* (Cambridge, Mass.: Harvard University Press, 1993), cited below by author.

8. Frederic Jameson, *Postmodernism, or, The Cultural Logic of Late Capitalism* (Durham, N.C.: Duke University Press, 1991), 25.

9. Cited in Ubiratan Castro Araújo, "Por uma história política da economia escravista," *Cadernos CRH* 20 (January–June 1994), 74–92.

10. Stuart Hall, *Critical Dialogues in Cultural Studies*, ed. David Morley and Kuan-Hsing Chen (New York: Routledge, 1996), 502; next quote in text.

11. Eduardo de Caldas Brito, "Levantes de pretos na Bahia," *Revista do Instituto Geographico e Historico da Bahia* vol. 20, no. 29 (1903), 91.

12. Francisco Oliveira, *O elo perdido* (São Paulo: Brasiliense, 1987).

TEN

Songs of Olodum
Ethnicity, Activism, and Art
in a Globalized Carnival Community

Piers Armstrong

The rapid development of the Carnival industry has generated a series of contradictions for the Afro-Brazilian community in Salvador, Bahia. In economic
terms, extreme marginalization contrasts with unprecedented communitarian
and individual opportunity.[1] In terms of social and ethnic status, stigmatization
through racism contrasts with a prestigious valorization of aesthetic expressions.[2]
As for the repertoire of symbols invoked by noted Afro-Bahian Carnival activists,
whether in formal manifestos, statements, and commentary, or in artistic expression, the discourse is again articulated on a broad axis: on the one hand, the immediate cultural realm of the city of Salvador with its various concrete manifestations: streets, squares, neighborhoods, cuisine, musical forms, traditions, and

peculiarities; on the other hand, beyond municipality, state, and nation, the international domain. The differing informants of the discourse are, respectively, a rich history of localized culture—largely restricted, even within the state of Bahia, to the region around Salvador and All Saints Bay known as the *Recôncavo*—and the developments of globalization, particularly in terms of two cultural paradigms: first, internationalized consumption of cultural goods, including the "world music" market, which facilitates dissemination of Bahian music, and the cultural tourism that brings foreigners to Bahia; and second, Afrocentric ethnic affirmation, encompassing pan-Africanism, the African-American struggle for social equity, and the separatism of Jamaican Rastafarianism as propagated in reggae music.

Abrupt juxtapositions of the archaic and the modern are characteristic of many Third World societies, which undergo industrialization at a speed and rhythm more rapid than in the organic development of capitalist society in Western Europe and the United States. Modernization now occurs in a context of economic development oriented by telecommunications and service industries rather than by the former model of industrial manufacturing that tended to restrict international contacts to links between (post)colonial states and the metropolis (the political or economic mother country or center—for example, Portugal, the United States). Communication and transportation barriers between Third World states and metropolitan Western society are receding rapidly, effecting a (sometimes virtual) reduction of distance and thus a new proximity and relationship of locations that formerly were separated spatially and psychologically. This new conjuncture is concomitant with the temporal juxtaposition of the archaic and the modern in these societies.

Bahian Carnival elicits constant aesthetic innovation and material expansion. Its evolving subculture integrates and reflects both social heterogeneity and speed of development. Largely inspired by international models, the ideological mission of the leaders of the Afro-Bahian Carnival groups known as *blocos afro* inevitably integrates aspirations to a new social order with insistent reminders of the rigidity and abuses of the past, as well as of their continuity into the present. The authenticity of Carnival music hinges on links with what is familiar—the archaic and the local—from the gestural repertoire of dance steps to rhythmic nuances and the referential domains of lyrics. The Carnival event, meanwhile, brings together the disenfranchised local masses and affluent tourists from Europe and elsewhere. The latter's reading of the ritual meaning of Carnival itself naturally differs from the local sense. The tourists, most often educated and progressive liberal types, generally differ from the local population with respect to both race and socioeconomic profile. Any hermeneutic model for reading the social, ethnic, and artistic meanings of Carnival is challenged by semantic ambivalences, differences between individual subject interests, and the successive modernizations of the event.

A crucial qualitative paradox of Afro-Bahian Carnival is that its international audience is essentially white and North Atlantic, while its ideological parameters are Afrocentric. The export of Carnival music and Carnival tourism facilitate constantly sought material expansion for the city and for *blocos afro* alike. This growth may be categorized as normative modernization, involving infrastructural improvements, rationalization of resource allocation, and increases in profit or turnover. On the contrary, the Afrocentric rhetoric of the *blocos afro* presents the aspect of non-normative modernization insofar as it focuses on ethnic differentiation. The invocation of "Mother Africa" infers such differentiation by insistence on the inalienable difference of cultural roots. The Rastafarian notion of black spiritual specificity and difference, widely disseminated in black Brazil through reggae, presents a radicalization of black identification as a response to the peculiarity of conditions in the Americas, the African diaspora created by slave society. The rhetoric of *blocos afro* integrated the mainstream African-American struggle for equity and genuine societal assimilation, which could be regarded as a "normative modernization." Yet the dissemination of African-American culture in Bahia also involves such anti-assimilation figures as Malcolm X (though not the Nation of Islam), as well as stylistic motifs marking civic dissent or simply disobedience (also along class lines, as evidenced in the popularity of gang attire such as low-hanging baggy shorts, with a Bahian accent in the form of exposed upper buttocks). The importance of a commercial, non-dissident notoriety within the entertainment industry should not be underestimated. The city's well-known Pelourinho Square has played host to such prominent recording artists as Paul Simon (United States) and Julio Iglesias (Spain), and the leading *bloco afro* Olodum welcomed Spike Lee and Michael Jackson to make a music video. The rhetoric, art, and consumption of Afro-Bahian Carnival culture must then be interpreted in terms of a heterogeneous series of generative semantic matrixes.

Olodum and the Emergence
of Interventionist Social Activism

Olodum was founded (1979) as a Carnival club for residents of the historic Pelourinho area. In the 1980s, the voice-and-drum ensemble began to animate regular street festivities, which were popular with the immediate locals, the poor suburban population, and tourists. Percussion director Neguinho do Samba became a key figure through the creation of the seminal cultural product, the *samba-reggae* rhythm. Though not the only genre practiced in Salvador, Olodum's percussion has come to dominate the market stylistically, particularly amongst adolescents.[3] With its reconstitution as the Grupo Cultural Olodum (in 1983), the group marked a transition from a recreational vehicle for Carnival to a year-round communitarian project with a dissident reform agenda. Olodum has worked between two fronts, artistic performance and social activism. With respect to the central activity of Carnival, the group's annual themes have presented a wide range of issues and made diverse references, such as to modern African states (Guinea Bissau, Nigeria, Tanzania, Mozambique, Madagascar); African legacies (Egypt, Tutânkamon, Ethiopia, Nubia); African diaspora states (Cuba); inspirational non-Afro countries (India); Brazilian artistic movements (*tropicalismo*); Afro-Bahian civil dissidence (the bicentennial of the Búzios revolt); and even the natural elements (sun and sea).

Olodum has grown to be a multifaceted cultural organization. The group is governed by directors (around twenty-five) in charge of areas such as cultural heritage, infrastructure, art, health, percussion, and finance. The directors, who receive healthy salaries, tend to remain in their positions indefinitely, though occasionally dissent leads to changes. Olodum maintains about 100 full-time employees. There are 400–500 band members (junior and adult), 150 school pupils, and about 75 dance and theater personnel. Apart from Carnival, Olodum maintains a journal, a theater company, a dance group, and a school for local poor youth. It is also the independent publisher of several titles. Olodum's community programs include the band as a source of (partial) employment, a school for children and adults, workshop factories, and a series of engagements in social programs (health, gay rights, sanitation). Olodum has maintained ties with various international organizations that provide support and/or have exchange programs, including academic institutions such as the University of Florida.

Olodum band performing in New York, 1995. Photo © by Jack Vartoogian.

The Carnival Community: Leaders; Artists;
Local Consumers; Tourists

Some of the current directors grew up as members of Olodum's core constituency, the poor of the adjacent districts of Maciel and Pelourinho, while others came from other areas of Salvador. The directors are both the highest administrators and the organic intellectuals. The organization has considerable financial needs, and revenue relies heavily on the sale of cultural products (sound recordings, performances, related items). In a marketplace of volatile tastes and styles, the issue of cultural articulation is fundamental at both the ideological and the pragmatic level. The evolving nature of Carnival expression (even for the *blocos afro* during their ascendance since the late 1970s) and changes in needs, opportunities, and logistics require an extraordinary capacity for adjustment. The directory must determine the annual theme, choose the songs (at times an issue of quality of lyric content versus popularity of melody), and also select the appropriate orchestration for the record (for example, pure percussion versus standard Western pop instrumentation). In this context, the approach of traditional community organizations (along which lines many Carnival groups have been launched) is often problematic if long-term survival is to be ensured. The *bloco* leaders must constantly have a command of discourses concerning aesthetics (the cultural products for sale), morals (the ideological foundation of the group), and material issues (management); and they must be prepared to analyze proposed modulations in such discourses.

The regular gathering of the Olodum band occurs on Sunday evening in the historical district of Pelourinho (*Pelô*). Here the sacred charge is in the implicit community investment. The rehearsal for Carnival is an opportunity for aspiring songwriters to present to the public works based on the designated theme for the year. If included in the limited repertoire of officially selected songs, they may become popular and be picked up by other groups or included on the next Olodum record. This part of the process presents a series of different semantic nuances in terms of community praxis. One important function is as a sort of parapolitical process. The selection of songs is largely based on popular reaction. The song that strikes a chord with the crowd is taken up and sung with enthusiasm, the lyrics are memorized (the refrain at least), other performers start to include it in their own repertoires, and so on. In the competitive world of artistry, a victory is achieved.

Olodum has attracted a good part of the local talent who concoct lyrics and melodies to propose as official repertoire for the year's theme. The songs are often picked up by commercial bands and turned into hits. While Olodum's own recordings were originally dominated by percussion, the Olodum band has increasingly moved, in its recordings at least, into the stylistic domain of the electrified commercial bands of *axé music*. This term denotes the entirety of Bahian Carnival music, recalling that there is little non-Carnival popular music; however, since records with instrumentation (e.g., bass, keyboards) sell better, there is a commercial connotation in this sense that excludes the roots sound of the unelectrified percussion which dominates live performance in the Pelourinho.

The songwriters themselves are numerous; hundreds have entered songs in general competitions. They are typically, though not necessarily, of humbler origins than the directors. A few have written a number of hits and thus made the transition to professionalism, either with the *bloco* or in the *axé music* industry. Perusal of the many hit songs in the period 1983–1998 reveals a great variety of contributors, indicating that the field is relatively open to newcomers and constitutes an exceptional opportunity. The Olodum rehearsal still offers the writers the chance to circulate their work in front of a very large audience. They bring nothing to the event other than the lyrics and the tune; the *bloco* provides the percussion backup, the microphones, and the stage. The key to success at this point is for the artist to strike a chord with the public; if the song is appreciated by the crowd it may move forward to the next stage of official selection. This context pressures the composers to produce something with ready appeal. Easy, catchy lyrics may thus be more conducive to success than difficult explications of theme (though the balance between strophes, generally not memorized by the crowd, and the chorus does afford a balance between a heavier and a lighter discursive space).

The artists who propose Carnival songs for Olodum's annual theme naturally adopt a less analytic explication of Olodum's mission than is found in official *bloco* literature. The songwriters of Olodum do not have the obligation to command the domains of pragmatism and intellect that the directors do, as seen above. As artists, their obligation is in a sense the opposite, to synthesize these discursive threads into a limited set of symbols within the space of the song lyrics (cf. examinations below). Oscillating between idealistic and ludic inflections, song texts present a more organic expression, touching on common experience as much as espoused identity, and evoking both familiar city locales and the landscape of the imagination, everyday camaraderie, and mythical African leaders.[4]

The crowd itself is a third element in Olodum's cultural production. Apart from their role in determining by their responses which songs become official, the local enthusiasts have a performative role. Their dancing often involves disciplined choreographies worked out by a small group in advance. They are in various ways the guarantors of authenticity. Far from being a homogeneous mass, the public consists of distinct layers of Bahian society. Finally, Carnival events attract a large number of tourists from the south of Brazil and overseas, mostly Europe. The tourists contribute substantially to the capitalization of the Pelourinho area. Just as important, they validate the aesthetic prestige of the celebration of negritude in a city whose history records periodical repression of such celebrations. Many of these tourists are motivated by genuine cultural curiosity and enthusiasm. They are sensitive to the communitarian dimension of the production and have some familiarity with the moral legitimization of the *negro-mestiço* community implicit in the aesthetic re-Africanization of the Carnival.[5]

A Constellation of Symbols: *Pelô; Negro; Olodum*

The lyrics of Olodum's Carnival songs often collapse into a single metaphor a series of distinct connotations pertaining to aspects of the group's identity. Three of the most frequently recurring motifs in the lyrics are the terms *negro* (black), the *Pelô* (Pelourinho area), and the word *Olodum* itself, used not merely as objective reference but as a poetic totem.

> Tem muita gente boa / Aqui tudo mudou / São quinze anos que brilhou / Olodum filhos do sol / Reluz e seduz o meu amor / Negros conscientizados / Cantam e tocam no Pelô / Pelourinho é primeiro mundo / Cartão postal de Salvador.

> [There's a lot of good people / Everything has changed here / It's been shining for fifteen years / Olodum, sons of the sun / Shine on and seduce my love / Blacks with awareness / Sing and play in the *Pelô* / Pelourinho is the First World / Salvador's postcard.]
>
> "Cartão postal" [Postcard] (Ithamar Tropicália-Mestre Jackson-Sérgio Participação)[6]

For the community, the *Pelô* remains a symbol of identity and a symbolic gathering place; it is considered to be charged with a particular Afro-Brazilian energy, both in the sense of recalling slavery and in the positive sense of musical expression. There is a constant ambiguity in the festivities between the aspects of ritual affirmation of community (local, municipal) and simple recreation. This is captured well in a Tuesday-night gathering known as "the blessing," which, like Carnival, derives from religious ritual, in this case, the showering of holy water on the poor (black) population at a local church famous for its gold-lacquered walls. This meaning of "the blessing" is unfamiliar to many of the poor young Afro-Bahians who flood into the *Pelô* in search of secular merriment.

Olodum me dá a luz / ilumina meu caminho Olodum/
quero andar na natureza.

[Olodum gives me the light / Illuminate my path, Olodum/
I want to walk in nature.]
"Águas" [Waters] (Ubiraci Tibiriçá-Eli Oliveira)

O país está no caos / E eu estou sem pé e sem meia / Há quinze anos toco no assunto / Alertando toda sociedade / O Olodum nos quatro cantos do mundo / Pregando a paz prá toda humanidade.

[The country is in chaos / And I don't have shoes or socks / I've been singing about it for fifteen years / Warning the whole society / Olodum in the four corners of the world / Preaching peace to all of humanity .]
"Careta feia" [Sour expression] (Reni Veneno-Ademário)

The constituency of Olodum presents great complexity. Olodum was founded to serve the local community, but has always looked beyond it, even to global dimensions. Maciel/Pelourinho is a mixed community in that even before its commercialization it comprehended both very poor locals and a bohemian, intellectual class with disparate roots. Consistent with the nature of this second group, Olodum has welcomed various lifestyles marginalized from the mainstream (gays, drug dealers, alternative musicians) as well as anyone sympathetic to the *negro-mestiço* struggle. Olodum's constituency is conceived as an axis of dissident solidarity.

Vem dizer para os negros / Que lembrar o passado ajuda a viver sem senhor / E aí reinará Olodum / Reinará o negão.

[Come tell the blacks / that recalling the past helps to live without a master / And Olodum will reign there / The strong black man will reign.]
"Mensagem" [Message] (Dude Santiago)

Raça negra emergindo fotografando o orgulho . . .

[The black race emerging, photographing its pride . . .]
"Palco da vida" [The stage of life] (Nêgo)

The most important word in the poetic repertoire is *negro*. The term captures ideological inflections based on differentiation, both positive (black pride and beauty) and negative (racist stigmas). Since these stigmas and the reactive valorization are products of the New World experience—slavery, and biracial or multiracial societies where blacks were disenfranchised by whites—the term *negro* relates to the experience of the diaspora despite its poetic recourse to the Mother Africa figure.

In ideological appropriations the meaning of *negro* becomes debatable. Risério noted mutual criticisms within the Afro-Brazilian fold between Ilê Ayê (Salvador's seminal *bloco afro*, still influential and highly respected), and the more orthodox leftist Movimento Negro Unificado [United Black Movement]. Examining Rio and São Paulo, Michael Hanchard provides an extensive evaluation of the problem of cultural versus political agendas from an African-American perspective.[7] Within Salvador the various *blocos afro* present a range of approaches.[8] Whereas Ilê Aiyê is essentially apolitical but emphasizes specifically African ethnicity, Olodum downplays race in its stress on societal reform and its acceptance of nonblacks as active participants. Olodum focuses on nonethnic moral issues and explicitly acknowledges the legitimacy of subalteries other than black (gays, prostitutes, the poor). For both *blocos*, racism is the original cause of the black community's alterity, but for Olodum this is an alert to the struggle against various other structural ills in society (eradicating oppressions and liberating creativity), whereas for Ilê Aiyê the issue is rather to mark positively the presence of a specific community (based around the home borough of the leader, Vovô, in the suburb of Curuzu).

While the term *negro* must be fully appreciated in the peculiarities of the local context, its use in Salvador cannot be disassociated from international black-consciousness movements that preceded and continue to inform organizations in Bahia. Insofar as *negro* means *afro*, it suggests a solidarity that extends across the African diaspora in the New World with a certain sociological consistency, invoking the African continent symbolically but vaguely. In terms of cultural specifics, *negro* is a modern term that is very flexible in terms of the cultural activities it connotes, as opposed to the classic local cultural doctrine of *baianidade*, which infers a series of exclusively Bahian and/or Brazilian praxes.

Intellectual Roots and Articulations

In his autobiographical account of the emergence of a dissident black intellectual consciousness in Bahia and Brazil from the 1960s, Olodum leader João Jorge Rodrigues dos Santos emphasizes an uneasy combination of assimilation of mainstream Left discourse and awareness of its problematic abstraction of ethnic affirmation "in raising the consciousness of a significant segment of the white population that needed to abandon the hypocritical position of being a Marxist, being on the left, but without ever having had a project that would integrate blacks and indigenous population into the future society they imagined."[9]

Bahian *negro-mestiço* intellectuals in the 1970s consequently found inspiration in socialist African national liberation movements. Denouncing local racism, they partially rejected the view, pervasive in Brazil, that class rather than racism per se is the real cause of the marginalization of blacks. However, its frame of cultural discourse, which diplomatically celebrates both the African heritage and the phenomenon of cultural miscegenation, was not abandoned. Olodum's presentation of the Palmares *quilombo* [runaway slave community] suggests a multiethnic gamut of oppressed groups—"an alliance between black Africans, Brazilian Indians, and poor whites,"[10] a parallel to today's *negro-mestiço*—rather than simply affirming the resistance of African warriors to slavery. The position of dos Santos includes dissatisfaction with a Bahian leftist intelligentsia that privileged black culture instead of the real civil rights of Afro-Bahians themselves, but it also rejects, as a binary reduction, a sort of Afrocentrist purism oriented toward the Nagô (Gulf of Guinea and Yoruba heritage), often preached by critics of cultural syncretism (some of them white):

> We created our own binary forms, helped a great deal by a Bahian intelligentsia who reinforced a Nagô-centrism that reinforced our limited vision, who pat us on the back saying "that's the path to follow, you have to mark the space of blacks in carnival. During the rest of the year, we will talk, we will interpret, we will do research, and we tell you what you should do."

Dos Santos's accommodating approach infers a view grounded in social engagement and pragmatism. He read both black and nonblack intellectuals in order to distill his own approach to share with others:

> We were never able to focus on only one part of Africa. We were unable to locate the mythical Africa we had imagined. We are from different places, and therefore we absorbed the ideas of Kwame Nkrumah, Sekou Toure, Amílcar Cabral,

Agostinho Neto, Samora Machel, Cheikh Anta Diop, and Franz Fanon, and we tried to take these ideas out of the classroom and lecture halls and share them with people who had been [abused] by the police many times.[11]

Artistic Perspectives

Olodum's songwriters position their work with varying degrees of faithfulness to the mission statement of the group and to the annual focus. They can develop a discursive lyric that pedagogically works through the specifics of a theme, adopt it as a loose metaphorical frame for a general celebration of Olodum, or simply praise Olodum's inherent virtues without regard to the theme. The third option typically includes acknowledgment of Olodum's moral qualities but is not restricted to this; the songs can address the fun of the event from the enthusiast's point of view or celebrate the aesthetic as opposed to the moral virtue of Olodum and/or the Olodum acolyte.

Songs demonstrate different conceptual approaches to integrating various elements of the discourse of the *bloco*. "Exposição cultural afro brasileira" [Afro-Brazilian cultural exposition] (Luciano Santos) expounds on a concrete topic (the country of Tanzania) and sounds like an encyclopedia entry or a pedagogical prose text, mentioning geographical locations, ethnic groups, languages, the foundation of the nation, names of politicians, and asserting the link to Olodum:

> Deus dos deuses é . . . O Olodum
> Laço familiar aldéias comunitárias
> Comunidade em estilo de vida
> Olodum acabou de narrar
>
> [The God of gods is . . . Olodum/ Familiar link communitarian villages
> Community in a life style / Olodum has just narrated]

Such texts, which display the influence of the discursive structure of Rio's *samba-enredo* (samba school theme song), were more common in the 1980s.

There was a growing tendency in Olodum lyrics of the 1990s to express directly an individual subject. These lyrics often evoke personal sentiments and adventures, describing the experience of participating in Olodum, including how this plays out in amorous encounters, as suggested in the following macaronic verse of "Verão no Olodum" [Summer in Olodum] (Rene Veneno-Ghermano Meneghel): "Um *weekend* odara com você ôba ôba" [An *odara* weekend with you, hey hey]. The verse also exemplifies another modality of intertextuality, or rather interdiscursivity, in its use of non-Portuguese words, juxtaposing English and Yoruba. *Odara* (basically "good" or "beautiful" in Yoruba; used in the Afro-Bahian Candomblé liturgy) suggests the local preservation of African tradition, while *weekend* infers modernity and leisure, the term being much more chic as a borrowed term in Portuguese than as a natural word in English. The final term (*ôba*) is standard Brazilian (though not continental Portuguese); it is of African origin, but unlike *odara* it has been fully integrated into common secular language (and has changed meaning, now being an informal salutation). The utilization of three linguistic codes suggests a cultural mobility that ranges from African legacy, to Afro-Brazilian experience, and to the global, represented by English, not so much as a language but rather as a stylistic marker of modernity itself, as an alterity in relation to local tradition.

Conclusion: Pragmatics over Ideology; Selective Negotiation of Globalization; Ethnic Preservation without Essentialism

In terms of rhetorical character, Olodum's affirmations of identity are built on a fundamental interdiscursivity that is apparent in the range of domains of symbolic and concrete reference. Song lyrics move from the local to the global, from the familiar to the exotic, and from the terms of traditional Bahian cultural heritage to those of an impending globalized future. The aspired future is simultaneously an ascendance to mainstream (Westernized) sophistication as a consumer and to an Afrocentric empowerment as a community.

Beyond the common aspect of valorization of negritude, the Afrocentric presents a series of distinct rhetorical currents and cultural constructs based on differing histories and experience. Within this range, at least four streams are prominent in Olodum's rhetoric: (1) the generalist pan-Africanism, which stresses fraternity and continuity between all blacks and designates the African continent as a sort of maternal, nurturing, spiritual matrix of origin without engaging in specifics of politics or culture; (2) the reactive Afrocentrism of the diaspora, based on the peculiar negatives of New World black experience (slavery, suffering, systematic racial division, marginalization, and moral devaluation of blacks), which generates a rhetoric marking racial difference in a new formulation favorable to blacks and which at the extreme, notably in Rastafarianism, is essentialist, exclusivist, and patriarchal; (3) the mainstream African–(North) American insistence on civil and material rights, which rejects racial differentiation and cultural essentialism (intellectually discredited as manipulations of white racism) in pursuit of socioeconomic parity; and (4) Brazilian *baianidade*, which celebrates Brazil as a paradoxical conjunction of both triangular miscegenation (white/black/indigenous) and the purity of the Gulf of Guinea heritage (most classically, the Yoruba continuity in Candomblé), and which functions as a political and cultural compromise that, without precluding essentialism, successfully defers resentment and separatism.

The ultimate tension between these positions remains unresolved in Olodum's song lyrics and to a large extent in its official literature. This seems inevitable given the group's disinclination to a doctrinaire platform and the insistence on individual right of opinion. Second, the notion of success per se has a new legitimacy for progressive intellectuals in the post-Marxist era. To a large extent, for *blocos afro* leaders, the point is simply that as a result of African heritage and the circumstances of oppression, "culture happens," inevitably: the role of leaders may be to facilitate popular expression rather than to dictate its meaning. Much of the leaders' energies is directed to pragmatic concerns and thus to managerial skills developed by capitalist culture, though the latter is not infrequently vilified in songs. In the poetic realm, the song lyrics construct analogies between the different streams of Afrocentricity by focusing on the common positive valorization of negritude.

If certain subjacent differences remain unresolved, what can be said of Olodum's ideology? Following the group's own concern for pragmatics, one must locate its position in terms of pertinent power relations. The rise of Olodum is morally premised on a movement of ethnic affirmation but materially inextricable from the increasing penetration of Salvador by global consumerism and corporate capitalism. While the *bloco afro* self-identifies as a direct expression of a concrete community, its conceptual constructs draw on different revelations of globalism: on the one hand, the Afrocentric agenda that draws and seeks links across the African diaspora; on the other, the structural imperatives of capitalization, which tend toward Westernization, whether seen as culturally marked as European, or as the dehumanized, ethnically indifferent hand of capitalism-as-process. In short, Olodum's paramount intellectual problem is not ideological position per se but rather the question of how to preserve a differential ethnic reality in the face of globalization.

Notes

1. See Tânia Fischer, ed., *O carnaval baiano: negócios e oportunidades* (Brasília: SEBRAE, 1996); and Petra Schaeber, "Um carro do ano já é sinal de uma vida melhor? Ascensão social de negros em Salvador através de grupos culturais," paper presented at V Congresso Afro Brasileiro, Salvador, Bahia, August 20, 1997.

2. See the various studies in *Ritmos em trânsito: socioantropologia da música baiana*, ed. Livio Sansone and Jocélio Teles dos Santos (São Paulo: Dynamis Editorial; Salvador: Programa A Cor da Bahia e Projeto S.A.M.B.A., 1997).

3. Larry N. Crook, "Black Consciousness, Samba-Reggae, and the Re-Africanization of Bahian Carnival Music in Brazil," *the world of music* vol. 35, no. 2: (1993), 90–108.

4. Milton Moura, "Faraó, um poder musical," *Cadernos do CEAS* 112 (1987), 10–29.

5. See Piers Armstrong, "The Cultural Economy of the Bahian *Carnaval*," *Studies in Latin American Popular Culture* 18 (1999): 139–58; and Marcelo Dantas, *Olodum—de bloco afro a holding cultural* (Salvador: Grupo Cultural Olodum / Casa Fundação de Jorge Amado, 1994).

6. Unless otherwise indicated, all translations are mine, and lyrics are from *A Música do Olodum 1983–1995*, ed. Tita Lopes and João Jorge Rodrigues dos Santos (Salvador: Lopes-Editora Olodum, 1996). All used with permission.

7. Michael George Hanchard, *Orpheus and Power: The Movimento Negro of Rio de Janeiro and São Paulo , Brazil, 1945–1988* (Princeton: Princeton University Press, 1994).

8. See Piers Armstrong, "The Aesthetic Escape Hatch: The Mutations of *Baianidade* under the Signs of Globalization and Re-Africanization," *Journal of Iberian and Latin American Studies* vol. 5, no. 2 (1999). The pioneering study is Antonio Risério, *Carnaval ijexá: notas sobre afoxés e blocos do novo carnaval afro-baiano* (Salvador: Corrupio, 1981).

9. João Jorge Rodrigues dos Santos, "Olodum," speech posted to the Olodum Web page, http://www.e-net.com.br/olodum/report.html; next quotes in text. See this site for discography as well.

10. In "Zumbi dos Palmares" at http://www.e-net.com.br/olodum/movim.

11. Kwame Nkrumah, first president of independent Ghana, had been a doctoral student at University of Pennsylvania; his thesis, "Mind and Thought in Primitive Society: A Study in Ethnophilosophy with Special Reference to the Akan People of the Gold Coast, West Africa," criticized Claude Lévi-Strauss's characterization of the savage; Sekou Toure, president of Guinea 1958–1984 and occasional political poet; Amilcar Cabral, revolutionary independence leader of Guinea-Bissau; Agostinho Neto, father of Angolan revolutionary independence struggle; Samora Machel, leader of revolutionary independence struggle of Mozambique and subsequent president; Cheikh Anta Diop, black African scholar who argued for Negroid ethnicity of the ancient Egyptians; Franz Fanon, seminal Caribbean and African black anticolonialist theorist. Many of these figures are profiled on Olodum's Web page also.

ELEVEN

"Fogo na Babilônia"
Reggae, Black Counterculture, and Globalization in Brazil

Osmundo de Araújo Pinho

Introduction: Edson Gomes, Reggae Singer

On a June night in 1996 I went to the Bar do Reggae in Salvador's historic Pelourinhho-Maciel district. The establishment was one of the territorial focal points for ongoing research on the reggae movement in Salvador, Bahia.[1] On that night, as usual, the bar was full of working-class black men and women swaying to the sounds of Bob Marley, Jacob Miller, and Alpha Blondy. At one point, the Bahian reggae singer Edson Gomes arrived and several people asked for autographs while the bar's sound system began to play his hit songs: "Esse sistema é um vampiro/ Ah! O sistema é um vampiro/ Esse sistema é um vampiro/ Todo o povo ficou aflito" [This system is a vampire/ Ah! The system is a vampire/ This system is a vampire/ Everybody is afflicted].[2] The son of a railroad worker and one of eight siblings, Edson Gomes was born July 3, 1955, to a poor family in the city of Cachoeira, a small historic city in inland Bahia. Upon his first encounter with the music of Jimmy Cliff, Gomes instantly knew that he wanted to express himself through reggae music.[3] Edson Gomes is a black artist in a country where Afro-descendants suffer systematic violence and exclusion.

Interest in reggae music has flourished in Salvador, a city of 2 million inhabitants, 74.8 percent of whom are black or *mestiço*, in a context of racial inequality. The songs of Edson Gomes reflect a concrete and real link between social status and symbolic practice. This pattern is repeatedly noted in ethnographic studies of reggae and other manifestations of black popular culture in Brazil, like funk in Rio de Janeiro, rap in São Paulo, and reggae in São Luis do Maranhão. Without proposing any economic reductionism, I would like to underscore the material circumstances from which particular forms of expression and taste emerge. Or, as Livio Sansone suggests, we might identify a racial habitus in Brazil, defined as contextualized variations of the forms of relationships between blacks and whites.[4]

Reggae in Brazil: Counterculture of the Black Atlantic

In this chapter I propose an interpretation of reggae as a global discourse incorporated as a symbolic practice among the Afro-descendants of Brazil. The bibliography on Brazilian reggae is limited. Beyond the numerous books about Bob Marley in Portuguese, academic studies have appeared in the 1990s: Carlos Bendito Rodrigues da Silva has written about reggae in São Luís do Maranhão, Olívia Cunha has written about Rastafarianism in Salvador, and Ericivaldo Veiga has contributed studies on the *bloco afro* Muzenza.[5] Extant research has established that the imbrication of reggae with the culture and musical traditions of Afro-descendants of Bahia dates to the late 1970s. This history is reflected in the history of the Bar do Reggae, founded in 1978 by an adolescent named Albino Apolinário, who now works as a promoter in the culture industry of Salvador. His mother ran a bar frequented by poor men and women in the historic center of Salvador who preferred to hear samba, *lambada*, and the Spanish-Caribbean form, merengue. After telling his mother that he needed money to buy a samba album, Apolinário bought instead Bob Marley's LP *Kaya* (1971), which he had heard for the first time several days before at a friend's house. Despite furious protests from his mother, indignant with Marley's dreadlocked, pot-smoking image, her clients enjoyed the record and the bar became a reference point for those who loved the music. Located not far from the Bar do Reggae was the headquarters of the traditional Carnival group, the *afoxé* Filhos de Gandhi [Sons of Gandhi], which attracted many people for weekly rehearsals. These fans spilled over into neighboring bars and wound up discovering the Bar do Reggae.[6] Following the formation of Olodum in 1979, a visit to this bar was practically obligatory for fans of reggae.

Both Cunha and Veiga confirm a close relationship between Afro-Bahian culture and reggae during the late 1970s. The latter underscores the mythic image of Bob Marley and the symbolism of Rastafari in the creation of the Carnival groups called *blocos afro* in Salvador. Muzenza, created in 1980 by dissidents of Olodum and residing today on Alvarenga Peixoto Avenue (known as Avenida Kingston in homage to the Jamaican capital) in the Liberdade neighborhood, identifies itself as the *bloco do reggae* and refers to Jamaica, Bob Marley, and Jimmy Cliff in its songs.[7]

The members of Muzenza present a socioeconomic profile similar to that of the clients of the Bar do Reggae. More than 50 percent earn between one half and twice the minimum wage per month and have not finished grade school. The *blocos afro* in general and Muzenza in particular represent important spaces for the formation of collective identity, constituting social allegiances primarily based on diversion, the pleasure of being together, and the creation of an objective identity based on the celebration of black culture. Muzenza offers alternative social opportunities for young poor blacks beyond the formal circuits of Salvador, and also creates conditions for black symbolic affirmation. In the case of Muzenza, this symbolism is associated with reggae and the figure of Bob Marley, who is invoked in the group's signature song as "the king."

> O negro segura a cabeça com a mão e chora
> e chora sentindo a falta do rei
> Quando ele explodiu pelo mundo
> ele cantou seu brilho de beleza
> Bob Marley pra sempre estará
> no coração de toda raça negra
>
> [Blacks hold their heads and weep / And weep, feeling the loss of the king / When he exploded around the world / he sang his brilliant beauty/ Bob Marley will always remain in the heart of the black race][8]

When Bob Marley visited Rio de Janeiro in 1980, he declared, "samba and reggae are the same thing, they have the same feeling of African roots."[9] Other major reggae artists, such as Jimmy Cliff, Alpha Blondy, and The Wailers, have visited Brazil in the last twenty years.

Reggae music was first referenced in a Brazilian song by Caetano Veloso ("Nine out of Ten," *Transa*, 1972). He and Gil had heard the emerging style while in exile in London between 1969 and 1972. They became the first nationally known artists to record, perform, and promote the style. In Bahia, the first record completely dedicated to reggae, *Reggae da Saudade*, by Jorge Alfredo and Chico Evangelista, was also released in 1972. The same duo performed the reggae song "Rasta Pé" in a 1980 music festival sponsored by the Rede Globo television network.

The emergence of *axé music*, which provides the sound track for the Bahian Carnival, likely created infrastructural conditions for the development of a local market for reggae music. This points to the importance of material aspects that support the expansion of musical markets, especially with regard to those musics considered "counter-hegemonic." In 1993, it was estimated that Bahian music generated more than 2,000 jobs, and that the number of records sold had already reached 5 million. The record label WR, which released Edson Gomes's first recording, would come to include more than 300 artists in its catalog.[10] The monetary stability induced by the implementation of the Plano Real [government economic program] in 1993 was also responsible for growth in the consumption of cultural goods and appliances. In 1997, some 104 million CDs, cassettes, and LPs were sold in Brazil. According to figures from the Fundação de Pesquisas Econômicas e Sociais do Governo Federal [Foundation for Economic and Social Research of the Federal Government], the poorest sectors of society were responsible for this surge in growth. In 1993, 50.1 percent of Brazilian households owned color television sets and by 1997 this number had reached 82.4 percent[11]

Reggae music could not have found acceptance and interest among the working-class sectors of Salvador and greater Brazil without the help of complex, sophisticated mechanisms of diffusion, reproduction, and circulation of messages. The integration of the world in terms of cultural markets on the one hand, and the constitution of a local structure for the production of symbolic goods on the other, provided the opportunity for young blacks at the Bar do Reggae to develop a relationship with the iconography and symbolism of a transnational reggae culture. This access, however, does not define the forms that the relationship assumes or the meanings these symbols come to hold locally. These meanings and relationships derived from a set of locally inscribed social practices defined by race relations in Brazil.

By means of a series of transnational connections, a cultural milieu arose in the 1970s in Salvador that created, or recreated, contemporary black identity in Brazil. For young Afro-Brazilians, international political and aesthetic struggles in Africa and the African diaspora, such as African decolonization, soul music, and the Black Power movement, had significant repercussions. Soul music dances were held in Liberdade and other working-class and black neighborhoods in Salvador. Risério first noted that the domestication of soul music in Afro-Brazilian culture led to the creation of the first *bloco afro*, Ilê Aiyê, in 1974.[12] Particularly noteworthy here is the transnational and multimediated construction of a modern black identity that defines itself locally, while employing a number of readings offered by globalization in order to engage in political and cultural activism. As Afro-Brazilians assimilated black culture and politics on a global scale, they entered into dialogue with international critiques of capitalism and oppression while at the same time critiquing the structures of racial politics in local and national contexts. Pan-Africanism and negritude, on the one hand, and dreadlocks and afros, on the other, were intellectual and aesthetic versions of dissent which in Brazil contributed to the rethinking of racial identity and offered models for the struggle against local discrimination and inequality. The omnipresent image of Bob Marley and the colors of the Ethiopian flag in Salvador clearly indicated a re-elaboration of black identity in the local context.

The creation of transnational loyalties and interpretive communities is best read in the context of cultural globalization, understood not as something univocal, but rather as a sort of conduit for local and relocalized narratives, oriented toward the negotiation of power and cultural legitimacy in contexts of social inequality.[13] Reggae enters into this "dance" between local/traditional and global/modern precisely as an element of mediation in a complex and multidetermined horizon of black identities.

Paul Gilroy's discussion of the Black Atlantic as a complex unit of analysis, which can be perceived as a field of interrelations as well as a real space of symbolic significance, is useful in understanding this process.[14] Gilroy understands the Black Atlantic as a space constructed by capitalist expansion, represented first by the slave trade and subsequently by the exchange of material and symbolic goods. Within this space, a "counterculture of modernity" is produced as a version inseparable from European modernity in which slavery and racism are constituent parts of Western history, rather than premodern or residual elements. Slavery and its aftermath are perceived as essential elements of modernity, located as an internal contradiction whose dialectics produce modern African and Afro-diasporic cultures.

As a symbolic articulation of this counterculture, reggae has developed as a means of constructing a perspective on Western modernity that would be a counterpart based on the experience of the slaves and their descendants. In Brazil the relationship between "Africanisms" and white hegemony follows this same dialectical model: racism and racial exclusion function as experiences that concretely structure blackness or transform diverse African peoples into blacks or Afro-Brazilians, in a process that continually engenders its own critique and contradiction.

Black Music in Brazil

Globalization is an idea that helps us to understand how a historical tendency of capitalism, present from its birth as an economic necessity, unfolds today as a support for the symbolic connection of various cultural differences. These differences reorganize themselves around images and symbols that traverse the planet with great speed, recreating local languages, identities, and senses of belonging, within and beyond national loyalties. We might understand globalization as a complexification of the relationships between the West and its Others, with Afro-descendants occupying a privileged place among the alterities constructed by modernity.[15] Conceiving of black music as a social phenomenon allows me to associate, despite many obvious differences, forms as different as Bahian *afoxés* from the first half of the century and funk dances in contemporary Rio de Janeiro. I am interested in understanding how music unites people and promotes a special type of communication experienced as social communion.[16] Reggae is a model of a collective, socially informed practice, organized around listening to music. Reggae in Brazil is not divorced from other forms of socially shared black musicality. The consumption of reggae cannot be understood as an isolated phenomenon occurring in an neutral space free of historical resonances and determinations. Samba, funk, rap, and other forms of music associated with Afro-descendant populations have established the contours for the phenomenon of reggae music. Reggae is another tradition of black culture in Brazil and is best understood through its links with other musical forms. The historical baseline for the identification of these vincula can be found in African music, present in Brazil since the arrival of slaves. Like religion, music was perceived as a means to preserve African values and identities in Brazil and other parts of Latin America.[17]

So distinctive and strong was the presence of African music in Brazil that at the end of the nineteenth century Nina Rodrigues asked himself: "Are Brazilian festivals occasions for true African practices that blacks add as their own equivalents, or are these practices already integrated or incorporated into our festivals as tradition and memory?"[18] We might rephrase Rodrigues's question in the following way: Do black festivities reproduce patterns of African socialization and symbolism, or are elements identified as African mere picturesque ornaments integrated into national culture? Can Afro-Brazilians be the subject of a dynamic and living tradition that is parallel to and even antagonistic toward national culture? The problematic relationship between the Africa represented in black songs and the West represented by hegemonic culture is a major constant in all historical registers.[19]

I am underscoring historic traces of continuity in the African musical tradition in Brazil because this history intervenes in the reception of reggae music by poor blacks and rich whites. I hope to demonstrate how historical and contemporary forms of collective listening to black music provide the necessary environment for the understanding of reggae music as a social phenomenon.

A common trait among black dances in Brazil is the *umbigada*, or navel touching, which, according to colonial-era and modern descriptions, privileges sexual gestures and the body. Licentious dance steps, hot lyrics, and sensual bodies are repeatedly noted. Why the body? Why sex? Florestan Fernandes has argued that the body serves as the final recourse for black expression in a context of privation and extreme brutality.[20] Other authors see a positive affirmation of corporality as a significant element in the construction of identity.[21] Strong references to the body, affirmations of a distinct identity, Afrocentric symbolism, and an emphasis on resistance to violence and racism are the common traits that characterize many forms of contemporary black music in Brazil, including reggae. One can imagine a common base for reggae, funk, or rap found somewhere between the material conditions of existence, access to the consumption of symbolic transnational goods, and the corpus of African cultural tradition.

Sociocultural Dialectics of Black Music

What other characteristics might illuminate the social and formal conditions that bring about these manifestations of black music in contemporary Brazil? Which traits will help us to better understand the sites that emerge between African tradition, global flows, and local living conditions?

First, the spontaneous initiatives that create conditions for the collective consumption of black music deserve mention. Various authors have called attention to the transgressions involved in procuring recordings (often contraband), the sound systems that will broadcast them adequately, and the public spaces in which to hold dances. For example, Vianna has noted the centrality of the sound systems for funk dances in Rio, and Silva has documented the importance of boom boxes for the production of reggae dances in Maranhão.[22] Seemingly out of nowhere, participants create the necessary conditions for the public broadcast of music that often arrives in Brazil through the musical expeditions of the DJs themselves to the United States.

Second, as Carvalho has argued, we might highlight the role of institutionalization that the consumption of music represents. Music has created the conditions for self-organization around a diacritical Afrocentric symbolic vocabulary, expressed mainly through dance, socializing, and leisure. According to Carvalho, the collective enjoyment of music among equals foments the creation of institutional alternatives to the white world as autonomous structures marked, as Gilroy has shown, in "Diáspora, Utopia," by a conflation of the aesthetic and the political.

Third, these manifestations organize themselves amidst intense repression and disapproval by the press, the police, and other dominant social actors. All of the aforementioned musical manifestations have met with the same discursive resistance: dances are hideouts for criminals; they promote vagrancy; they do not reflect national culture; they are foreign invasions; they represent the degradation of culture; they are aesthetically deplorable; and so forth. This repression has molded a continuity of cultural contradiction that is found in many concrete forms. Though containing differences amongst themselves, all of these manifestations constitute identities when mobilized in relation to white hegemony precisely because this very hegemony has elected them as the *bête noire* of national culture.

This last point is fundamental. Despite the clarity with which the social sciences have identified the historical construction of black subjectivity, the location of race as a defining factor in the construction of social borders, and the maintenance of racial privilege, a lack of understanding still persists. Rather than suggesting that African music and culture were repressed because they were African, we ought to recognize that, as racialist thought "created blacks," anti-African violence and repression dialectically produced black music as a site of resistance, thereby defining the borders of an internal Africa which has been maintained in Brazil, as in the rest of the diaspora, for five centuries.

Reggae culture does not exist as a generalized abstraction, whether in Bahia or in Maranhão. What exists are social discontinuities organized around music. As a given historical fact, reggae culture only exists as a generality insofar as it exists as a set of particularities that merge in a global process of production and reproduction of social spaces and forms of symbolic struggle. Music provided the language for the expression of positions which are in themselves contradictory.

It is not surprising that contestation arises from reggae and other forms of black music. Likewise, it comes as no surprise that these forms constitute the site for the creation of subjects of resistance and objects of repression. The tradition of black music is related to this oppression as a dialectical counterpoint to racism and exclusion, independent of the particular vision that the agents involved may have. In all of the aforementioned contexts, poverty and violence occur along racial lines. It is important, in this way, to consider that culture might not form an integrated whole, a package or fixed set of elements. Culture might be better understood as a series of interactions and developments that never stabilize, but rather continually reinstate themselves in a dynamic whose parameters are defined by struggles in the field of political hegemony.[23]

Setting Fire to Babylon

As exemplified by Edson Gomes's story, investigations of black musical cultures suggest a connection of race and socioeconomic condition with the consumption of black music. The fact that young Afro-Brazilians do not conceptually formulate an explicit ethnic or political link between the social consumption of funk or reggae and their own racial condition does not relieve us of the responsibility to seek explanations, especially considering the prevalent racial ideology in

Bahian reggae star Sine Calmon, 1996. Photo by Lázaro Roberto, Zumvi Arquivo Fotográfico, Salvador.

Brazil, based on *mestiçagem* [racial mixing], whitening, and the denial of racism and racial inequality.[24]

The question that Suylan Midlej posed to her subjects regarding their introduction into funk dance culture might illuminate this issue. According to the author, the majority of the young people interviewed were brought to the dance by older siblings or friends.[25] The majority did not hear about the dance on radio or television, but rather because the immediate coparticipants of their sociocultural experience brought them. In the immediate network of relationships constrained by racial oppression we can seek paths that lead from the funk dance to the reggae show. In the concrete social environment where agents effectively interact, practices linked to the collective consumption of black music take root. On this level the link between social and racial conditions and black music can be found. It is here that globalized messages arriving by means of mass media reverberate. As Vianna has suggested, those who frequented the funk dance were black residents of the neighboring *favela*. It was a friend who gave Albino his first

Bob Marley record. It was a neighbor who taught Carlinhos Brown how to play percussion.

Considering the ideas examined here, I would like to present a provisional interpretation of the social significance of reggae as a collective symbolic practice in Brazil. Reggae is a historical and contingent phenomenon, relative to the social structure that is, ultimately, the context in which the agents define themselves as listeners.[26] My experience at the Bar do Reggae in Salvador has led me to believe the following: first, the principal inspiration for attending the Bar do Reggae is the desire to dance and socialize. Dancing synthesizes a certain use of the body, a dialogue with tradition, and a path toward the construction of alterity. Second, the social origins of those who frequent the Bar do Reggae itself are marked by the general conditions of poverty and exclusion common to most Afro-Brazilians.

Reggae in Brazil might be understood as a social phenomenon analogous to other forms of musical tradition of African origin in its capacity to create symbolic links among those who might access a common tradition in a similar social space. It constitutes a channel for the expression of rebellion and nuanced social critique on various levels by means of collective manifestation. The global character of these discourses of rebellion is evident, yet it is not necessarily something new. Is it a true historical discontinuity? Is cultural globalization a new and determinant factor in this construction of new identities? Or could it be that black cultural tradition in Brazil was always transnationally oriented? We must remember the explicit reference to Africa in the Bahian Carnival at the beginning of the century, the significance of the Indian liberation movement to the creation of the Filhos de Gandhi in 1949, and the influence of 1970s Black Power on the founders of Ilê Aiyê.

As Gilroy has shown, black culture is a countercultural practice of modernity that allows Afro-descendants to reconstitute a historical link which, from the very interior of Western modernity, critiques it from its foundation and questions its univocality as a legitimate and universal inheritance. It also permits the construction of a symbolic link between socioracial condition and forms of expression, creating a channel through which dense, particular, and concrete forms flow in the creation of a transnational, critical identity. According to George Yúdice, the idea of nationality in Brazil is being questioned in an increasingly global cultural landscape through hip-hop and funk. By claiming links with other transnational identities formed in the African diaspora, young people who consume hip-hop and reggae have rejected the official cultural identity offered by the nation and have found, in music, a way of articulating the specificity of their own social experience.[27] The local context is reinterpreted by means of transnational or globalized readings. The allegiances among diasporic Africans are a result of the global integration of capitalism, the Babylon invoked by the Rastafarians. The contradiction of modernity produces its own critique which, in Yúdice's analysis, is manifested in the rejection of the idea of a singular nationality, people, or territory.

Mobilized from the perspective of the Black Atlantic, the metaphor of Babylon has had a significant impact in Salvador. During the 1998 Carnival, the song "Nayambing Blues" by Sine Calmon & Banda Morrão Fumegante was one of the most popular, possibly suggesting the definitive implantation of reggae music in the culture industry of Bahian Carnival. One of the best known refrains of the song goes: "I'm setting Babylon on fire." Babylon is a metaphor, like "the system," for the modern, capitalist, racist world as interpreted by Rastafarian philosophy.[28] The phrase is ambivalent initially, as setting Babylon on fire is often interpreted as lighting a joint, marijuana being an important element in Rastafarian culture. Setting fire to Babylon also means, however, attacking or destroying the oppressive system. In reality, both meanings coincide in the general rejection of the status quo. A segment of the Afro-Brazilian youth even believes that smoking marijuana openly or defending its legalization is a form of attacking the system. To play or to listen to reggae, by some measure, is to set Babylon on fire. Culture, or symbolic forms, lend themselves as mediators between agents and social structures. Creating collective territories for the reception of reggae, these adolescents, most of them black, appropriate spaces and symbolic forms in order to create objective and collective forms of dissent. Through this dissent they visualize a structure—symbolized by Babylon—which oppresses them. The slogan "fire in Babylon" has an aspect of defiance that unfolds in two ways: defiant behavior linked to the use of drugs, and political defiance, linked to the critique of the system. We ought not, naturally, to overestimate the countercultural aspects of the dissemination of reggae music in Brazil. We observe, however, in Pelourinho, the poorest of the poor, as I did for several months, dancing and enjoying themselves listening to reggae, while knowing that the larger society perceives them as potheads and potential criminals. In recognizing the defiant aspects of song lyrics, we also find revolt manifested in the dances, arms raised to the sky in praise of Jah Rastafari.

Notes

1. I would like to thank Christopher Dunn, Ari Lima, and Humberto A. Silva Jr. for their comments on the present essay and suggestions; any eventual errors, of course, are mine alone. My previous research has appeared as follows: Osmundo de A. Pinho, "The songs of freedom: notas etnográficas sobre cultura negra global e práticas contracultur- ais locais," in *Ritmos em trânsito: sócio-antropologia da música baiana*, ed. Livio San- sone and Jocélio Teles dos Santos (Salvador: Dynamis Editorial/ Programa A Cor da Bahia/Projeto SAMBA, 1997), 181–200, cited below by title of book; see also "Descen- trando o Pelô: narrativas, territórios e desigualdades raciais no centro histórico de Salvador," master's thesis in anthropology, Universidade Estadual de Campinas, 1996.

2. "Sistema vampiro" (Edson Gomes), Edson Gomes e Banda Cão de Raça, *Reggae resistência* (EMI 364791024 Z, 1988), recorded at WR Studio in Salvador.

3. Drawn from a profile of Edson Gomes published in *Folha do Reggae* 2 (February 1997).

4. Livio Sansone, "As relações raciais em *Casa grande & senzala* revisitadas à luz do processo de internacionalização e globalização," in *Raça, ciência e sociedade*, ed. Marcos Chor Maio and Ricardo V. Santos (Rio de Janeiro: Editora Fiocruz / Centro Cultural Banco do Brasil, 1996), 207–218. "Habitus" as referenced in Pierre Bordieu, "Gostos de classe e estilos de vida," in *Bourdieu sociologia* (São Paulo: Ática, 1983).

5. Carlos Benedito Rodrigues Silva, in *Da terra das primaveras à Ilha do Amor: reggae, lazer e identidade cultural* (São Luís: EDUFMA, 1995), cited by author's name later; Olívia M. Gomes da Cunha, "Fazendo a coisa certa: rastas, reggae e pentecostais em Salvador," in *Revista brasileira de ciências sociais* [São Paulo] 23 (October 1993), 120–137; Ericivaldo Veiga, "O errante e apocalíptico Muzenza," in *Ritmos em trânsito*, 123–144, and others cited below.

6. On the filhos de Gandhi, see Anamaria Morales, "O afoxé filhos de Gandhi pede paz," in *Escravidão e invenção da liberdade: estudos sobre o negro no Brasil*, ed. J. J. Reis (São Paulo: Brasiliense, 1988), 264–274, cited below by title of book; and Amélia T. Maraux, "Sindicato dos estivadores: um espaço negro?" in *Análise e dados* [Salvador], issue *O negro*, vol. 3, no. 4 (March 1994), 23–26.

7. Ericivaldo Veiga, "Rastafari e cultura em Salvador," in *Olodum, estrada da paixão*, ed. João J. S. Rodrigues (Salvador: Fundação Casa de Jorge Amado, 1996), 88–92; and "Afro Muzenza: organização, ideologia e estratificação social no bloco do reggae," in *Analise e dados* [Salvador], issue *Carnaval* vol. 5, no. 4 (1996), 105–109.

8. From Muzenza, "Brilho e beleza" (Jorge Participação), on *Muzenza do reggae* (Continental LP 1-01-404-332, 1988).

9. Leo Vidigal, "Bob Marley no Brasil," in *Massive reggae* 6 (January–March 1996), 12–15.

10. Geraldo Mayrink and J. G. Lima, "Os tambores ardem na nação baiana," in *Veja* vol. 26, no. 8, February 24, 1993, 21–25.

11. *Mais!*, supplement of *Folha de São Paulo*, April 12, 1998.

12. Antonio Risério, *Carnaval ijexá* (Salvador: Corrupio, 1981), 38 ff.

13. The idea of interpretive community is similar to the idea of social identity based on opinion, taste, and cognitive orientation. Paul Gilroy, "Diaspora, Utopia and the Critique of Capitalism," in *There Ain't No Black in The Union Jack* (London: Hutchinson, 1987), cited later by chapter title. On globalization, especially its decentering impulse, see Mike Featherstone, "A globalização da complexidade: pós-modernismo e cultura de consumo," in *Revista brasileira de ciências sociais* 32 (1996), 105–124, cited below by author.

14. Paul Gilroy, "The Black Atlantic as a Counterculture of Modernity," in *The Black Atlantic* (London: Verso, 1993).

15. On this point, readers are referred to Livio Sansone, "O local e o global na Afro-Bahia contemporânea," in *Revista brasileira de ciências sociais* vol. 10, no. 29 (October 1995), 65–84; Anthony Giddens, *As conseqüências da modernidade* (São Paulo: Editora UNESP, 1991); and Featherstone.

16. Renato Ortiz, "Estado, cultura popular e identidade nacional," in *Cultura brasileira e identidade nacional* (São Paulo: Brasiliense, 1985).

17. See such sources as José Ramos Tinhorão, *Os sons dos negros no Brasil: cantos, danças, folguedos: origens* (São Paulo: Art Editora, 1988); and Isabel Aretz, "Música y danza (América Latina e Continental, excepto Brasil)," in *África en América Latina*, ed. Manuel M. Fraginals (Mexico City: Siglo XXI, 1977), 238–278, cited below by editor.

18. Nina Rodrigues, *Os africanos no Brasil* (São Paulo: Companhia Editora Nacional, 1977), 179.

19. See, for example, Jocélio Teles dos Santos, "Divertimentos estrondosos: batuques e sambas no século XIX," and Raphael Vieira filho, "Folguedos negros no carnaval de Salvador (1880–1930)," in *Ritmos em trânsito*, 15–38; Peter Fry et al., "Negros e brancos no carnaval da Velha Republica," in *Escravidão e invenção*, 232–62; and José Jorge Carvalho, "La música de origen africana en el Brasil," in Fraginals, cited later by author of article.

20. Florestan Fernandes, vol. 1, *A integração do negro na sociedade de classes* (São Paulo: Editora Ática, 1978), 151.

21. For example, Ari Lima, "O fenômeno Timbalada: cultura musical afro-pop e juventude baiana megro-mestiça," in *Ritmos em trânsito*, 161–180; and "Espaço, lazer e música e diferença cultural na Bahia," in *Estudos afro-asiáticos* 31 (1997), 151–168.

22. Hermano Vianna, *O mundo funk carioca* (Rio de Janeiro: Jorge Zahar Editor, 1988).

23. Cf. Néstor García Canclini, "Do primitivo ao popular: teorias sobre a desigualdade entre as culturas," in *As culturas populares no capitalismo* (São Paulo: Brasiliense, 1983), 17–41.

24. See Anthony Marx, "A construção da raça e o estado-nação," in *Estudos afro-asiáticos* 29 (1996), 9–36; Lilia Scharcz, "Complexo de Zé Carioca: notas sobre identidade mestiça e malandra," paper presented at eighteenth meeting of ANPOCS, Caxambu, Minas Gerais, 1994; Roberto DaMatta, "Digressão: a fábula das três raças, ou

o problema do racismo à brasileira," in *Relativizando: uma introdução à antropologia brasileira* (Rio de Janeiro: Rocco, 1987), among others, especially France Winddance Twine, *Racism in a Racial Democracy: The Maintenance of White Supremacy in Brazil* (New Brunswick, N.J.: Rutgers University Press, 1998).

25. Suylan Midlej, "Sociabilidade contemporânea, comunicação midiática e etnicidade no funk do Black Bahia," in *O sentido e a época* (Salvador: Federal University of Bahia, 1995), 49.

26. On the construction of socially mediated spaces of listening, see Jody Berland, "Angels Dancing: Cultural Technologies and the Production of Space," in *Cultural Studies*, ed. L. Grossberg and C. Nelson (London: Routledge,1992), 38–55.

27. George Yúdice, "A funkificação do Rio de Janeiro," in *Abalando os anos 90: funk e hip-hop, globalização, violência e estilo cultural*, ed. Micael Herschmann (Rio de Janeiro: Rocco, 1997), 24–49.

28. On Rastafarianism, see E. Cashmore, "Encounters in Babylon," in *Rastaman: The Rastafarian Movement in England* (London: Allen and Unwin, 1979); and Gilroy.

Eu ando aqui! Pela Babi!
Eles me chamam de brasileiro
Porém eu me sinto um estrangeiro

[I walk around here, Babylon
They call me Brazilian
But I feel like a foreigner]
—Edson Gomes, 1990

TWELVE

Reggae and *Samba-Reggae* in Bahia
A Case of Long-Distance Belonging

Antonio J. V. dos Santos Godi

It should be noted at the outset that I don't intend to set the capitalist Babylon on fire, because the present moment is one of crisis and the contemporary flames affect our notions of time and space, and this cannot be solely attributed to the agents of reggae. At any rate, the Bahian reggae band Morrão Fumegante [Smoking Weed] set fire to the already hot Salvador summer of 1998 with its album *Fogo na Babilônia* [Fire in Babylon]. Despite these musical flames, the Bahian capital remains as it has always been. Reggae arrived, remained, and became Bahian.

It is not difficult to understand the globalizing surge of reggae and its localized manifestations in the Bahian capital. One might consider the emergence of reggae as another end-of-the-century novelty. Reggae is a cultural expression of a localized disorder, of a chaos with its own temporal and territorial context, even though this locality is not limited to Jamaica, its place of origin. Reggae is a product of the international recording industry and, as such, is reproduced beyond the boundaries of Jamaica, reflecting different notions of place as it develops in other nations and continents. Despite its cohabitation with reggae, the city of Salvador is not Jamaica, much less the Jamaica of the 1930s, which created Rastafarianism, or the Jamaica of the 1960s and 1970s, which gave birth to reggae.

One must bear in mind, however, that the markedly electronic and mediated contemporary moment can make long distances seem short. Jamaica can appear to be here and the mythified Ethiopia can be anywhere where the Rasta-reggae presence is found. As David Harvey suggests, new technologies of transportation and communication have created a compression of time and space.[1] Jamaica and Ethiopia remain where they have always been and the roots of reggae and Rasta remain geographically secure. However, these aesthetics and beliefs have had ramifications throughout the world as a pop-music style.

Between the 1960s and the 1970s, reggae and its embryonic forms, ska and rock steady, took root in diverse and distant locations. The British culture industry provided the first point of departure for these musical styles since Jamaica was an English colony until 1962. On the other hand, the electronic atmosphere that characterizes contemporary culture obeys neither national-geographic nor social-generational patterns.

Not coincidentally, the emergent expressions of electric pop of the 1970s and the 1980s, represented by the irreverence of punk rock, would find a curious complicity with the Jamaican musical aesthetic, most specifically with ska.[2] Both explicitly expressed a refusal of the established order and called for the destruction of the system. Reggae artists, in particular, announced the apocalyptic destruction of the capitalist "Babylon" and supported the return of blacks to a mythic Africa.

Punk rock and ska-reggae shared a certain social identity, the former being the electric expression of rebellious London youth and the second the musical expression of black immigrants from Jamaica.[3] That is to say, both were social presences marked by exclusion and lack of legitimate power. Despite this similarity, punk and ska-reggae evidence differences beyond the color of their practitioners. Punk spoke in a vocabulary of violent destruction and sadomasochism, while reggae spoke of peace and love. Despite such philosophical differences, these British and Jamaican musical expressions would find similarities in the critical character of their lyrics.

How does one explain the insinuating presence of Rasta-reggae expression today, and what are the cultural roots that justify its existence? How is this phenomenon, marked by the crossing of different traditions with contemporary sociocultural implications, articulated in the construction of this movement? Which cultural variables suggest a feeling of long-distance belonging? How do we explain the affinities between the Rasta-reggae culture in Jamaica and the aesthetic behavior of the *blocos afro* of the contemporary Bahian Carnival?

Reggae: Tradition, Youth, and Electronic Ethnicity

The mythical and theoretical narratives that attempt to explain the emergence of Rastafarianism underscore the prophetic discourse of Marcus Garvey: "Look to Africa, where a black king will be crowned, because the day of liberation will come next."[4] One could interpret as coincidence or prophecy the fact that, three years later, in 1930, a black king was indeed crowned in Ethiopia. Ras Tafari Makonnen would be referred to from then on as Haile Selassie, the "King of Kings" and the "Lion of the Tribe of Judah." According to some, Haile Selassie was the direct descendant of King Salomon and the Queen of Sheba, two important figures in Judeo-Christian history. However, Garvey's apparent prophecy was neither a coincidence nor a premonition, but rather the perception of a black militant profoundly in step with his time and with the ideas of an Ethiopianism that mythically constructed Africa as the cradle of Christianity.

By the middle of the 1970s, Jamaica already had close to 75,000 Rastas.[5] More recent data suggest that the Rastas represent 10 percent of the population of the island, constituting a group of about 250,000.[6] The biblical stories that justified and legitimated African slavery in the Americas would be reinterpreted by Jamaican Rastas so as to emphasize instead the liberation of black people, thought to be the manifestation of Jah, their supreme God. Reading the Old Testament in some unusual ways, the Rastas refused to cut the hair on their heads or bodies, leading to the creation of dreadlocks as one of their most important symbols of identity. Likewise, they refused to eat meat, in particular pork, adopting instead a diet based on fruits, vegetables, and grains. The Rastas are also known for their rejection of the laws and social behavior of "Babylon," opting instead for a radically alternative outlaw lifestyle.

Besides being based on the Africanized traditions of Christianity in Jamaica, the behavioral aesthetic of Rasta-reggae would assimilate elements of international youth culture of the era, especially electric pop music. Another characteristic of young people of that generation was the adoption of a free, adventurous lifestyle based on the love of nature and the rejection of moralizing hypocrisy and the unbridled consumerism of the capitalist world. The most seminal representation of youth culture during this time, the hippies, had a profound, worldwide influence, and shared many similarities with the Rasta-reggae movement. Music associated with social rebellion and spiritual revival was essential to both movements.

The youth of the 1960s and 1970s had attained a certain cultural autonomy that would substantially influence youth cultures in the following decades. The electronic dissemination of the behavioral aesthetic of rock was a determining factor in the cultural revolution of this period.[7] Likewise, the appearance of reggae in Jamaica and of *samba-reggae* in Bahia were phenomena engendered by irreverent, black youth cultures, contextualized in new social experiences for which music would be the most fundamental reference.

Livio Sansone, concerned with understanding the local and the global in relation to Brazilian funk, underscores the idea of cultural globalization and emphasizes the importance of youth culture. For the Italian anthropologist, "homogenization" and "massification" are not useful concepts in understanding the peripheral expressions of a globalized youth culture. Far from the old ethnocentric pretensions, the relationship between the local and the global engenders the construction of contextualized expressions.[8] Jamaican reggae and Bahian *samba-reggae* represent local reconstructions of originary representations of "Anglo-Saxon" youth cultures that have music as their crucial expression. I agree in part with Sansone, although to see these local presences as peripheral manifestations of a centralizing, determinant, and global "Anglo-Saxon" culture presents a flagrant paradox. The music that influenced both the development of reggae and the *blocos afro* [Afro-Bahian Carnival groups] was produced by African Americans. However, as blacks living in a world of racial inequality, these aesthetic agents maintained a certain feeling of transnational belonging, making it difficult to label their cultural expressions "Anglo-Saxon."

In the global context, in which the music of the African diaspora represents a crucial reference, there exists neither center nor periphery, but rather a space without borders. We are in a virtual dimension, characterized by a cultural environment without a determined space that adopts multiple global positions as sites of belonging and references of identity. Reggae might "originate" simultaneously in Jamaica and Brazil, as well as anywhere else in the world where electronic pop music is disseminated.

In its electronic and cultural aspects, globalization is an incontestable fact. However, with regard to geographic mobility and social contact among individuals across distant borders, the situation is different. The local press has noted various cases in which Brazilians have been violently denied entrance to other countries, even though they had appropriate legal documentation and proof of personal financial requirements. This suggests that, while long-distance electronic and cultural contact is easily exercised, people often have a difficult time crossing geographical borders.

John Naisbitt, a defender of free economy between nations and, consequently, a supporter of local privatization, suggests that the more globalized the economy, the more power acquired by its minor protagonists—nations, businesses, and individuals.[9] Certainly the Brazilian individuals who suffer disrespect in the airports of other nations would disagree with Naisbitt's ideas regarding the democratization of tourism. On the other hand, these same people could hardly disagree with him when he affirms that technological innovations allow people to "visit" any part of the world in the comfort of their own homes.

One should keep in mind, however, that not everybody possesses a home with the comfort that modern technology offers. The number of disenfranchised people in the world continues to rise. Contemporary globalization reflects the old contours of political and economic order with an increase in social inequalities on a local and international scale. This deserves careful attention. Brazilian ethnomusicologist Jorge José de Carvalho notes that intellectuals from other countries have critiqued globalization as the dissemination of capitalist imperialism, while Brazilian studies, focused on culture and communication, have overlooked issues of power and domination which are at the core of end-of-the-century international relations.[10]

On the other hand, the presence of reggae introduces mythic notions of a type of social globalization, expressed in the idea of "Babylon," which represents a predatory capitalist imperialism. The many seemingly disconnected stories of reggae suggest a chaotic multiplicity of time and space, combining past history with contemporary experience. Discussions about contemporary cultural globalization and the phenomena of long-distance contacts and identifications can be discerned in reggae, where questions related to power and domination are considered in a new dimension characterized by the relationship between local and global connections.

Long-Distance Belonging

Despite a lack of materials in Portuguese about Rasta-reggae culture, one notes in Brazil a remarkable growth of aficionados and followers of this behavioral and aesthetic complex. In greater Salvador, the appropriation of Rasta-reggae culture is notable in the suggestive presence of the many individuals who proudly wear dreadlocks, or in the production and consumption of reggae music. One might go so far as to say that the presence in Salvador of Ubaldo Uharú, Geraldo Cristal, Dionorina, Gilsan, Jorge de Angélica, Edson Gomes, and Sine Calmon, just to note a few of our most important reggae performers, is revealing proof of a sociocultural singularity that has been constituted at long distance. This might lead us to believe that the notion of belonging at the end of the century does not adhere to the same patterns of concepts such as "social identity" and "cultural identity," which have been essential to sociological and anthropological theory in the last few decades. Increasingly, feelings of belonging have been redimensionalized.

The formation of an electronic cultural market created by radio, television, the recording industry, and, most recently, information networks is essential to understand the complexity of contemporary society. The popularity of reggae would not have been possible without shortwave and AM radio transmissions from the southern United States, which were received in Jamaica in the 1960s and 1970s. During this time, distinct locations all over the planet were influenced by African-American popular music, leading to new ethnic and cultural expressions in various areas.

We might say that the utilization of African-American music and contemporary communication technologies led to the development of Jamaican reggae and the subsequent emergence of the Bahian *blocos afro*. Antonio Risério suggests that the musical movement of African-Americans was "the great catalyst" in the creation of the Carnival aesthetic introduced by the first *bloco afro*, Ilê Aiyê, in 1974. In this period there was a weekly television show with the Jackson Five, and the influence of this soul group on the contemporary behaviors of the black youth of Bahia was intense. In addition to this group, origin of the polemic megastar Michael Jackson, Risério emphasizes the presence of James Brown, who profoundly affected the "engineering" of popular culture in Salvador.[11] From there on, record and radio markets became determinant factors in the creation of long-distance cultural identifications.

The construction of an Afrocentric aesthetic in the Carnival of Salvador was one of the major cultural developments in recent Bahian history, and music was the fundamental expression of this phenomenon. Initially, this presence gained visibility and audibility in the localized dimension of the Carnival masses, and thereafter began its conquest of the mass media. From the outset, the local phenomenon of the *blocos afro* was related to Afro-diasporic musical forms with global projection. Though African-American music influenced the general elaboration of these entities, it would not determine the form of local musical expressions. Subsequently, traditional samba was filtered through contemporary and globalized musical motifs. *Samba-reggae* would come to represent a determining example of the mix between the local roots of samba and an already global reggae.[12]

The establishment of *samba-reggae* as the rhythm that generated a new musical movement in Bahia in the mid-1980s reveals the force of reggae in the new aesthetics and behaviors seen in the most predominantly black city in Brazil. The *bloco afro* Olodum and its former musical director, Neguinho do Samba, were the principal protagonists in the recent success of *samba-reggae*. However, other *blocos afro* were dedicated to the aesthetic of reggae, during the period before the construction of this hybrid Afro-Bahian musical form.

Malê Debalê and Muzenza are two *blocos afro* that provide early examples of an intense Bahian affinity for Jamaican reggae. Malê Debalê appeared in 1979, as the local cult of reggae, especially of Bob Marley, was beginning to emerge. The group pioneered the incorporation of reggae with its song "Coração Rastafari" [Rastafari heart] (1982), written by Djalma Luz and recorded by Lazzo Matumbi, another reggae artist in Salvador. Muzenza received attention for being the first to adopt a Jamaican behavioral aesthetic as a central theme. The group would later become known as Muzenza do Reggae.

The long-distance affinities between the *blocos afro* and Jamaican reggae can be explained by the fact that both movements arose from very similar political, cultural, and historical conditions. Both represented movements of young, dispossessed blacks fighting against social injustice. During this time cultural production became increasingly more global by means of multinational recording industries. It was not coincidental that both reggae and *bloco afro* aesthetics were cultivated with reference to a very specific conception of Africa. Africa was constructed by both groups as a mythic locus that provided a feeling of origin, dispersion, and symbolic reunion. The notion of black diaspora reflects strong associations with the development of new ideas of time and space within the electronic cultural market in which music plays a central role.[13] Ultimately, what was far away would appear close and points of reference of identity could be revisited by historic and geographic memory.

Death in the Trajectory of Belonging

Death does not always signal the end. The passing of Robert Nesta Marley on May 11, 1981, led to the definitive incorporation of this date into the calendar of events of the black movement in Bahia. The month of May in Salvador ceased to be solely a time to commemorate the abolition of slavery (May 13, 1888) and became the month of tributes to Bob Marley. Images of the musical hero would adorn the T-shirts of thousands of youths, including whites, blacks, and *mestiços*. If May 13 represented a historical-ideological construction based on the official decrees of the past, May 11 would come to represent the invention of a recent tradition made possible by a mass-mediated and globalized cultural context that was determined primarily by black music.

The introduction of reggae in Bahia did not exactly coincide with the death of Bob Marley, even though the event brought greater attention to the reggae style. The event contributed decisively to the aesthetic re-elaboration of Muzenza, which was founded as a dissident group of Olodum in 1981. This phenomenon would lead to the creation of other *blocos afro* with reggae influences. In the Carnivals of 1997 and 1998, for instance, several reggae-influenced groups appeared, including the Amantes do Reggae, Ska Reggae, and Resistência Ativa.

Jamaican reggae led to the appearance of a new musical style in Bahia, *samba-reggae*, and a new Carnival subcategory. It should be noted that the Carnival scene had already been the primary site for the social and aesthetic innovation that revitalized the city each year. The 1970s saw the opening of reggae bars, beginning in the Maciel-Pelourinho neighborhood and spreading throughout the area. During the 1980s, reggae would be progressively disseminated in Salvador by means of extremely popular radio programs dedicated exclusively to the reggae genre. How was the insertion of reggae in Bahia processed, and what were the historical conditions that led to this new form of cultural belonging?

One of the first manifestations of Jamaican music in Brazil occurred in 1968 when reggae singer-songwriter Jimmy Cliff performed at the International Festival of Song in Rio de Janeiro. The festival was cosponsored and aired by TV Globo, an important national television network, which provided Cliff exposure to the Brazilian public. Reggae music was later introduced by Caetano Veloso and Gilberto Gil, who had first heard the new Jamaican music while exiled in London between 1969 and 1972.

Initially, reggae in Bahia was regarded as a marginal cultural movement, appearing in the working-class black neighborhoods. At this point, reggae was still rarely played on the radio, and scarcely available in record stores. In spite of this, reggae appeared in the bars and brothels of the historic downtown, Maciel-Pelourinho. Likewise, the music composed and performed by the *blocos afro* had yet to penetrate the radio or recording markets, despite its widespread performance by informal percussion groups during leisure time.

Spanish-Caribbean rhythms, referred to generically in Salvador as "merengue," were also widely heard in the brothels and at the weekend house parties of Maciel-Pelourinho. The long-distance connection between Bahia and the Caribbean existed before the recorded presence of reggae, and Maciel-Pelourinho, the emblematic territory of the Filhos de Gandhi and Olodum, was an important neighborhood in terms of racial and ethnic re-elaboration.

In the late 1970s, Pelourinho also came to be the subcultural territory of Salvador for artists and black militants. The first reggae bar opened in 1978, the same year as the creation of the Unified Black Movement (MNU), and of the establishment of the *festa da benção* [blessing party], which occurs every Tuesday evening in Maciel-Pelourinho.[14] The late 1970s and early 1980s was a period of profound changes in the ethnic and aesthetic image of the city. Afro-diasporic music, with its attendant cultural styles and political discourses, would play a determining role in this crucial process of local transformation.

In 1979, amidst the political opening of the military dictatorship and the founding of the *bloco afro* Olodum, Gilberto Gil would release a version of Bob Marley's "No Woman, No Cry," under the title "Não chore mais." The song would become an anthem of the struggle to end military rule in Brazil. From then on, reggae in Brazil would be sung in clear Portuguese and would progressively move from certain tribal territories to the dimension of electronic mass mediation throughout the nation.

On March 18, 1980, Bob Marley, the avatar of the Rasta-reggae style, visited

Brazil, establishing important contact with local artists. On May 26, 1980, Gilberto Gil and Jimmy Cliff played a concert in Salvador that inaugurated a successful tour through the principal Brazilian cities. About 50,000 people came to
see them at the main soccer stadium in the Bahian capital. In the same year,
Peter Tosh came to Brazil to participate in the Second International Festival of
Jazz in São Paulo, and was featured on an extremely popular soap opera. These
local events led to the dissemination of reggae in Brazil, inspiring a growing
sense of identity and long-distance belonging in Bahia.

Rasta-Reggae and Electronic Media

Reggae is a contemporary behavioral and aesthetic invention. Despite its connections with mento, calypso, and other Carribean musics, it is also the direct
descendant of rock music, soul, and rhythm and blues. These musical forms
emerged with new electronic media markets connected to radio, television, and
recording industries. Marshall McLuhan sees the invention of radio as a "tribal-
izing drum." For radio has a cloak of invisibility that is manifested intimately
from person to person, striking remote and forgotten chords.[15] The recent success of Bahian music is a perfect example of the "magical power" of the radio to
broadcast hot information and encourage the acceptance of new musical and
behavioral languages.

The cooperation between Rádio Itapoan FM and the pioneering WR recording studio in Salvador led to the popularity of *samba-reggae* and so-called *axé
music* in the late 1980s. Until that time, local radio rarely aired reggae, despite
popular acceptance. Several FM stations currently have weekly reggae shows,
which reflects changes in public taste and radio programming. The story of
reggae and the radio market of Salvador has as its principal protagonist DJ Ray
Company. Ray was a passionate fan of Jamaican music and collaborated on the
"Roots Program," which aired in 1979 on Rádio Cruzeiro. He contributed to the
pioneering program "Rock, Reggae, and Blues," on Rádio Piatã FM, in 1982 and
1983.[16]

In 1986, Ray Company organized two programs for Rádio Itaparica FM,
"Mama Africa" and "Reggae Specials," the latter devoted entirely to reggae. Besides presenting an extensive and rare repertoire of music, "Reggae Specials" featured interviews with artists and devotees of reggae music. Lino de Almeida, a
member of the black movement, would regularly visit the show, stimulating pro-

Dressed in the Carnival attire of *bloco afro* Ilê Aiyê, Gilberto Gil (right)
welcomes Jimmy Cliff to Bahia at the international airport of Salvador,
1980. Archive of *A tarde*.

vocative discussions around the issue of ethnicity and its link to the Rasta-reggae
movement.

It should also be noted that 1988 marked the commemoration of the centen-
nial of the abolition of slavery in Brazil, an event that would focus media attention on black culture. In the 1980s, while *samba-reggae* was in its formative stage,
a particular type of roots reggae with a local inflection was also being constructed
in Salvador. Initially, this musical style would be reconstructed by means of local
versions in which the deep pulsations of the bass guitar would be replaced by a
pop-rock attack, as in Gilberto Gil's cover of Bob Marley's "No Woman, No
Cry." However, Bahian performers would soon achieve success in the recording
and radio markets with specifically local elaborations of roots reggae.

The local social and spatial context of the *blocos afro*, the reggae bars, and the
Rasta groups, interfaced with the chaotic and infinite universe of the masses, was
transformed by radio and recording markets in Salvador. In addition to the radio
programs, Bahian reggae would enter the mainstream recording market in 1988
with the release of albums by the Banda Terceiro Mundo [Third World Band]

and Edson Gomes, who would gain considerable attention in Bahia and the northeast of Brazil in the 1990s. More recently, Sine Calmon's album *Fogo na Babilônia* would achieve formidable success between 1997 and 1998. In 1998, the radio-push song of this album, "Nayambing Blues," was a huge hit during Carnival, the principal thermometer of Bahian music. During ten years of Bahian reggae production, only a few bands were commercially successful in the recording market. This may reflect a certain mistrust among black youth in relation to local media.

In 1998 the city of Salvador had approximately ten FM radio stations, and a third of these stations had weekly reggae programs. Itaparica FM and Salvador FM still kick off the weekend with reggae shows, and Rádio Cidade has a Saturday program called "Cidade reggae" [Reggae city]. The fact that the reggae programs all air during the weekend is telling. In fact, the term "reggae" is currently used by Bahians to mean "party." This leads us to conclude that reggae was culturally assimilated in Salvador not only as a musical genre, but also as a lifestyle marked by pleasure. Beyond these theoretical elaborations, Jamaica is not here, but reggae is here, persisting as a local presence.

Notes

1. David Harvey, *A condição pós-moderna: uma perspectiva sobre as origens da mudança cultural* (São Paulo: Loyola, 1989).

2. Roberto Muggiati, *Da utopia á incerteza (1967–1984)*, vol. 2 (São Paulo: Brasiliense, 1985), 80.

3. See Steven Connor, *Cultura pós-moderna: introdução às teorias do contemporâneo* (São Paulo: Loyola, 1992); and Dick Hebdige, *Cut 'n' Mix: Culture, Identity and Caribbean Music* (London: Routledge, 1987).

4. Quoted by Stephen Davis and Peter Simon, *Reggae, música e cultura da Jamaica* (Coimbra: Centelha, 1983), 62.

5. Davis and Simon, 59.

6. Otávio Rodrigues, "Os rastas," fascicule of *Revista Planeta*, n/d., 7.

7. Eric J. Hobsbawm, *Era dos extremos: o breve século XX (1914–1991)* (São Paulo: Companhia das Letras, 1995), 318.

8. Livio Sansone, "Funk baiano: uma versão local de um fenômeno global?" in *Ritmos em trânsito: sócio-antropologia da música baiana*, ed. Sansone and Jocélio Teles dos Santos (São Paulo: Dynamis Editorial; Salvador: Programa A Cor da Bahia e Projeto S.A.M.B.A., 1997), 137; cited below by editors.

9. John Naisbitt, *Paradoxo global: quanto maior a economia mundial, mais poderosos*

são os seus protagonistas menores: nações, empresas e indivíduos (Rio de Janeiro: Campus, 1994), 137.

10. Jorge José de Carvalho , "Imperialismo cultural hoje: uma questão silenciada," in *Revista USP* 32 (1996–1997), 68.

11. Antonio Risério, *Carnaval ijexá: notas sobre afoxés e blocos do novo carnaval afrobaiano* (Salvador: Corrupio, 1981), 20–28.

12. Antonio J. V. dos Santos Godi, "Música afro-carnavalesca: das multidões para o sucesso das massas elétricas," in Sansone and Santos, eds. 73–96.

13. Paul Gilroy, *The Black Atlantic: Modernity and Double Consciousness* (London: Verso, 1993).

14. Osmundo de Araújo Pinho, "The songs of freedom: notas etnográficas sobre cultura negra global e práticas contraculturais locais," in Sansone and Santos, eds., 182–184.

15. Marshall McLuhan, *Understanding Media: The Extensions of Man* (New York: New American Library, 1964), 339.

16. Antonio J. V. dos Santos Godi, "Reggae na Bahia: história de uma presença recente," in *Folha do Reggae* 3 (1997).

THIRTEEN

Black or *Brau*
Music and Black Subjectivity in a Global Context

Ari Lima

In the state of Bahia, Brazil, popular music since the 1970s has moved well beyond the conventional boundaries of the musical universe.[1] The affirmation of identity, and the hegemony of a set of signs appealing to both the consumer public and the music industry, have been put into play, attracting national and even global audiences. The music of Bahia has appealed to a young, poor, semischooled, black and *mestiço* audience, avidly consuming symbolic and material goods. These musical codes derive from such sources as funk, rap, salsa, samba, romantic music, and the Afro-Brazilian religion, Candomblé. Extra-musical concerns that encompass individualistic sentimentalism, the search for a mythical and pure Africa, global discourses on race, the exploration of body languages, and the crystallization of a Bahian identity associated with black cultural production also play a significant role. In this chapter, the band Timbalada and its founder, Carlinhos Brown, offer a point of departure for a discussion of how black music and subjectivity are constituted and transformed in a context of cultural globalization.

A Globalized Diaspora

Though the term *globalization* has a strong economic connotation, it also has important political and cultural components that have received attention in various areas of inquiry. The phenomenon of globalization is characterized by the international integration of capital, the stretching and virtualization of the frontiers of time and space, the development of transnational political power, and the intensification of global social relations by means of sophisticated networks of communications. The music and subjectivities engendered by performers and young blacks living in the state of Bahia are also located within the structure of a global culture characterized by the superimposition of local and worldwide values and symbols, and by the aestheticization and spectacle making of daily life.

Featherstone believes that global culture does not function in the same way as the culture of the nation-state.[2] Rather, we might think of a global culture in terms of the processes of cultural integration and disintegration that occur on transnational and trans-social levels, crossing nation-state boundaries and permitting the flow of information, products, ideologies, images, and people. These various forms of transnational communication acquire a certain autonomy on the global level, becoming third cultures, subject to cultural flows beyond the bilateral norms of the nation-state and transcending dichotomies of homogenization/heterogenization and integration/disintegration.

Smith affirms that emerging global culture is not linked to any time or place.[3] Unlike national cultures, it is essentially one without memory, one that does not respond to real necessities or to formative identities. It is artificially put together at great cost, taken from numerous extant folk/national identities into which humanity was divided for so long. There is no real universal memory that can be used to unite humanity; the most global experiences only serve to remind us of our historical divisions.

Global culture is transnational, mass-mediated, and artificial; it lacks a specific locus and memory and it has a logic of material and symbolic consumerism as its fundamental perspective. According to this logic, socially structured means for the deployment of consumer goods demarcate social relations. The symbolism of this consumerism is not only evident in the design and imaginary of production and marketing, but also in the symbolic associations of different products that can be used and renegotiated in order to emphasize lifestyle differences that demarcate social relations. This involves the evocation of narcissistic dreams and desires, as much as the control or lack of control of behaviors and emotions engendered in a flexible productive structure that is clearly based in economic power.[4]

With respect to diasporic black cultures, Paul Gilroy claims that music, above all, permitted blacks to make alliances, assert themselves, resist, and develop a consciousness in the West.[5] A product of exchange, dislocation, assimilation, "simplification," and ethnic affirmation, music would come to function for blacks as a model of cognition for their experiences of continuity and rupture in relation to a past in which ethics, aesthetics, politics, culture, and religion were present.

This Afro-Atlantic movement presupposes memory, the need to belong, and a constant mobilization of identities. It is relived in endless flows that are local and at the same time transnational, denationalized, and independent of social relations based on a consumer logic. However, if we think of this diaspora in terms of a current global culture as Featherstone and Smith understand it—also keeping in mind ethics, aesthetics, politics, culture, and religion—a consumer logic (based on the aestheticized distinction between lifestyles), social prestige, and class all emerge. This ensemble creates a new movement of relational ethnicity that transcends emotional ties and traditional forms of socialization. The new ethnicity is marginal, but is also integrated into the city via media technologies that communicate the symbols of the modern culture industry. Such symbols are particularly manifest in music, whether rap or funk.[6] The mediation and global spread of this Afro-Atlantic complex is centered around African-American culture, which operates within hegemonic U.S. capitalism. Thus it is no coincidence that, whether in Bahia or Amsterdam, black culture should be conceived and produced as much for its symbolic power as for its economic power, and that this power should possess a homogenizing tendency.[7]

Music and Black Subjectivity

In Bahia, the two diasporic processes intersect in a very complicated way. I believe that, in this context, the regular notion of ethnic identity loses authenticity, transparency, and authority. There are constant ruptures and discontinuities that do not permit a specific "black Bahian identity" to crystallize. Thus, instead of understanding such an identity as an established fact that is represented by new cultural practices, perhaps we should see it, following Stuart Hall, as a perpetually incomplete "production" that is always in progress and is constituted within representation and not outside of it.[8] With respect to the meaning of ethnic identity in Bahia, various flows of black subjectivity occur, and I will represent them through specific subjects. These are best understood in three fundamental ensembles: the *bloco afro* Ilê Aiyê, founded in 1974 by the *dono* [owner] Antônio Carlos Vovô; the *bloco afro* Olodum, whose principal name has been João Jorge dos Santos Rodrigues since 1980; and the band Timbalada, formed in 1992 by its creator, Carlinhos Brown. I will summarize the first two and the principal meanings and actions they inspired in young blacks. Then I will endeavor to construct Carlinhos Brown as a black Bahian subject.

Vovô is from the neighborhood of Curuzu, João Jorge is from Maciel-Pelourinho, and Carlinhos Brown is from Candeal Pequeno. With this in mind, I would like to discuss something common to the three cases: the manipulation of myths of origin in Salvador. If, on the one hand, all three neighborhoods are niches of poverty, inhabited by illiterate or semiliterate blacks, they are, on the other hand, also repositories of different ethnomusical discourses. That is to say, if Curuzu represents Afro-Bahian tradition, and Maciel-Pelourinho suggests a new, media-driven ethnic identity, then Candeal Pequeno is a musical laboratory.

Influenced by the U.S. American Black Power movement as well as by antiracist movements in Brazil, Ilê Aiyê evoked an essential vision of Africa in its neighborhood of Curuzu by assigning value to Candomblé iconography and creating a space where only blacks of the most Negroid phenotype would belong. The pioneer ethnomusical discourse of Ilê Aiyê elaborated a "black world" in opposition to the racist white world. Since then, Ilê Aiyê has become the signature of blackness in the Bahian Carnival. The members of Ilê Aiyê are somewhat like African-Americans in that they respond explicitly to a context of socially racialized relations. Upon assuming a "black" physical appearance in Carnival, the group demythified the notion of racial democracy in Bahia. In an aesthetic or ludic register, a public space was created for a black identity that had been confined to an inner existence.[9] Vovô, who articulates this process of blackening or re-Africanization of the Bahian Carnival, is the son of Mãe Hilda, a priestess of Candomblé.[10] With dreadlocks and dark skin, and versed in the rhythms of the religion, Vovô has come to represent the ethnic archetype for the ideology and myth of the traditional Afro-Bahian subject.

In the early 1980s, Olodum emerged from Maciel-Pelourinho, a marginalized neighborhood stigmatized as a haunt for prostitutes and transvestites. The new *bloco* was formed by previous members of Ilê Aiyê and militant members of the Unified Black Movement (MNU). Olodum would quickly come to occupy an important role in the Bahian Carnival. Olodum innovated with its beat (*samba-reggae*), its multiracial composition, and its search for visibility by means of cultural marketing. Without compromising its anti-racist position, Olodum accepted the challenge of creating relations between socioeconomically diverse groups, knowing that they would never have absolute control over the consequences of this mix. The next step was to locate symbolic as well as economic value in Afro-Bahian culture. João Jorge's group became a cultural holding that gathered, unified, and commodified black culture.[11] With the massification of its image, black culture became more accessible to scattered and heterogeneous constituencies. The copying and reproduction of Olodum's style allowed for the integration of Bahians and foreigners, and blacks and whites, around symbols that referred less to the black appearance, and more to the black origins of Bahia. That is, in Olodum, one is black if one feels that he or she is black and wishes to be recognized as such and identifies with the demand for full-fledged citizenship for Bahian blacks.[12] This integration is fluid and reflects a politicized, albeit fragmented discourse. João Jorge, better educated than Vovô, spoke English, and, beginning in 1990, arranged tours for Olodum in Europe and the United States, as well as recordings with global pop stars Paul Simon and Michael Jackson. Critical of the hierarchical and polarized models of Ilê Aiyê, João Jorge was active in the production of an aestheticized and globalized identity disseminated by the mass media.

Black or *Brau*

According to some of its elder citizens, Candeal Pequeno was the property of a family of wealthy free Africans who had come to Bahia to look for expatriated family members. Frustrated in their search, they acquired the land of Candeal Pequeno and initiated the worship of Ogum, the Yoruba deity of iron, represented by a stone brought from the coast of Africa. Today, local inhabitants who identify themselves as direct descendants of these black pilgrims guard the stone and maintain the cult. At the end of every year they hold a festival for Ogum, the patron saint of Candeal. In the past, the festival began Christmas week and ended after Mass on January first, with breakfast and a table of sweets. In 1995 Carlinhos Brown tried to reconstitute the splendor of the festival with a Mass and an offering of popcorn, candy, and *acarajé* [bean fritters]. Timbalada performed at the festival.

Carlinhos Brown and the local community brought back to life this history of Candeal to share it with the mass media and anthropologists, in hopes of reestablishing a direct link between Africa and Candeal Pequeno. In fact, the truthfulness of the story was of little importance. What seemed more important was the calling forth of a vague, undocumented, fragmented history, more than its actual revival. This reclaiming allowed the inhabitants of Candeal Pequeno and Carlinhos Brown to tell their own story, whose continuity was elaborated in relation to the festival and, more importantly, the music of their community. In 1995, upon agreeing to enliven the tradition of the festival, Carlinhos Brown called upon his family and his percussionists to help him in a task that was originally up to the founders of community.

In this way, music and religious tradition are linked in Candeal. Music engenders this alliance by inspiring a reflective attitude. Thus, the time and space that the inhabitants of Candeal reappropriated are a mythical territory, crystallized in oral memory and the tradition of the body. As Muniz Sodré has written, this territory is "related to personal space, like the body itself and the space adjacent to it—an invisible delimitation of space which accompanies the individual, capable of expanding or contracting itself according to the situation and characterized by flexibility."[13]

Timbalada, like the majority of important bands in Salvador, is the result of a collective effort. However, the individual work of its creator, head percussionist, and songwriter Carlinhos Brown (b. 1963) was decisive in the process of its formation. Working as a street musician after dropping out of school at a young age, Brown learned to play the most common percussion instruments with Osvaldo Alves da Silva, a retired driver better known as Pintado do Bongô. Brown inherited the musical tradition that survived from the Bahian Candomblés and the streets. Since the early 1980s, he has been part of the Bahian music scene, having played anonymously in *trio elétrico*, participated in bands led by others, and contributed to the consolidation of a new Bahian musical product that would come to be known as *axé music*. Brown's work gained national acclaim when he played

Timbalada performing in the streets of Salvador, 1994. Photo by Lázaro
Roberto, Zumvi Arquivo Fotográfico, Salvador.

on Caetano Veloso's albums *Caetano* (1987) and *Estrangeiro* (1989). Contact
with Veloso gave credence to Brown's name in the local and national media, attracting the attention of such other figures in Brazilian popular music as Djavan,
João Bosco, João Gilberto, and Gilberto Gil. Brown performed around the world
with other renowned musicians, accumulating and recycling musical information and acquiring recordings and such musical instruments as *kloters* from Af-
ghanistan and the *barbuca* and *adofo* of Arabic origin.

Traveling the world, relating to foreign audiences, learning from more mature performers, and doing percussion arrangements for diverse original musicians all influenced Brown's conception of percussive music and inspired him to
incorporate sounds uncommon in traditional Bahian music. Today Timbalada
has a strong leaning toward codified public tastes and the commercial directions
of the music industry, but its origins are in Carlinhos Brown's experimental work
with a previous band called Vai Quem Vem, which earned a Grammy for its 1992
participation on Sérgio Mendes's acclaimed album *Brasileiro.*

The success of Timbalada beginning in the summer of 1993 brought Brown
even more attention. The respect that he had acquired in the restrictive and in-

fluential world of mainstream popular music was fundamental to the band. Carlinhos Brown also consciously assumed leadership of the group, serving as a model of success to the band members. Little by little, Brown developed a musical project. Besides Timbalada, he formed an all-female band called Bolacha Maria as well as a youth band called Lactomia, and built a professional school for street musicians that opened its doors at the end of 1996.

The Carlinhos Brown we know today, however, came into existence before all of this, with James Brown and the Black Power movement. In the 1970s, the U.S.-American Black Power movement was disseminated to several cities in Brazil via Rio de Janeiro, spreading the idea of "soul power," and the "I am somebody" slogan of pop star James Brown, the idol of the movement. The movement was characterized by the strong rhythmic appeal of soul music, an exuberant choreography, extravagant costumes, an emphatic rhetoric of protest against racial discrimination and American politics, and the construction of "soul" as an open signifier.[14] Carlinhos Brown, who experienced Black Power in the working-class neighborhoods of Salvador, described the movement to me via his impressions of James Brown:

> I didn't understand anything he was singing, but I understood how he acted, and everyone understood that, because his dancing, the way he danced, dragging himself along, you know, was like a *drible* [dribble, faking others out, avoidance], like a dribble around social things, going down to the floor, using his whole body like a movement. When you came to Liberdade [the largest black neighborhood in Salvador], some guy would always challenge you: Draw a line! And he'd dance a circle. So if you danced cool, if you did a novel step, it was all right. If not, everyone messed with you and stuff—"You aren't *brau*, man!"

In this context, boundaries and limits of ethnicity and identity could, to a certain degree, be formalized. Although it was most often expressed at the aesthetic level, it also had psychological, historical, economical, religious, and political repercussions.[15] In Brazil, the English words *black* and *brown* (i.e., *brau*) have been appropriated to express specific cultural affinities. In general, *black* connotes a more politicized racial identity, while *brau* refers to the consumer of African-American soul culture in Bahia. These two terms appealed to different feelings of identity that could be recodified in gesture, dress, dance, and discourses of affirmation and social critique.

Thus it was possible to share attitudes and feelings in an institutional sense, as when Ilê Aiyê translated Black Power, or to reinterpret the political vigor and the aesthetic of the movement, as Carlinhos Brown did in the 1990s by reviving the movement's supreme avatar, individualized in his very name through a basic mechanism of distinction and belonging. What made Carlinhos Brown venture beyond his home territory, Candeal Pequeno, to dance in other neighborhoods, was his desire to be a *brau* among equals in terms of class and cultural experience. Since the ethnic and racial identity of its members seemed quite obvious, it made less sense to identify as black.

To be discussed, the issue of identity would have to appear as a problem or a limit of action imposed by some determining Other.[16] Black Power, Ilê Aiyê, and Olodum inspired in Carlinhos Brown the recognition, the affirmation of the black element in the myth of the three races so sophisticatedly entrenched in the social imaginary, without leading to the racialization of behavior.[17]

Carlinhos Brown affirms that he was interested in the "leftovers," the diluted information, of Ilê Aiyê and Olodum. He thus inverts the position of music and of musicians in the ethnomusical discourses of these vestiges, emphasizing what we might call, to elaborate on concepts of Roberto DaMatta, the *person of the individual*.[18] This refers to those musicians who were bound by the social totality, submitted to hierarchical power, committed to the collectivity, yet had the power to choose and to decide. Instead of investigating African cultures, Brown explored musical rhythms popularized in Bahia for the consumption of whites and blacks, rich and poor.

Another difference between Carlinhos Brown and the others is that he proves to be more conscious of the existence of a political limit for the representation of black music, expressed in the ways in which musical producers and media figures have domesticated the music:

> If Timbalada loses something when captured on tape, it loses in the sense that the recording is not created with Timbalada in mind. Not just for Timbalada, either. The same is true for everyone: Muzenza, Araketu. They are not prepared to record what everybody today calls "unplugged." We've been unplugged for a hundred years, my friend. We're acoustic. Now what can I do if the system is like this? We don't have a vocabulary to talk about our music. There's ethnic, there's "world music," but that's so limiting. They want to see a toothless face, so that when you hear the song you imagine rotten teeth and hunger. That's what I refuse to do. We need to get away from that.[19]

While Brown didn't develop the experience of the militant black, he possesses the experience of the musician who establishes contact with audiences and performers of the most varied tendencies in Brazil and the entire world. He perceives that his music and behavior are pressured by representational models of "white supremacy" that do not possess the analytical categories to translate a way of seeing, thinking, and feeling that gets beyond the terms in which black alterity is conceived—that is, in terms of victimization and an incomprehensible "primitivization."[20] Thus, if Carlinhos Brown were to "go ethnic," to make "world music," to expand his music in a certain way, he would confine his past, his future, and the affective black materiality crystallized in the imaginary of Candeal Pequeno.

Similarity and Imagination

Michel Foucault suggests that a discontinuity between representation and the social world characterized modernity from the beginning of the eighteenth century. First, he argues that until the sixteenth century, similarity played the most important role in the knowledge systems of the Western world. Language was a mirror of the world. In the sixteenth century, language was studied as a part of nature, rather than as a set of independent, singular things. It was something opaque, mysterious, and enigmatic that mixed with and imbricated itself in the things of the world. Since then, without similarity to fill them out, words have wandered aimlessly without stable content. Representation acquires a dark power of making a past impression suddenly present, something that can appear similar or dissimilar to what precedes it. Foucault affirms that the importance of the power of memory, a type of imagination that implies at least the possibility of making two impressions appear almost similar (neighboring, contemporaneous), ceased to exist.[21]

Carlinhos Brown possesses a powerful imagination. He once defined himself to me as a concrete poet. I see him as an allegorical defender of subterranean similarities—the history of Candeal, of the Bahian Carnival, of Bahian music, of his personal history without words and without discourses by means of this power to imagine:

I'm a street musician. Am I an urban musician? Yes, I am. So I know how a trowel or a shovel can sound. All of this is music that I have and that's what makes me strange. Sometimes I make a shovel sound, and nobody knows what I'm doing, they think I'm singing badly, but today people understand this language. But it was tough, because people know where I came from and I, for my part, claim that place. So when you go to Candeal, mention the things that I'm telling you.

While Afro-Atlantic music is a modern, Western experience, it is at the same time within and outside of conventions, presuppositions, and aesthetic rules that distinguish modernity. This music becomes important in revealing how blacks understand themselves and what global culture means to them. In today's Bahia, the Timbalada movement probably most characteristically incorporates a global panorama in which the local is dispersed in homogeneous flows, deterritorializations, and syntheses of exotic images that upset the politics of racial confrontation and capitalist "white supremacy."

At the same time, it is by means of a modern and privileged invention, the musician, that subjects such as Carlinhos Brown are part of this context. He enters with a truncated, verbose, and ironic political discourse, and a social critique that is not racially based. He does not reproduce a diacritical ideology that, upon rejecting the black versus white polarity, reifies the condition of the *mestiço*, an ideology that situates itself within the interminable debates regarding race in Bra-

Gilberto Gil and Carlinhos Brown, ca. 1997. Photo by Cristina Granato.

zil and updates the myth of Brazilian racial democracy. A new discontinuity in modern and ultramodern Bahian music is registered when improvisation, self-reflexivity, citation, rationality, and simultaneity of narratives exist in the same space and in the same person.

This insertion creates potential for music in all of its expressive capacity, transforming it into an argument for those who "don't know how to speak" or "can't read well." Their agent, Carlinhos Brown, devours funk, rap, reggae, samba, lowbrow pop, and rock. He mixes politics and aesthetics, the vulgar and the refined. By gathering bits of information through his musical memory and recycling them in media flows, transforming their appearances into phenomena adjusted to the means of communication, he dazzles the media. This helps guarantee his permanence, though it also foments fragmentation, spectacle making, and the primitivization of a percussive sound full of extramusical content that evokes a Bahia reified as the myth of black originality, celebrated as cultural difference, transformed into an aesthetic taste that orients consumerism.[22]

Notes

1. See Jefferson Bacelar, *Etnicidade, ser negro em Salvador* (Salvador: Yanamá, 1989); Antonio Godi, "De índio a negro ou o reverso," in *Caderno CRH: cantos e toques, etnografias do espaço negro na Bahia* (1991), 50–71; Ana Maria Morales, "Blocos negros em Salvador. Reelaboração cultural e símbolos de baianidade," *idem*: 73–93; and Livio Sansone and Jocélio Teles Santos, eds., *Ritmos em trânsito. sócio-antropologia da música baiana* (São Paulo/Salvador: Dynamis Editorial/ Programa A Cor da Bahia e Projeto S.A.M.B.A., 1997).

2. Mike Featherstone, ed., *Cultura global, nacionalismo, globalização e modernidade* (Petrópolis: Vozes, 1994). Cited below by editor and title.

3. Anthony Smith, "Para uma cultura global," in *Cultura global*, ed. Mike Featherstone, 189–192.

4. Mike Featherstone, "Teorias da cultura do consumo," in *Culturas de consumo e pós-modernismo* (São Paulo: Studio Nobel, 1995), 31–50.

5. Paul Gilroy, *The Black Atlantic: Modernity and Double Consciousness* (London: Verso, 1993).

6. See Livio Sansone, "Pai preto, filho negro: trabalho, cor e diferença de geração," in *Estudos afro-asiáticos* 25 (1993), 73–97.

7. See Livio Sansone, "A produção de uma cultura negra (Da cultura 'creole' à subcultura negra. A nova etnicidade negra dos jovens 'creoles' surinameses de classe baixa em Amsterdam)," in *Estudos afro-asiáticos* 20 (1991), 121–134.

8. Stuart Hall, "Identidade cultural e Diáspora," in *Revista do Patrimônio Histórico e Artístico Nacional* 24 (1996), 68.

9. Michel Agier, "Etnopolítica—a dinâmica do espaço afro-baiano," in *Estudos afro-asiáticos* 22 (1992), 99–115.

10. Antonio Risério, *Carnaval ijexá* (Salvador: Corrupio, 1981), 38–46.

11. Marcelo Dantas, *Olodum: de bloco afro a holding cultural* (Salvador: Grupo Cultural Olodum/Casa de Jorge Amado, 1994).

12. Manuela Carneiro da Cunha, "Etnicidade: da cultura residual mas irredutível," in *Antropologia do Brasil*, ed. da Cunha (São Paulo: Brasiliense/ EDUSP, 1986), 97–108.

13. Muniz Sodré, *O terreiro e a cidade* (Petropólis: Vozes, 1988), 37.

14. Ulf Hanerz, "The Significance of Soul," in *Soul*, ed. Lee Rainwater (New Brunswick, N.J.: Transaction Books/Rutgers University, 1973), 15–30.

15. Anthony Cohen, *The Symbolic Construction of Community* (London: Tavistock, 1988).

16. Gerhard Kubik, "Ethnicity, Cultural Identity and the Psychology of Culture Contact," in *Music and Black Ethnicity: The Caribbean and South America*, ed. Gerard Béhague (Miami: North-South Center, 1992), 17–46.

17. On the myth in question, see Roberto DaMatta, "Digressão: a fábula das três raças ou o problema do racismo à brasileira," in *Relativizando, uma introdução à antropologia social* (Rio de Janeiro: Rocco, 1997), 58–85.

18. On the distinction between *person* and *individual*, see Roberto DaMatta, *Carnavais, malandros e heróis* (Rio de Janeiro: Zahar, 1978).

19. Quoted by Gideon Rosa, "O universo é aqui," in *A tarde* [Salvador], August 18, 1993, Caderno 2, 1.

20. Cf. bell hooks, *Black Looks. Race and Representation* (Boston: South End Press, 1992); Franz Fanon, *Pele negra, máscaras brancas* (Rio de Janeiro: Fator, 1983); and Antônio Sérgio Alfredo Guimarães, "Raça, racismo e grupos de cor no Brasil," in *Estudos afro-asiáticos* 27 (1995), 45–63.

21. Michel Foucault, *As palavras e as coisas* (São Paulo: Martins Fontes, 1990).

22. Osmundo Araújo Pinho, "A Bahia no fundamental: notas para uma interpretação do discurso ideológico da baianidade," in *Revista brasileira de ciências sociais* vol. 13, no. 36 (1998), 109–120.

FOURTEEN

Turned-Around Beat
Maracatu de Baque Virado and Chico Science

Larry Crook

Recife's music scene exploded onto the map of Brazilian popular music in the mid-1990s as a young generation created a new artistic movement called *mangue beat*.[1] Artists identified with the northeast's cultural roots but refused to remain "premodern" and thus also identified with global youth culture, cyberspace, and international pop. Spearheading the movement was the band Chico Science & Nação Zumbi. A key component of *mangue beat* was the desire to universalize regional heritage through the application of global pop ideas. The *mangue beat* movement explicitly sought to forge a new musical aesthetic by mixing U.S. popular music forms (funk, rock, metal, punk, rap, and hip-hop) and world-beat influences with a variety of musical traditions from northeastern Brazil, especially the percussion-heavy Afro-Pernambucan Carnival tradition known as *maracatu de baque virado*, or the turned-around beat. This form is generally acknowledged to be the oldest and most Africanized element of Pernambuco's Carnival and to comprise an essential component of its unique regional identity within Brazil.[2] As such, it provided a highly potent symbol for constructing a modern identity for Recife's youth. In this chapter I explore the history of the *maracatu de baque virado* and how Chico Science utilized the tradition to construct a modern musical identity for Recife.[3]

The History of a Royal Form

The *maracatu de baque virado* has its origins in the institution of the Rei do Congo [King of the Congo], or Rei de Angola [King of Angola], which involved the crowning of black kings and queens in colonial Brazil. The earliest record of this institution, which is closely linked to black Catholic fraternal orders, is the coronation of a king and queen of "Angola" in 1666 at the Church of Nossa Senhora do Rosário dos Pretos [Our Lady of the Rosary of the Blacks] in Recife, Pernambuco.[4] These elected black kings and queens served as intermediaries between white masters and the enslaved and helped keep order as they presided over religious and secular activities of the black population. The separation of black and white churches in colonial Brazil became a mechanism for blacks to maintain African practices under the cloak of Catholicism. The Catholic Church's early policy toward blacks was founded on the belief that Africans had the mentality of grown-up children and "must be attracted by music, which they loved; by dancing, which was their great diversion; and by their liking for titles and grandiose positions."[5] As long as African practices did not directly conflict with Church dogma, African traditions were used to attract blacks in Brazil to the true faith. Outside of church grounds, on special occasions such as the day of the annual celebration for the patron saint of the brotherhoods, festivities were held in which blacks processed with their kings and queens dressed in regal attire and held danced dramas with African drumming and singing. The processional dramatic dance included many of the elements that later would comprise the *maracatu de baque virado*: an African king and queen with a royal court, royal slaves, drummers, dancers, and singers. When colonial authorities discouraged and even banned African costuming, the dance processions incorporated European-style dress for the king, queen, and the royal court.

During the nineteenth century, the Catholic Church looked on the "African" processions with increasing disfavor. In Pernambuco, African-based religious houses took over the ceremonies surrounding the King of the Congo festivities.[6] The diversity of African ethnic groups in Brazil and the maintenance of their associated religious practices and cultural identities along ethnic lines led to the designation of these processional groups and to specific Afro-Brazilian houses as *nações* [nations]. The term *maracatu* possibly originated as an iconic representation of the sound of the drumming that accompanied the processions[7] and the groups came to be called *nações de maracatu* [maracatu nations]. With the increasing number of such groups and with their direct link to African religion, public outcries against the *maracatu* became common. The following excerpts appeared in a story in the major newspaper of Recife in the late nineteenth century:

> *Maracatu,* the stupid African merrymaking for which a certain segment of our society shows itself to be insatiable, notwithstanding appearing in the municipal register and police records, has been growing in this city and in its outskirts, and it seems that, if not with their collusion, at least with the permission, of police authorities. Meanwhile, this alleged entertainment—where abjectly immoral scenes are observed, devoid of any good customs—is the motive for fights, and it is not rare for the participants to leave with knife wounds. Moreover, as we have already said, and we will repeat, the [*maracatus*] are extremely inconvenient for the neighbors of the locations where they hold the meetings, not only because the beating of the barbaric instruments and the out-of-tune voices of the singers are deafening and go on for hours, but also because when the participants leave the area they occasionally shout obscenities and dirty sayings. . . .
>
> Just the day before yesterday [at a *maracatu*] on Atalho street in Boa Vista, there was a giant uproar and disturbance in which knifes were drawn. Luckily, no one was injured but it was not far from happening. We urge that order be restored, that such savage instruments disappear, and that the Chief of Police, who has turned his attention to gambling houses, should also turn his attention to the *maracatus.*[8]

The identification of the drumming as "barbaric beating" and the singing as "out-of-tune" and "deafening" leaves little doubt that the *maracatu* was seen by some members of Recife's dominant society not as an artistic cultural expression but rather as noise. And going a step further, the instruments themselves are demonized as savage and drumming as a threatening activity. Approximately 100 years later, it would be precisely the powerful, even menacing, quality of the drumming that would attract young Pernambuco musicians and audiences.

With the abolition of slavery in Brazil (1888), *maracatu* nations entered Recife's yearly Carnival street parades. The processing of royal courts of various *maracatu* nations, dressed in European regal attire, and the deep sound of the powerful drumming became fixtures in Recife's annual event. The clash of cultural/artistic aesthetics and the association of the *maracatu's* loud drumming with immoral activity, as revealed in the quote above, led to many confrontations between the police and *maracatu* groups.

Singing, Drumming, and Black Consciousness

Over the course of the twentieth century, *maracatu* nations, like the religious houses to which they were attached, were subjected to severe racial and religious discriminations. Until recently, the close association of the groups with African religion in Recife has been cause for many socially mobile blacks to shun the *maracatu* in favor of other Carnival traditions not overtly associated with African culture.

While the musical instruments, song texts, costumes, and characters mix European, African, and even indigenous elements, the *maracatu de baque virado* has come to represent the most African component of the Pernambuco Carnival. Song texts like the following, "Nagô, Nagô," link the groups to their African origins and to the coronations of their African kings and queens.

Nagô, Nagô	[Nagô, Nagô
Nossa rainha já se coroou	Our queen has already been crowned
Nosso rei que veio de Mina	Our king who came from Mina
Nossa rainha já se coroou	Our queen has already been crowned]

This is one of the most popular songs from the repertoire of the Maracatu Nação Porto Rico.[9] *Nagô* is a generic term in Brazil used to identify Yoruba groups originally from south-central Dahomey (Benin) and southwestern Nigeria. During colonial times, *Mina* referred to the Fanti-Ashante as well as their African territory in present-day Ghana. Other *maracatu* songs have recently come into the repertoire that overtly mention the history of slave resistance. While song texts symbolically link *maracatu* groups to an African past and serve to articulate group solidarity and, perhaps, even resistance to European domination, it is the specific performance practice of *maracatu* drumming, singing, and dancing that created the strongest sense of African identity for both the members of the *maracatus* and Afro-Pernambucan Carnival revelers. The performative style of drumming, dancing, and singing—so disturbing to some segments of Pernambucan society—became a means to enact and maintain knowledge about African heritage, about the legacy of slavery, and about post-abolition discrimination and socioeconomic inequality.

The powerful nature of the drumming (both acoustically and physically) is itself a likely origin of the name *maracatu*. The imposing sonic presence created by the large drum orchestra (with up to twenty-five drummers) announces a *maracatu* group well before its physical arrival in a given location during Carnival. Long before the advent of amplification and the performative power of electric music styles such as rock, *maracatu* drumming asserted similar acoustic power in the streets of Recife. When a *maracatu* is near, drumbeats vibrate the bodies as well as the eardrums of the participants. As a street music, the *maracatu de baque virado* creates a powerful aura and arena of blackness within the Recife Carnival. The no-apology drumming style links up with the general association that drumming in Brazil has with African heritage, with Afro-Brazilian religious practices, and with Afro-Brazilian cultural values that delight in dramatic shows of personal and collective style.

The characteristic *maracatu* beat centers on a rhythmic schema similar in concept to African-based percussion traditions throughout the Caribbean and Brazil. Largely West and Central African in origin, the drumming is based on several interlocking rhythmic patterns that combine to produce a strong groove. In *maracatu*, groove is everything. A metal bell known as *gonguê* articulates a syncopated organizing rhythm around which are layered set and variational/improvised drum parts.[10] A constant stream of notes is played on the *mineiro*, a metal shaker, and on the *tarol*, a shallow snare drum, while a deceptively simple but highly syncopated against-the-beat groove is performed on large double-headed bass drums known as *alfaia*[11] or simply *bombos*. When the pattern is firmly established, the lead *bombos* cut across the other parts *virando* (spinning or turning things around).

Maracatu and Black Consciousness

By the 1970s, Brazil's black population became increasingly conscious of the historical legacies of slavery and post-abolition racial discrimination in the country.[12] Inspired by cultural and political movements throughout the African diaspora, a renaissance of African culture spread in Brazil that highlighted Afro-Brazilian traditions and encouraged the formation of African-inspired cultural expressions. The center of this activity was Salvador da Bahia, where the long-standing Afro-Bahian Carnival tradition known as *afoxé* was revived and where a new form of Carnival association, the *bloco afro*, emerged. A distinctive musical style termed *samba-reggae* developed in the 1980s among the drummers of the influential Olodum group.[13] During the 1980s the *blocos afro* and the *samba-reggae* musical style became potent symbols of black identity among young Bahian blacks and quickly spread to other Brazilian cities. Bahian groups such as Olodum also became players in the world-music scene through collaborations with Paul Simon, Jimmy Cliff, Michael Jackson, and other international music luminaries.

In Recife and Olinda, percussion-based groups patterned on Bahian *blocos afro* and *afoxé* groups (such as Ilê Aiyê, Filhos de Gandhi, Olodum, Muzenza, Ara Ketu, and Badauê) began emerging in the 1980s. The first of these new Pernambucan groups was Afoxé Povo de Odé, founded in 1982, and by 1991 there were some twelve groups participating in Carnival.[14] The Afro-Pernambucan journal *Djumbay* (no. 2, May 1992) listed four *afoxés*, six *blocos afro*, and fifteen *bandas afros*. The differences among these three types of organizations is important. Both *afoxés* and *blocos afro* were constituted as not-for-profit Carnival organizations with social and political agendas while the *bandas afro* were musical bands, constituted as commercial enterprises. All drew substantially on the new Afro-Bahian musical sounds of the late 1980s, but the *bandas* were less inhibited

Musical example: A basic rhythmic scheme of the *maracatu de baque virado*.

and mixed modern electronic instruments into their format. Within the Pernambucan context, all of these groups were met with criticism and xenophobic opposition from local conservatives who saw their cultural activity as a "foreign" invasion from Bahia. There was even a failed attempt to legislate a ban on Bahian music during Carnival.[15]

But until the influx of the new Bahian musical sounds and models of artistic social awareness linked to issues of race and class, most middle-class blacks in Recife were hesitant to participate in the area's *maracatus* because of the strong links with African-based religious practice and lower-class aesthetics. The formation of *blocos afro* and *afoxé* groups in Recife and Olinda helped stimulate middle-class Pernambucan musicians, artists, and dancers to revisit their own homegrown traditions and led directly to the formation of new *maracatu* groups.

The most prominent of these new *maracatus* was the Maracatu Nação Pernambuco, formed in 1989 with the intent of reviving and popularizing the *maracatu* tradition and making it more accessible to the general public. And, unlike the other *maracatu* nations of the area, Maracatu Nação Pernambuco comprised primarily well-educated, middle-class musicians and dancers. The influx of middle-class white and black Brazilian youth who now saw the *maracatu* as a participatory option for their Carnival activities also introduced musical and choreographic change. Led by artistic director Bernardo José, this group began performing stage shows and presentations throughout the year and mixing the *maracatu de baque virado* with other folk traditions from the area. Nação Pernmabuco also released a self-titled CD (1993) and began traveling throughout Brazil and Europe.

Members of traditional *maracatu* nations have reacted both positively and negatively to commercial development, increased international exposure, and the rapid change of a tradition over which they hold a sense of ownership. The Maracatu Nação Pernambuco was criticized as a *maracatu de branco* [white man's maracatu] because many of its drummers and dancers were in fact white. Aesthetically, the drumming and dancing has also been criticized on grounds of being too "stylized." On the other hand, members of traditional *maracatus* have also embraced the changes and new attention given to the tradition. The increased involvement of women in groups such as the *maracatu* Estrela Brilhante is a case in point. International exposure for two of Recife's venerable *maracatu* nations (Nação Porto Rico and Nação Elefante) came via organized tours to Europe in 1988 and 1989 and helped increase both local and international interest in the tradition. The community of the *maracatu de baque virado* in Recife was working its way through a dynamic process as local musicians, dancers, and artists utilized the *maracatu* tradition in new ways.

Maracatu and Mangue Beat

The advent of *mangue beat* coincided with the emergence of Recife from an extended period of economic and cultural stagnation, as the artistic community of the area was awakening to new creative possibilities. During this time many of the northeast's folk traditions such as *maracatu, côco, embolada, ciranda, quadrilhas,* and the use of folk instruments such as the *rabeca* [fiddle] and *pífano* [cane fife], were being revived and reinvented.[16] It was also within the general context of the renaissance of African cultural forms in Brazil, led by the popular sounds from Bahia (*blocos afro, samba-reggae,* and *axé music*) that *mangue beat* first appeared.

According to various press accounts, Internet site histories, and personal remembrances of musicians, Chico Science (Francisco de Assis de França) met percussionist Gilmar Bola Oito of the *bloco afro* Lamento Negro in 1991 and attended several of the group's rehearsals. He was impressed with the power of the percussion-based music (Lamento Negro played primarily *samba-reggae* style) and decided to experiment mixing it with his own background in U.S. black music (James Brown, Grand Master Flash, and the Sugar Hill Gang were his favorites). He put together a band mixing local percussion styles with electric guitar, and bass. Experimenting with several Pernambucan styles, he finally settled on the *maracatu de baque virado* to combine with his funk, soul, hip-hop, and rock background. As Recife's oldest, most venerable Carnival tradition, something that was unique to Pernambuco, that had a sonic presence of power, and that symbolically represented the history of black resistance, the *maracatu de baque virado* provided the perfect local vehicle for Chico Science to mix with electric guitars. At first the group was called Chico Science and Lamento Negro, later changing to Chico Science & Nação Zumbi. The name Nação Zumbi indicated a link both to the *maracatu de baque virado* tradition (*nação* is the designation indicating a *maracatu's* link to a Candomblé house) and to the history of black Brazilian resistance symbolized by Zumbi, the legendary Afro-Brazilian leader of the Quilombo de Palmares runaway slave society.

The influence of the *maracatu de baque virado* became most visible in the live performances of Chico Science & Nação Zumbi through the use of the distinctive *maracatu* drum itself. During stage presentations the group included a lineup of three drummers with large *maracatu bombo* drums performing in the middle of the stage.

The *maracatu de baque virado* was also highlighted through CD packaging. The graphic layout on the back cover of Chico Science's influential CD *Afro-ciberdélia* (1996) prominently features the images of band members framed inside the rim of a *maracatu* drum. While the visual impact should not be diminished, it was through the near-ubiquitous sonic presence of the characteristic *maracatu* drumbeat that *mangue beat* became a distinctive musical style and through which it was able to take its place as Recife's entry into the world-music scene. As Timothy Taylor has noted, the international marketing category of world music has been founded largely on Western notions of the premodern authenticity of selected Third World musical styles.[17] In the case of *mangue beat*, this authenticity was provided primarily through the use of the *maracatu* drums and the distinctive "primal" nature of its rhythmic patterns.

In an interview with Walter da Silva, Chico Science emphasized the importance of the group's live shows and how its members have struggled to translate the energy of live performance quality to the recorded format. Responding to a question about the difference between the group's first and second CDs, Chico spoke of giving "weight" to the recording, "a consistent kind of weight with every thing in its place."[18] What was the weight that was missing? He goes on to stress that it was the timbre of the drums, the *maracatu* drums: "Listening to the first CD, playing shows, we saw how we could improve the sound by giving a new timbre to the drums." It was the acoustic power of the large *maracatu* drums that created the distinctly Pernambucan accent to Chico Science's music and made it appealing to the world-beat scene.

The sound of the *maracatu* drums and the *maracatu de baque virado* patterns, mixed with other rhythms, run throughout Chico Science & Nação Zumbi's two CDs. But equally important for the construction of *mangue beat* were the performance aesthetics, production values, and musical influences that linked the music to global youth culture. The distortion-timbres of Nação Zumbi's lead guitarist Lúcio Maia were reminiscent of Jimi Hendrix and heavy-metal tinged. The recitative-like rap vocal delivery and hip-hop physical stage presence of Chico Science, the unabashed love of electronic and computer technology, and the sampling all linked the *mangue beat* movement to postmodern aesthetics of the local/global context of artistic production. It was the creative fusion of these with local realities that made Chico Science's importance extend well beyond the music.

Da lama ao caos (1994) includes a manifesto of the *mangue beat* movement, coauthored by Chico Science and Fred Zero Quatro (Fred Rodrigues Montene-gro).[19] Written in three sections—"Mangue: the concept," "Manguetown: the city," and "Mangue: the scene"—the manifesto links issues of ecology and bio-logical diversity to the social, cultural, and economic realities of the greater Recife area. The term *mangue* refers to the mud-swamp estuaries common in the network of rivers crisscrossing Recife where the ocean tide meets river cur-rents. The importance of estuaries is the central component of "Mangue: the concept." It is estimated that 2 million species of microrganisims and vertebrate and invertebrate animals are likely associated with the vegetation in the *mangue*. The estuaries supply areas of spawning and creation for over two-thirds of the annual fish production in the entire world.

In "Mangue: the city," the history of Recife is located within the context of the ecological impact of living out of harmony with the natural forces of the local estuary system. Historically, Recife grew in an indiscriminate manner without concern for the consequences of invading, covering over, and destroying its *mangues*. The so-called progress of Recife in becoming a regional metropolis in northeastern Brazil in the 1960s revealed both ecological and economic fragility. As the manifesto puts it, during the last thirty years the syndrome of stagnation, linked to the permanent myth of the "metropolis," has only brought about the accelerated aggravation of misery and urban chaos. Today, Recife has the largest percentage of unemployed people in the country. More than half of its inhabit-ants live in slums and flooded swamp areas. According to a Washington-based institute of population studies, Recife is now considered the fourth-worst city in the world to live in.

A call to action is articulated in the section "Mangue: the scene."

> Emergency! A quick shock, or Recife will die from clogging! You need not be a medical doctor to realize that the easiest way to stop the heart is to clog its veins. The quickest way also, to glut and drain the soul of a city like Recife, is to kill its rivers and cover up its estuaries. What can be done so that we don't worsen the chronic depression that paralyzes the city's people? How can we bring back the spirit and delobotomize and recharge the batteries of the city? Simple! Just inject a little of the energy of the mud and stimulate what is left of the fertility of the veins of Recife.

In mid-1991, a nucleus of research and production of "pop" ideas began to be generated and articulated in various parts of the city. The objective is to engender an "energy circuit" capable of linking the good vibes of the *mangues* with the global networks of the circulation of pop concepts. Symbol image, a parabolic satellite dish stuck in the mud.

One of the primary ways in which the *mangue* movement has injected energy into Recife is by taking full advantage of the robust *maracatu de baque virado* and translating it into a modern format. The national and international impact of singer/composer Chico Science was meteoric, as his career was tragically cut short when he died in an automobile accident (February 2, 1997) during Carnival. Though his time was short, Chico Science made indelible marks on Recife's and Brazil's musical scenes.

Notes

1. I gratefully acknowledge the support of the University of Florida's Fine Arts and Humanities Scholarship for funds to travel to Recife in June and July of 1998. I also wish to thank Sérgio Gusmão for his generosity and willingness to share his extensive knowledge of the artistic community of Recife.

2. Another genre, the *frevo*, is generally acknowledged as the most typical music/dance style of the Pernambuco Carnival and its associations cut across class and race lines in Recife. The *maracatu de baque virado* is associated exclusively with Recife's black population. For general descriptions of the *maracatu de baque virado* and other types of groups that comprise Pernambuco's Carnival, see Katarina Real, *O folclore no carnaval do Recife*, 2nd ed. (Recife: Editora Massangana, 1990).

3. I do not mean to diminish other important regional influences on *mangue beat* such as *côco*, *maracatu de baque solto*, *embolada*, and *baião*. However, the *maracatu de baque virado* stands out as its most important regional influence, both symbolically and musically.

4. Leonardo Dantas Silva, "Elementos para a história social do carnaval do Recife," in *Antologia do carnaval do Recife*, ed. M. Souto Maior and L. Dantas Silva (Recife: Editora Massangana, 1991), xxxii; cited below as Silva.

5. See Roger Bastide, *The African Religions of Brazil: Toward a Sociology of the Interpenetration of Civilizations* (Baltimore: John Hopkins University Press, 1978), 119.

6. In Bahia and in Pernambuco, the African-based religious houses that persist to today were established during the first half of the nineteenth century. The houses were dominated by the late influx of slaves from Yoruba- and Fon-speaking peoples from West Africa. Mixture with other African religious systems (primarily from the Congo-Angola region) produced a rich variety of traditions in Brazil. In Recife, where the Yoruba deity Xangô was particularly strong, the African religious houses came to be generically

referred to as Xangô. In Bahia, religious houses known as Candomblé frequently had secular festival procession groups known as *afoxé* that were similar to the *maracatu* of Pernambuco.

7. See Guerra Peixe, *Maracatus do Recife*, 2nd ed. (São Paulo: Irmãos Vitale, 1980), 28. The term *maracatu* was also used for almost any social grouping of blacks in Pernambuco involving dancing to the accompaniment of drumming.

8. *Revista Diária*, May 18, 1880, quoted by Silva , xxxiii. My translation.

9. I first heard the Maracatu Nação Porto Rico perform this song during Recife's Carnival in 1987. I interviewed Shacon, the leader of the Porto Rico drummers, in July 1998, and he told me that this continues to be one of their most popular pieces.

10. The term *gonguê* is possibly related to the Ewe term *gakogui* [iron bell], a musical instrument that accompanies a variety of Ewe musical ensembles.

11. *Alfaia* (from Arabic) is a term also meaning adornment. As applied to the drums of the *maracatu*, the term is used for the entire ensemble set of bass drums. *Maracatu* drummers emphasize the elaborating role of the *alfaia* lead drums in the ensemble.

12. See Larry Crook and Randal Johnson, eds. "Introduction," in *Black Brazil: Culture, Identity and Social Mobilization* (Los Angeles: UCLA Latin American Center Publications, 2000), 1–13.

13. See Larry Crook, "Black Consciousness, Samba-Reggae, and the Re-Africanization of Bahian Carnival Music in Brazil," in *the world of music* vol. 35, no. 2 (1993). See also Coli Guerreiro, *A tràmà dos tambores: a música afro-pop de Salvador* (São Paulo: Editora 34, 2000).

14. Alzenir Nascimento, "Afoxé ganha espaço na terra do frevo," in *Jornal do comércio* (Recife), January 27, 1991, section Cidades.

15. Sérgio Gusmão, personal communication, July 9, 1998.

16. On northeastern musical traditions see Larry N. Crook, "Brazil Northeast," in vol. 2, *The Garland Encyclopedia of World Music* (New York: Garland Publishing, 1998), 323–339.

17. See Timothy D. Taylor, *Global Pop: World Music, World Markets* (New York: Routledge, 1997), passim.

18. See Walter da Silva, "Chico Science: do mangue para o mundo," Brazilian Music UpToDate, http://www.uol.com.br/uptodate/up3/interine.htm.

19. On *mangue beat*, including the original text of the manifesto, titled "Caranguejos com cérebro" [Crabs with brains], see the liner notes to CSNZ CD 1994, or www.emprel.gov.br/mangue or www.elogíca.com.br/users/zinhore/mangue.

Discography

Chico Science & Nação Zumbi. *Da lama ao caos*. Chaos CD 850.224/2–464476, 1994.
———. *Afrociberdélia*. Sony Music CDZ–81996 2–479255, 1996.
Nação Pernambuco. *Nação Pernambuco*. Velas 11–Vo16, 1993.

FIFTEEN

Self-Discovery in Brazilian Popular Music
Mestre Ambrósio

John Murphy

A sense is emerging from the growing body of literature on the relationships between local musics, on the one hand, and musics that are commercialized on a global scale, on the other, that no single set of concepts can adequately explain their interaction.[1] The diversity and interconnectedness of musical styles, and their reception at both global and local levels, make generalization difficult. Reebee Garofalo, for example, has shown how the concept of cultural imperialism hides as much as it reveals: "In addition to underestimating the power of local and national cultures in developing countries, this tendency [to privilege the role of external forces] assumes audience passivity in the face of dominant cultural power and neglects the active, creative dimension of popular music consumption."[2] Steven Feld has explored the unequal dynamics of musical appropriation in the context of world beat and adaptations of the musics of Central

African forest peoples.[3] Mark Slobin has adapted Appadurai's various "scapes" (e.g., ethnoscape, ideoscape, mediascape) and given examples of the interaction of musical sub-, inter-, and supercultures.[4] Rather than interpreting local responses to global styles as resistance that stands outside the world-music system, Veit Erlmann views these differences as a part of the system: "It is this tension between a total system and the various local cultural practices that opens up a space for ethnography. Thus, musical ethnographies will increasingly have to examine the choices performers worldwide make in moving about the spaces between the system and its multiple environments."[5] Most recently, Ingrid Monson uses the organizing role of interlocking riffs and repetition in musics of the African diaspora to reconceptualize music and globalization: like the contrasting riffs in a musical texture that combine to form a groove, "[r]epeating social variables, ideologies, and binaries, continue to form layers in the very complex constellations of multiplicity that we observe in our ethnomusicological work.[6]

In the case of one band from northeastern Brazil, an inquiry into the interplay of the global and the local reveals a process of musical self-discovery, in which the multiplicity of musical styles its members had performed was carefully filtered by the choices they made as they explored a variety of local musics. Mestre Ambrósio was formed in Recife and is now based in São Paulo. After coming to regional prominence in the 1990s through live peformances and an independently produced CD, the group emerged on a national level and released a second CD on the Sony label in 1999. Mestre Ambrósio's music draws on a variety of traditional musical sources; members of the group describe the result as *forró pé-de-calçada*, or *forró* with an urban, rock-influenced sensibility.

This band is part of the recent wave of new music from Recife, known as the *movimento mangue* or *mangue beat* (or *bit*), which includes musicians who blend local musics with a wide range of global popular styles. The late Chico Science (Francisco França) and journalist/musician Fred Zero Quatro of the band Mundo Livre S/A, together with a group of artists and intellectuals dubbed *caranguejos com cérebro* [crabs with brains], envisioned the movement as a fusion of global cultural influences with the fertile local artistic scene, symbolized by the tidal mudflats or *manguezais* that surround central Recife:

> In mid-1991, a nucleus of research and production of pop ideas began to be generated and articulated in various parts of the city. The objective is to generate an "energy circuit" to connect the good vibrations of the tidal mudflats with the

global network of circulation of pop concepts. Symbolic image: a satellite antenna stuck in the mud.[7]

The *mangue* movement is musically diverse. In the music of Chico Science, for example, the mix of *maracatu* and other local styles is roughly equal to that of hip-hop and funk. Other bands, such as Mestre Ambrósio, Cascabulho, and more recently, Comadre Florzinha, reinterpret local musical traditions.

The selections on Mestre Ambrósio's first self-titled CD (1995) draw on several northeastern traditional musics, some of which have had little exposure at the national level: *forró, maracatu, cantoria, côco*, and forms associated with *umbanda* and *bandas de pífano*. One special source is *cavalo-marinho*, a musical play that portrays life on a sugar plantation in song, poetry, dance, and dramatic action.[8] The band's name is taken from that of a character in *cavalo-marinho*. Mestre Ambrósio is a traveling salesman who opens rural performances of the play by selling the costumes of the rest of the characters, imitating each one as he does so. The band's live performances open with Hélder Vasconcelos dancing this role. The principal melodic instrument in *cavalo-marinho* is the *rabeca*, a fiddle of Portuguese origin, which accompanies the singing and provides instrumental dance music between scenes.[9] The *rabeca* is the principal melodic voice of the northeastern Brazilian dance genre known as *baiano*. Adaptations of this and other regional genres for accordion by Luiz Gonzaga became known as *baião* in the 1940s, and later as *forró*. *Baiano* is a staple of the repertoire of *rabeca* players in Pernambuco. The *rabeca* style of band member Siba on *forró* songs such as "Mensagem pra Zé Calixto" reveals a new aspect of music that most listeners outside of northeastern Brazil have encountered as an accordion-based style.

Two different musical practices share the name *maracatu*. What is called *maracatu de nação africana* [of African nation] or *maracatu de baque virado* [turned-around beat], long a part of Carnival in Recife, features an elaborate procession and ensembles of large drums.[10] The second variety is *maracatu rural*; it is practiced primarily in the small towns in the sugar-growing region north of Recife. The music alternates between improvised verses and frenetic percussion on snare drums and metal bell along with trumpets or valve trombones. *Maracatu rural* percussion can be heard in Mestre Ambrósio's "Se Zé Limeira sambasse maracatu."

Cantoria refers to a variety of poetic genres that are performed with accompaniment by the *viola*, a double-coursed steel-string guitar. Mestre Ambrósio's "A roseira" draws on this style. "Usina" is a well-known *côco*, a responsorial song accompanied by *pandeiro* or *ganzá* [shaker], which is included in Mário de Andrade's noted collection.[11] Mestre Ambrósio's version adds *maracatu* drumming. *Samba-de-mestre*, a traditional drum pattern used in *umbanda*, the syncretic spiritualist religion, can be heard in "José." "Três vendas" uses it along with the *umbanda* patterns called *samba-de-angola* and *quebra-louças*. The *banda de pífano*, made up of the *pífano* [sideblown flute], snare drum, cymbals, and bass drum, is heard at religious processions, fairs, and other public events in the northeast.[12] Mestre Ambrósio's "Jatobá," "Pipoca moderna," and "A feira de Caruaru" use this instrumentation and rhythmic style.

These sources are interpreted with varying degrees of transformation and combination in Mestre Ambrósio's live and recorded performances, in a self-conscious process that has included a sustained relationship with traditional performers, including Mestre Salustiano, Mestre Inácio Lucindo da Silva, and the late Mestre Batista. The band members describe the process as one of *autodescobrimento*, or self-discovery, and *limpeza*, literally cleaning or cleansing, not unlike R. Murray Schafer's notion of ear cleaning.[13] These processes will make more sense once the path that brought each band member to the project has been described.

Mestre Ambrósio began in projects by Siba, Hélder Vasconcelos, and Éder "O" Rocha that mixed *maracatu* with thrash metal in 1991. Later additions of Mazinho Lima, Maurício Alves, and Sérgio Cassiano completed the group. Siba was born and raised in Recife to artistic parents: his late father was an amateur musician, and his mother is a painter. He was interested in music as a child and was playing guitar and studying music at the Federal University of Pernambuco when we met in 1990. As part of my research on *cavalo-marinho* in 1990–1991, we traveled regularly to the interior together to watch performances and visit musicians. Later Siba carried out research on the *rabeca* and became a skilled player, eventually becoming able to complete night-long performances of *cavalo-marinho*.[14] He has participated actively in *maracatu rural*, and since the band's move to São Paulo he has become involved with the lively northeastern musical scene there, especially with *cantoria*.

Hélder Vasconcelos was born and raised in the interior of Pernambuco, then moved to Recife at age eleven. His childhood in the interior was filled with musical activity, which decreased when he moved to the capital. He met Siba at around age sixteen, when both began playing guitar. As he was finishing his engineering degree, he became interested in percussion, and he and Siba played rock together. Since forming Mestre Ambrósio, Hélder has concentrated on percussion and rediscovered the *fole de oito baixos* [eight-bass button accordion], an instrument he heard frequently as a child. Like Siba, he feels closely drawn to the performance traditions of the interior, and together they have participated in *cavalo-marinho* and *maracatu rural*.

Percussionist Éder "O" Rocha was born in Recife, but only went to live there twelve years later. Growing up in the 1970s, he listened to disco and rock and began studying drums at a state music school. In his first year of playing he formed a group whose goal was to make enough money playing *forró* to be able to go to the Rock in Rio festival (1985). His subsequent musical experiences included playing rock, blues, thrash metal, *xote*, *forró*, samba, and classical music. While he has participated in *maracatu de nação*, *maracatu rural*, and *cavalo-marinho*, Éder feels more strongly drawn to the urban musics.

Éder, Siba, and Hélder brought a wide set of musical influences to the collaboration, adding local traditional music and Caribbean and African musics to a mix of rock, jazz, and *forró* in acoustic and electric formats. When they needed someone to sing for São João [St. John] feast-day engagements, they invited bassist Mazinho Lima to join. At thirty-seven the oldest member of the band, Lima was born in southern Brazil and has lived in Recife since his teens. He was prompted to start playing rock after watching the Led Zeppelin film *The Song Remains the Same*. A self-taught musician, Mazinho has played rock guitar and bass extensively around Recife. He met the other members of Mestre Ambrósio when they were putting together a *boi de carnaval* [an abbreviated version of the folk pageant, *bumba-meu-boi*], which developed into a *cavalo-marinho* in which Mazinho played *mineiro* [metal rattle] and *rabeca*.

Percussionist Maurício Alves de Oliveira was born and raised in a suburb of Recife, and became involved at an early age with Afro-Brazilian music and dance, including various forms associated with Candomblé, *maracatu*, samba school, *capoeira*, and *afoxé*. Like the rest of the group, Maurício listens to a wide variety of music, but his principal musical identification is with the Afro-Brazilian genres ("o lado mais afro da coisa," or the more African side of things, as he puts it). He joined Mestre Ambrósio through his acquaintance with Éder Rocha (they played in a percussion group together), knew Siba from the university, and joined the band shortly after bassist Mazinho Lima.

Percussionist Sérgio Cassiano is also a Recife native. As a youth he listened to the radio and explored his family's record collection, which ranged from MPB [Música Popular Brasileira] to rock. His early experiments with homemade percussion instruments were followed by a wide range of performance experiences: working as an actor and musician in theater projects, and playing *trio elétrico*, MPB, rock, and other Latin American styles. He met Siba at the university and knew Éder from thrash-metal bands and Maurício from *trio elétrico* groups.

The members of Mestre Ambrósio identify *autodescobrimento*, or self-discovery, for themselves and for their audiences, as one reason for their critical and popular success. Their experiences have demonstrated the wide appeal of music that is rooted in local traditions. Siba's experiences with Mestre Ambrósio have demonstrated "the universality of music as a language, not in the sense of the universal being music that's played everywhere, but as music that speaks of a specific kind of truth. If you find people open enough to perceive this, then the message can be understood anywhere in the world."[15]

In further reflections on the notion of self-discovery, Siba writes:

Self-discovery is, among the infinite things that depend on the individual who embarks on such a journey, to respond inwardly to universal questions such as "who am I?" "where have I come from?" and "what sort of person am I?"

In Brazil—a country on the verge of completing its 500th year of existence, which took shape amid the intense blending of diverse races and peoples and where a huge bombardment of foreign cultural references coexists with basic problems of income distribution and education—the question of self-discovery can acquire dramatic twists and nuances. It implies a process of recognition, acceptance, and valorization of such basic things as one's physical aspect, way of speaking, dressing, walking, dancing, singing, playing music and self-expression in general.

Culture and the ways it manifests itself therefore assume a fundamental role as a source of references for the search for identity. Brazil in the 1990s is still waking slowly from 20 years of military dictatorship (1964–1985), and as it seeks its self-image in the mirror it has begun to value music more highly. This process, which began by increasing drastically the percentage of Brazilian music heard on radio (most of which is excessively commercial), has also served to bring greater prominence to the music of Carlinhos Brown, Chico César, Marlui Miranda, Antônio Carlos Nóbrega, and Mestre Ambrósio, among others.

Finally, we are beginning to view traditional cultural performances of each region with more respect, and to understand more readily that there, in rural performance venues, in the diverse street performances, in religious events, dances, instruments, poetic forms and special ways of playing and feeling music, dance, theatre, visual arts and even human relations, the essence of Brazilianness is revealed as alive and dynamic (1998).

The process of self-discovery occurs for both performers and audiences, as Hélder Vasconcelos explains:

This base [of public support] is quite strong. It comes from an identification with what we are doing. There is a strong relationship of respect for what we are doing, a relationship of personal rediscovery. We work with various elements that affirm us. It's a process that both we and the audience are involved in, at the same time. You're discovering yourself, simultaneously with the audience (1996).

At a show in Curitiba, in southern Brazil, a listener approached the band members and spoke about the new appreciation for Brazilian music that their performance had awakened in him, saying, "Man, your music made me remember . . . a Brazil that I know belongs to me, but I didn't realize I still had, [and] that it's not so far from Curitiba to the Northeast" (1996).

Mestre Ambrósio, ca. 1996. Photo by and courtesy of Marco Oppido.

This strong identification with regional roots styles comes after a prolonged and self-conscious process of *limpeza*, or ear cleaning. The outside stylistic references were removed not because the band members disliked them, but in order for them to discover their own most basic musical references. Siba explains:

> To be truthful, for the music that we play today to be possible, we've been through a long process of self-cleansing. Cleaning ourselves of rock, of jazz, of art music. Cleaning not in the sense that these things are good or bad, but in the sense that as we grow up with these other styles, living with them on a daily basis, we completely lose our meaning, our specific references, as musicians, as persons, and even as Northeasterners and Brazilians (1996).

Siba discovered in this process how estranged he had become from the music of his own region:

> And suddenly you see yourself, as I saw myself in my early twenties, studying at the university, where there was only room for art music, where I only played rock guitar and was starting to learn jazz. Everyone goes through this here. The process the band went through illustrates this. We started out with a very diverse sound, full of references, and started cleaning, cleaning, cleaning, until we arrived at a music that reflects the place where we live very well, and despite this still has references to jazz, to rock — it's all there, in small proportions, for better or worse. But we had to clean ourselves. Not to put down or bracket off the other styles, but to be able to see the real importance of each element (1996).

Band members have a self-conscious way of referring to information, and to the direction of information flow into their artistic project. In the words of Hélder Vasconcelos, "It's natural today, especially for our generation, for information from the outside to predominate" (1996). Siba explains that there are many musical styles ready for one to adopt, to put on as if they were new clothes: "At this stage in our musical development there are lots of things readymade for you" (1996).

While the members of Mestre Ambrósio are often grouped with the *movimento mangue* or *mangue beat* by the media, they see their process differently. They make a distinction between those groups which, like them, build on a basis in regional traditional styles and add global musical references, which they refer to as "from the inside out" ("de dentro para fora"), and groups which add regional flavor to a predominantly global style, such as heavy metal or rap, "from the outside in" ("de fora para dentro").

Mestre Ambrósio's work progressed during 1996 and 1997, according to Siba:

With respect to the "cleaning process": it is more or less "inherent" with us these days; that is, we have already incorporated the results of the "cleaning" so much that we don't think so much about the necessity and importance that it had (and has). I think we've developed a musical concept and the new projects that we are developing here flow from this concept in a very natural way (1997).

After its arrival in São Paulo in November of 1996, Mestre Ambrósio became nationally known through frequent television appearances and newspaper coverage, and by playing concerts in São Paulo, Santos, Rio de Janeiro, Parati, Brasília, Belo Horizonte, Ouro Preto, Curitiba, Natal, Fortaleza, João Pessoa, Recife, and numerous smaller cities, as well as festival appearances in São Paulo (Heineken Concerts), New York (Central Park Summerstage), and Lisbon (Expo 98).

In the two years since, besides the growth of the band's reputation among a larger public in a country that is increasingly interested in understanding and expressing itself in its own way, there has been profound artistic growth on the part of all of the group members, which became obvious as we began creating the material for our second CD, *Fuá na casa de Cabral*, to be released by Sony Music.

The responsibility for musical direction, which used to be mine alone, has been assumed by the group as a whole, a natural consequence of the maturation that time and stage experience have made possible. The compositions are shared among most of the group members, and several creative partnerships have formed. Sérgio Cassiano, who had been responsible for percussion and background vocals, now sings lead occasionally. The instrumentation is basically the same, with a larger presence of the electric guitar on some songs.

The collaboration with producers Mitar Subotic and Antoine Midani and greater access to technological resources (the CD was recorded at the studios Nota por Nota and Wah-Wah in São Paulo and mixed at Looking Glass Studios in New York) have helped us attain a quality sound that we hope will enable us to receive radio airplay—without, however, losing the individual character of our music.

Finally, we are now preparing for the national release of *Fuá na casa de Cabral*, with the exciting prospect of making our vision of the Northeast and of Brazil more easily visible by a larger public both within and outside of Brazil (1998).

Band members have also collaborated on cinematic projects and notable sound recordings. Mestre Ambrósio, Chico Science, Fred Zero Quatro, and others performed the sound track of *Baile perfumado* [Perfumed dance], the 1997 film by Paulo Caldas and Lírio Ferreira set in the time of Padre Cícero and Lampião. Mestre Ambrósio also appeared on the second CD of the internationalized ensemble Karnak, *Universo umbigo* [Universal navel].[16] Siba's *rabeca* can also be heard on the sound track of the Oscar-nominated 1998 film *Central Station*, by Walter Salles.

The creative response by the members of Mestre Ambrósio to both local and global musics illustrates one facet of the construction of what is musically local.[17] Global musical influences have been filtered and carefully reintroduced. The resulting style is called *forró-pé-de-calçada*, a transformed *forró* that includes other local musics, such as those of *cavalo-marinho* and *cantoria*, which is made possible by the band members' previous immersion in a wide variety of global popular styles, including rock and jazz. This filtering of influences might be labeled resistance, but the band's concepts of self-discovery and ear cleaning more aptly describe their process of artistic self-determination and their ongoing negotiation between local and global modes of expression.

Notes

1. Field research on which this chapter is based was undertaken with the support of a U.S. Department of Education Fulbright Fellowship in 1990–1991, and grants from the Western Illinois University Foundation and the WIU College of Fine Arts and Communication for travel to Brazil in 1996. This chapter began in conversations with Sérgio "Siba" Veloso and the other members of Mestre Ambrósio in 1996, took shape as a conference paper in 1996, and was expanded with additional comments by Siba in 1997 and 1998. I am grateful to have learned from this dialogue, and the responsibility for any errors is mine.

2. Reebee Garofalo, "Whose World, What Beat: The Transnational Music Industry, Identity, and Cultural Imperialism," *the world of music* vol. 35, no. 2 (1993), 18.

3. Steven Feld, "From Schizophonia to Schismogenesis: On the Discourses and Commodification Practices of 'World Music' and 'World Beat,'" and "Notes on 'World Beat,'" in *Music Grooves: Essays & Dialogues*, ed. Steven Feld and Charles Keil (Chicago: University of Chicago Press, 1994), 257–289, 238–246; "Pygmy POP: A Genealogy of Schizophonic Mimesis," *Yearbook for Traditional Music* 28 (1996), 1–35.

4. Mark Slobin, *Subcultural Sounds: Micromusics of the West* (Hanover, N.H.: Wesleyan University Press/University Press of New England, 1993).

5. Veit Erlmann, "The Aesthetics of the Global Imagination: Reflections on World Music in the 1990s," *Public Culture* 8 (Spring 1996), 474.

6. Ingrid Monson, "Riffs, Repetition, and Theories of Globalization," *Ethnomusicology* vol. 43, no.1 (1999), 31–65.

7. Chico Science & Nação Zumbi, liner notes to *Da lama ao caos* (Chaos/Sony 850.224/2–464476, 1994).

8. John Murphy, "Performing a Moral Vision: An Ethnography of Cavalo-Marinho, a Brazilian Musical Drama." Dissertation, Columbia University, 1994.

9. John Murphy, "The *Rabeca* and Its Music, Old and New, in Pernambuco, Brazil," *Latin American Music Review* vol. 18, no. 2 (1997), 147–172.

10. Tiago de Oliveira Pinto, "Musical Difference, Competition, and Conflict: The Maracatu Groups in the Pernambuco Carnival, Brazil," *Latin American Music Review* vol. 17, no. 2 (1996), 97–119.

11. Mário de Andrade *Os cocos*, preparation, introduction, and notes by Oneyda Alvarenga (São Paulo: Duas Cidades; Brasília: INL, Fundação Nacional Pró-Memória, 1984), 141–143.

12. Larry Crook, "Zabumba Music from Caruaru, Pernambuco: Musical Style, Gender, and the Interpenetration of Rural and Urban Worlds." Dissertation, University of Texas at Austin, 1991.

13. R. Murray Schafer, *Ear Cleaning: Notes for an Experimental Music Course* (Don Mills, Ontario: BMI Canada, 1967); *The Tuning of the World* (New York: Knopf, 1977).

14. Sérgio Roberto Veloso de Oliveira (Siba), "A rabeca na zona da mata norte de Pernambuco: levantamento e estudo, " manuscript at Departamento de Música, Centro de Artes e Comunicação, Universidade Federal de Pernambuco, Recife, 1994.

15. Siba 1996; all following quotations are from interviews with the author or from personal correspondence, years in parentheses. Original Portuguese given in appendix.

16. See Bruce Gilman, "Guerrilla Sound" [on the group Karnak], in BRAZZIL online magazine, http://www.brazzil.com/musfeb98.htm (1998); and "Recife's Repercussion Unit" [on Mestre Ambrósio], in BRAZZIL online magazine, http://www.brazzil.com/musjan99.htm (1999).

17. Veit Erlmann, "How Beautiful Is Small? Music, Globalization, and the Aesthetics of the Local," in *Yearbook for Traditional Music* 30 (1998), 12–21.

Discography

Mestre Ambrósio. n/t. Rec Beat [Recife, Brazil] 107.984, 1995.

———. *Fuá na casa de Cabral.* Sony Chaos 758.491/2–492195, 1999.

Appendix

Quotations in the original Portuguese are included here in order to preserve as much of the original voice as possible; unless otherwise indicated, texts in Portuguese are by Sérgio "Siba" Veloso, and translations are by the author.

1. . . . a universalidade da música como linguagem, não no sentido de que universal é música que toca em todo lugar, mas universal é música que fala de uma verdade específica . . . e aí se você encontra as pessoas abertas o suficiente para perceber, então ela pode falar em qualquer lugar do mundo (1996).

2. Auto-descobrir-se é, entre infinitas coisas que dependem do indivíduo que se lança na busca, responder em si mesmo perguntas universais como: "quem sou eu?" "de onde eu vim?" "Como sou?" etc.

No Brasil, país às vésperas de completar 500 anos de existência, formado no intenso cruzamento e relacionamento de raças e povos diversos e onde um enorme bombardeio de referências culturais exteriores convive com problemas básicos de distribuição de renda e educação, auto-descobrir-se é uma questão que ganha contornos e nuances às vezes dramáticos. Implica num processo de reconhecimento, aceitação e valorização de coisas básicas como aspecto físico, modo de falar, vestir, andar, dançar, cantar, tocar e expressar-se de um modo geral.

A cultura e suas formas de manifestar-se assumem aí papel fundamental de fornecedoras de referências para a busca de identidade. O Brasil, adormecido nos anos 80 por 20 anos de ditadura militar, acorda lentamente na década de 90 e vai em busca de sua imagem no espelho da cultura voltando a valorizar a música. Esse processo, que a princípio elevou radicalmente a porcentagem de música brasileira executada nas rádios (geralmente de cunho excessivamente comercial), também serviu para trazer à tona, em diferentes níveis de evidência na [música] de Carlinhos Brown, Chico César, Marlui Miranda, Antônio Carlos Nóbrega e Mestre Ambrósio, entre outros.

Finalmente, começamos a olhar com mais respeito para as manifestações culturais tradicionais de cada região, entendendo com mais facilidade que ali, nos terreiros, nos diversos folguedos de rua, eventos religiosos, danças, instrumentos, formas poéticas e maneiras especiais de tocar e sentir música, dança, poesia, teatro, artes plásticas e até relações comunitárias e humanas está viva, atual, dinámica e exposta a semente da brasilidade (1998).

3. Essa base que . . . é muito forte. Ela vem de uma fidelidade muito grande com o que a gente está mexendo. Existe uma relação de respeito muito grande com que está mexendo, uma relação de afinidade muito grande, uma relação de redescoberta pessoal. A gente mexe com vários elementos que nos auto-afirmam. E é um processo, tanto pro público como pra gentê; é ao mesmo tempo. Você tá se autodescobrindo. Isso é um processo quase que simultáneo com o público (Hèlder Vasconcelos, 1996).

4. Rapaz, tua música me faz lembrar . . . um Brasil que eu sei que eu tenho, mas que eu não tenho mais, que o Brasil não é tão distante de Curitiba pro Nordeste (quotation from an audience member, recounted by the band, 1996).

5. Na verdade, para a música que a gente faz hoje ser possível, a gente vem de um processo longo de se limpar. Se limpar do rock, se limpar do jazz, se limpar da música erudita. Se limpar não no sentido que aquilo seja ruim ou bom, mas que da forma como a gente vai crescendo, convivendo com isso, a gente perde completamente o sentido, a referência específica nossa, como músico, como pessoa até, de nordestino, brasileiro (1996).

6. E de repente você se vê, eu me vi com vinte e poucos anos, dentro da universidade, onde só tinha lugar pra música erudita, onde eu só tocava guitarra, rock, começava a tocar jazz. Todo mundo passa por isso aqui. Até o próprio processo da banda

já foi uma ilustração disso. A gente começou com uma coisa muito variada e cheia de referências, e foi limpando, limpando, limpando, até ter uma música que reflete muito bem a realidade do lugar em que a gente vive, e que apesar disso traz todas as referências do jazz, rock, tudo tá ali—duma maneira que a gente conseguiu dosar—bom ou ruim, tá lá dosado. Mas a gente teve que se limpar. Não desprezar ou colocar de lado, mas tentar ver qual a importância mesma dos elementos (1996).

7. O natural hoje da gente, principalmente na nossa geração, é a informação externa predominar (Hélder Vasconcelos, 1996).

8. Nesse meio de caminho tem um monte de coisa pronta pra você (1996).

9. Quanto ao "processo de limpeza," conceito que ocupa parte muito importante do seu trabalho, ele hoje está entre nós meio que "inerente," ou seja, já incorporamos tanto as conseqüências da "limpeza" que já nem pensamos tanto na necessidade e importância que ela teve (e tem). Acho que já desenvolvemos um conceito musical e os novos trabalhos que estamos desenvolvendo aqui já fluem a partir deste conceito de forma muito natural (1997).

10. Após a vinda para São Paulo em novembro de 1996, o Mestre Ambrósio já se faz conhecido nacionalmente. Seja por estar presente com freqüência nos meios de comunicação de abrangência nacional (principalmente TV e Jornais), seja fazendo shows pelo país: São Paulo, Santos, Rio de Janeiro, Parati, Brasília , Belo Horizonte, Ouro Preto, Curitiba, Natal, Fortaleza, João Pessoa, Recife, diversas cidades do interior, além dos festivais Heineken Concerts (SP), Summerstage (NY), e Expo 98 (Lisboa).

Nesses dois anos, além da solidificação do nome do grupo para um público mais abrangente num país cada vez mais ávido por descobrir-se, entender-se e expressar-se de maneira própria, houve um profundo crescimento artístico em todos os integrantes, que se manifestou a partir do momento em que iniciamos os processos de criação do material do segundo CD (*Fuá na casa de Cabral*), a ser lançado pela Sony Music.

A direção musical, que antes era meu encargo, passou a ser assumida pelo grupo todo, numa conseqüência natural do amadurecimento que o tempo e o palco nos trouxeram. As composições também são divididas entre boa parte dos integrantes, registrando-se também muitas parcerias. Sérgio Cassiano, antes responsável por percussão e coro, agora assume também a voz principal em algums momentos. A instrumentação usada é praticamente a mesma, com a presença maior da guitarra em algumas canções.

A parceria com os produtores Mitar Subotic e Antoine Midani e um acesso maior a recursos tecnológicos (o disco foi gravado nos estúdios Nota por Nota e Wah-Wah em São Paulo e mixado no Looking Glass em New York) nos ajudou a chegar mais perto de uma qualidade sonora que esperamos que nos possibilite atingir o rádio sem no entanto descaracterizar nossa música.

Finalmente, nos preparamos agora para o lançamento nacional de *Fuá na casa de Cabral,* com a expectativa estimulante de fazer nossa visão de Nordeste e de Brasil mais facilmente visível a um maior número de pessoas no país . . . e fora dele (1998).

The idea is: from the particular to the general
From the general to the local gang
Good blood in the veins of this Brazilian Rio
Amplifying its beat to the whole world
To the entire world
— (Fernanda Abreu-Chacal-Chico Neves, *Raio X*, 1997)

❊❊❊ SIXTEEN ❊❊❊

"Good Blood in the Veins of This Brazilian Rio" or a Cannibalist Transnationalism

Frederick Moehn

The work of certain contemporary Brazilian pop musicians expresses an identity that stresses transnational links while engaging with local histories, traditions, and values. The music makers considered here draw on styles that range from the national and regional Brazilian traditions of samba, *maracatu*, and *côco*, to the now-international genres of disco, rap, reggae, and rock. These Brazilian artists tend to view the varied effects of the trend toward global interconnectedness from an optimistic yet critical perspective. In their interpretations of popular musical trends, such artists as Fernanda Abreu, Chico Science, and Carlinhos Brown often draw on two of the central discourses on Brazilian identity: miscegenation and *antropofagia*, anthropophagy or cultural cannibalism. The celebration of miscegenation, the best known expression of which is Gilberto Freyre's *The Masters and the Slaves* (*Casa grande e senzala*, 1933), is essentially a discourse on Brazilian national culture. Freyre was one of the first members of the elite to champion racial mixing in Brazil and to recognize that Afro-Brazilian culture was one of Brazil's greatest resources, a source of national pride. *The Masters and the Slaves* was the most forceful statement of the elite's growing awareness of the uniqueness of the country's population, and of the importance of the African and indigenous contributions to its culture. This was a general trend which, in music, culminated with populist president Getulio Vargas's successful adoption of samba as Brazil's national music.[1]

In the song lyrics and other articulations about popular music examined here, Brazil's miscegenated culture is often cited with pride. Yet while the emphasis on *racial* mixing remains central, equally important is a notion of transnational miscegenation of musical styles, as we will see in the case of Fernanda Abreu's "Esse é o lugar" [This is the place]. Part of Abreu's work, and that of other contemporary artists of MPB [Música Popular Brasileira], is to continue the process—begun by the Tropicalists in the 1960s—of destroying stereotypes such as the one engendered by the nationalist discourse that championed the samba of Rio de Janeiro. On the flip side of this coin, of course, are the Brazilian stereotypes propagated outside the country. This is one issue broached in the lyric of the celebrated song "Chiclete com banana"—". . . when Uncle Sam . . . learns that samba isn't rumba . . ."—and it is also part of what MPB artists since Tropicália have continued to work to change.

One of the ways of working against both the localized and the more transnational stereotypes of Brazilian culture is to "cannibalize" international pop music styles within the discourse of *antropofagia*. This artistic philosophy was inspired by the history of certain indigenous Brazilian tribes that supposedly cannibalized their vanquished in order to gain their strengths and virtues. In the late 1920s, modernist thinker Oswald de Andrade elaborated this notion as a symbol of a search for new Brazilian art that did not simply copy European and North American models but which *adapted* specific elements of foreign cultures and art in the creation of uniquely Brazilian works. Andrade's text, the "Cannibalist Manifesto" (1928), was the original expression of this idea, an aesthetic that continues to resonate in discussions of Brazilian art today. This cultural metaphor entered the world of Brazilian popular music through the Tropicália movement in the late 1960s. The two central figures of the movement, Caetano Veloso and Gilberto Gil, adopted cultural cannibalism as a framework through which they could adapt, for example, the electric guitars of rock 'n' roll to Brazilian popular music. Certainly, the history of Brazilian music has always been one of absorbing and adapting varied cultural influences. What sets the Tropicália movement apart in this long history is its deliberateness, and the seemingly heightened awareness of its members that a new era of popular culture was emerging and that the relationship between the local and the global needed to be rethought. Significantly, the Tropicalist maneuver that caused the greatest stir was the use of electric guitars at a televised MPB festival; that is to say, it was the imported electronic technology that seemed most threatening to the public at the time. The clothes, the hairstyles, even the lyrics were not as iconically potent as was the electric guitar. One of the central ruptures for which the Tropicália movement was responsible, then, was the cannibalization of foreign music technology.

The stylistic mixing foreseen in "Chiclete com banana" (e.g., "bebop in my samba") was wholeheartedly celebrated by the Tropicalists. Today such hybridization has become a normal feature of the process of music production, facilitated by expensive studio technology and by the rapid dissemination of stylistic trends through international media and distribution networks. MPB artists embrace the possibilities offered by the media and technology for exploration of new musical pathways. Yet this optimistic techno-cosmopolitanism enters into a tension with a construction of identity that asserts a greater role for Brazilian musicality in a world of cultural hypermiscegenation.

For Fernanda Abreu, whose lyric manifesto from the album *Raio X* [X ray] serves as epigraph to this chapter, not only is Brazil central in world groove production, but within Brazil, Rio de Janeiro is the crucial conduit for groove circulation. The city is likened to a heart connecting the nation's cultural arteries with the veins of the international music industry ("amplifying its beat to the entire world"). Her music is a mix of disco with funk, hip-hop, rap, reggae, and samba. Abreu "was born and grew up listening to disco."[2] In "Esse é o lugar" [This is the place], from *Da lata* [Of cans, 1996], Abreu expresses her hybrid musical identity: "With my feet here and my head there / My vision here but my look from there / Jorge BenJor is from here, James Brown is from there / Carlinhos Brown is from everywhere/ I go on living mixed, mixed." Abreu isn't singing about cultural imperialism here; she is a global citizen, from Brazil. The title of the song is instructive. Abreu is a traveler—"when I go there, I miss here, when I return here, I miss things from there"—but her reference point is clear: Rio de Janeiro. We know, without being told specifically, that "there" is the United States, whether

Fernanda Abreu and daughter, ca. 1997. Photo by Cristina Granato.

literally or only in an imagined sense. Here, to which Fernanda returns, is the city of Jorge BenJor, and the country of Carlinhos Brown (from Bahia), whom she compares to James Brown. And although she only sings about Brazil and the United States, she has a cultural visa to the world: "the things that I say are from anyplace," she sings. Her transnational compatriot is Carlinhos Brown, who she asserts has a passport from the universe. The trick to survival in this state of affairs, says Fernanda Abreu, is to "go on living, mixed, mixed."

Abreu is especially articulate about the new role of Brazilian musicians in the global music industry. About her work *Raio X* (1997), Abreu writes:

> To begin the recording with the Old Guard of Mangueira [the famous samba school], and to finish with the sound of Funk'n Lata [a local pop/funk group that includes percussionists from Mangueira] synthesized for me the whole idea of the disc. The idea that, in this miscegenated and cannibalistic country, our cultural and racial tradition comes from the verb "to mix." A disc that mixes *tambor* and *maracatu*, *timbau* from Bahia, electric *bumbo* and the *surdo* from samba in service of Brazilian dance music. I don't even need to mention the use of Pro-Tools,

Samplers, Macintoshes and technology in general in this cauldron, because these are already an organic part of my work and the universal pop language. I feel that this disc affirms the idea that, starting in the 90s, Brazilian Pop Music mixes, in a more effective manner, "Brazil" in its language. To be Brazilian, to be of the world. From the particular to the general. Good blood in the veins of this Brazilian Rio [double meaning: Rio literally means "river"], amplifying its beat to the entire world (press kit).

While Abreu, like all Brazilian music makers, uses the English names of imported technology (e.g., Pro-Tools, Macintosh), she says that both technology and the sampling process are an "organic" part of her work, as if technology has literally been *incorporated*, that is, brought into the living body of her dance groove.[3] The technology is part of the "universal pop language," while Brazil provides the good blood, the samba, and the miscegenated groove of cultural cannibalism—"good blood in the veins of this Brazilian Rio, amplifying its beat to the entire world." The lyric conjures the image of Rio as a cardioid center of transnational groove production whose beat travels through rivers and veins (the media organicized) to a global pop-music community. In Abreu's music, the importance of the local is clear; she refers to "the universal pop language," yet she is nevertheless confident that her contribution to the global circulation of grooves represents a unique dialect.

Like Fernanda Abreu, Chico Science (d. 1997), from Recife in the northeastern state of Pernambuco, was very explicit about the use of technology in his music. He is considered the founder (with his band, Nação Zumbi) of what has been termed the *mangue beat* (or *mangue bit*) movement. *Mangue* [mangrove or marsh] *beat* is a mixture of the northeastern rhythms *maracatu* and *côco*, among others, with such international genres as rock, funk, raggamuffin, or rap.[4] Using mostly instruments from a typical rock or funk band—drums, electric bass, and guitar, occasional brass, in addition to percussion, Chico Science created a highly original mixture of rhythms that has earned an enthusiastic public within Brazil and abroad. Chico Science's interpretation of the possibilities facilitated by the world of technologically assisted groove mixing is suggested on the disc *Afrociberdélia*:

(Taken from the Galactic Encyclopedia, volume LXII, 2102 edition)
AFROCIBERDELIA (from Africa + Cybernetics + Psychedelicism)—s.f.—The art of mapping the primal genetic memory (which in the 20th century was called

"the collective unconscious") through electrochemical stimulation, verbal automation and intense bodily movement to the sound of binary music.

Practiced informally by tribes of urban youths during the second half of the 20th century; only after 2030 was it officially accepted as a scientific discipline, together with telepathy, pataphysics, and psychoanalysis. For *afrociberdelic* theory, humanity is a benign virus in the software of nature, and can be compared to a Tree whose roots are the codes of human DNA (which originated in Africa), whose branches are the digital-information-electronic ramifications (Cybernetics) and whose fruits provoke altered states of conscience (Psychedelicism).[5]

This passage, complete with organic and biological metaphors (e.g., the tree of life), an evolutionary timeline, and the central place of Africa in a diffusionist cartography (while modern "tribes" are part of an urban diaspora), claims that the creed of *mangue beat* is to embrace technology as an aid in the art of mapping the "primal genetic memory." In the song "Etnia" [Ethnicity], Chico Science begins with a reference to ethnic and racial miscegenation: "We are all together a miscegenation and we can not escape from our ethnicity / Indians, whites, blacks and *mestiços* nothing wrong in their principles /Yours and mine are equal, runs through our veins without stopping." But this is simply a prelude to a celebration of musical and cultural miscegenation, and to a Brazilian adaptation of technology: "It's hip hop in my *embolada* . . . . psychedelic *maracatu* . . . *Bumba* my radio . . . electric *berimbau.*"

The aesthetic of mixing/miscegenation extends even to phrases and words, part of what Chico Science refers to as "pataphysics." Pataphysics is a "French absurdist concept of a philosophy or science dedicated to studying what lies beyond the realm of metaphysics, often expressed in nonsensical language."[6] However, Chico Science's pataphysical word plays, though often obscure, are not entirely nonsensical. "*Bumba* my radio," for example, recalls the northeastern ritual *bumba-meu-boi* [buck my bull], a folkloric play in which the character of an ox parodies figures from the local community. One of the Brazilian northeast's most characteristic folk traditions becomes mediated (by radio) through an efficient word game. Chico Science's play here recalls the famous Tropicalist song-manifesto "Geléia geral" [General jam] (Gilberto Gil-Torquato Neto, 1967), which sings, "It's *bumba-iê-iê-iê,*" referencing the folk dance and British yeah-yeah-yeah pop. Charles Perrone has pointed out that Gil's voicing contrasted an electrified instrumental accompaniment with the "traditional rhythmic base of a Northern variety" featured on his recording.[7] This is precisely what Chico Science did in his music.

Chico Science's liner-note passage on *Afrociberdélia* and the *"bumba* my radio" lyric effectively organicize technology and incorporate it into discourses on race and evolution, as well as into regional folklore (e.g., *bumba-meu-boi*). Similarly, the "electric *berimbau"* adapts electronic technology for amplification of one of the quintessential instruments of Brazilian folklore. By cannibalizing technology and inserting it into a discourse of miscegenation that emphasizes blood and genes, and by "electrifying" *berimbau* and mediating *bumba-meu-boi*, Chico Science finds a space within Brazilian national discourse from which to view globalization critically. The CD liner notes include the following instructions written in the style of a computer (or audio equipment) manual:

ENTER—Subversive technology, the grand library of cyberspace, symbiotic viewpoint, fractals in the cure for stress (plug in and chill out [sic]), afrociberdelia, theater of chance, impressive cinema, copied literature, fractal poetry, sampled culture, telecracy, interactive community, science-fiction, revival sense and musicracy.

DEL[ete]—Fraud, *midiotia* [media+idiocy], illicit wealth, false doctrine, misery, evil space, religious commerce, fanaticism, huge corporations striving in cerebral deformation, racism, exploitation of child labor, suffering from death and hunger shame the planet.

On the positive side ("Enter"), we find high-tech interactive *community*, while it is suggested that with the press of a button ("Delete"), dogmatism, intolerance, and transnational exploitation can be erased.[8] It is an idealistic but not a utopian stance. Globalization, here to stay, has both positive and negative consequences; the challenge of popular music is to understand fully these distinctions.

An artist whose lyrics recall Chico Science's method of lyrical "pataphysics" is Carlinhos Brown, who, Fernanda Abreu said, is "from everywhere." Brown, born in Salvador, Bahia, recorded his last two CDs transnationally, in Brazil, Paris, and New York. His compact disc *Omelete Man* (1998) was pieced together in no less than nine studios in three cities. Brown mixes English, French, and Portuguese words and syllables in a manner difficult to decipher. Nearly every track on the disc features such mixing, as does the title of the disc. "Hawaii e you" is Brown's play on "How Are You?" Brown sings, "I am happy / Io Iô és you / My son as you / My sun és you / My som is you," a tricky play on the pronouns "I" and "you," on the verb "to be," and on the nouns "son," "sun," and "sound." This "omelet man" is so transnationally culturally miscegenated that he seems almost incapable of singing an entire phrase in Portuguese without mixing in Yoruba, English, or even, occasionally, French. In the song "Tribal United Dance," Brown sings, "I'm eternal matter / succulent cannibal / ether now." Brown is an omelet of syllables, words, and musical styles; now and eternally ethereal. He ironically calls himself a succulent cannibal and offers himself up for consumption *em caso de fome* [in case of hunger].

This type of transnational cultural production, in which a recording is pieced together in stages in several different locales, even in different countries, and in which lyrics mix different languages—in short, a musical omelet—suggests that popular music is adapting to new transnational identities. Addressing postmodernist claims that individual identities are getting lost in a world of so-called pseudo-difference (a claim most notably theorized by Jean Baudrillard),[9] Gage Averill argued for Haitian popular music that "the global circulation of expressive culture doesn't render it incapable of addressing identities, nor does it assign all the signifiers to the category of pseudo-difference. Rather, these cultural symbols better represent identities that are at once both local and supra-local." Averill concluded that "Haitian identities are at once spatial and non-spatial phenomena: local, diasporic, global, national and transnational, and Haitian popular music has come to symbolize that complex state of being. The increasingly global influences in Haitian popular music correlate with Haiti's increasingly integrated status in the global system. . .and an increasing desire to take part in global discourse."[10]

When Grammy-award winner Milton Nascimento cries over a bed of intense percussion based on local rhythms from Minas Gerais, "I will not be a foreigner! I will not be a foreigner! I'm a citizen of the world! I'm a citizen of the world!" it is apparent that he is affirming an identity that cannot be based simply on nationality. For their parts, the Brazilian musicians discussed above, like the Haitian popular musicians Averill researched, are forging localized conceptions of transnational identities. However, the case of Brazil is complicated by the fact that Brazil's music industry is so vast and is, in fact, largely *self-contained*. Indeed, the expression of an identity that is at once Brazilian and "of the world" is in tension with a local music industry that sells much more domestic *pagode* or *axé music* product (primarily romantic samba and dance music) than it does Fernanda

Abreu or Chico Science. In contrast, then, with the Haitian popular music that Averill discusses, the MPB artists that I cite here are in fact a minority in terms of sales within the Brazilian industry. At the same time, it is the music of this minority that attracts the most attention outside Brazil, and it is this music that tends to have lasting appeal to both critics and musicians. The recent discovery among young North American audiences of the music of the Tropicália movement, and of Tom Zé and Os Mutantes (see John Harvey's chapter here), is evidence of the more international appeal of this cannibalist pop in relation to the dance-oriented and romantic genres such as *pagode* and *axé music*. This points to the class base of Brazilian music's international public, and to the lack of a large working-class Brazilian population outside of Brazil. While in New York City, the large Latino population put the salsa and merengue station La Mega (97.9) in first place in listenership among all radio stations in the city in 1998, Brazilian music in the United States is most notably promoted by art-rocker David Byrne, whose transnational affinity lies primarily within the MPB camp.

This dichotomy—a large domestic consumer base in Brazil's lower classes for *pagode, axé music*, and *música sertaneja* and the primarily middle-class audience of the artists discussed above—contrasts with the nature of the music industries of the United States, Europe, and Japan, where the largest consumer base is a relatively well-educated middle class. At the same time, it distinguishes Brazil from the far smaller economies that are also peripheral to world centers of capital and media. One could say that Brazil represents, in essence, a "middle case," but this runs the risk of implying an evolutionary progression of industrial development with, say, Haiti and the United States representing two extremes. Rather, popular musicians in all three places are contemporaneously shaping unique identities rooted in their particular material circumstances and cultural histories.

A large economy such as Brazil's will naturally present the researcher with several different spheres of cultural production. For example, while Chico Science and Fernanda Abreu celebrate miscegenation and racial pluralism, a very different transnational affinity is stressed in the *blocos afro* of Salvador, and in much of the *samba-reggae* of that city. Larry Crook noted that in the re-Africanization of the Bahian Carnival beginning in the 1970s, "[r]ather than a romanticized return to an idealized 'tribal' Africa or a frozen folkloric Africanity, this process involved the reinvention of Africa and the construction of a socially engaged image of black Brazilian identity that celebrated African heritage and black distinctiveness but that was rooted in the social, cultural, and economic realities of blacks in contemporary Brazil."[11] A similar identification is evident in Brazilian rap today; rather than celebrate the miscegenated *mulato/mulata*, blackness is celebrated, and identification with foreign artists is strengthened through a sense of common struggle. This is a turning away from Freyrean idealism and from the myth that a supposedly fully miscegenated Brazil is free of racism.

Marcelo D2, a rap artist from Rio (formerly of the group Planet Hemp, now disbanded), looks outside of Brazilian national culture for an affirmative racial identification with a black transnationalism. In "Eu tiro é onda" [I'm kiddin' around], D2 shares the lyric with New York rapper, Shabazz: "I came from Rio de Janeiro to New York, attracted by the sound," sings D2. "In Andaraí [D2's neighborhood in Rio], in Brooklyn, there's only good blood ('sangue bom'). . . . In Portuguese or English, the fight is the same, stay alive, in peace."[12] Here, the reference to good blood takes on a poignant significance when one considers how much of that blood flows tragically in ghettos and *favelas*.

In a thoughtful analysis of the international appeal of Bob Marley's music, Michelle Stephens writes:

> . . . black transnationalism is not a universalist doctrine, but a vision of the liberation of a very particular, historical racial and class community. This vision seeks to overcome racial division by overthrowing systems of unequal power relations between races and peoples. This vision never assumes that cultural intermingling across lines of difference will occur until peoples can interact with each other on a level social, political and economic playing field. This was the true body and soul of "one nation under a groove," the bass beat that makes artists such as James Brown and George Clinton still so useful for black musicians.[13]

In this vision, the level playing field in which Uncle Sam might play *tamborim*, the line from the original "Chiclete com banana" lyric, is still a long way off. As researchers of the various popular musics of the world, we need to be aware of the peculiarities of locale, race, class, and gender, and of the varied *motivations* for transnational affinities. The pronouncement of a progression toward global musical homogenization, if true, is premature—for now, we need to learn better to understand where difference hides in the transnational culture industries.

In the recording studio, when a producer wants to hear more of a particular musical part in the monitors, he or she may ask to have it "brought up" in the mix. I suggest that the music makers I discuss here are asking to have Brazilian musical values and styles "brought up" in the "global mix." By reinterpreting local musics into transnationally hybrid styles, they are literally increasing the presence of local Brazilian genres in the international popular music scene. Rather than viewing local musical traditions and values as unchanging, or as losing ground to some type of homogenized global mass culture, they assert that the way in which Brazilians "mix" will always be unique. For artists such as Fernanda Abreu, to be Brazilian is not in contradiction with being of the world, it is precisely to be of the world. Each artist's work presents a unique interpretation or combination of global trends and influences. Samba, *forró*, and *maracatu*, for example, are in a constant process of change through encounters with international pop musics, but they are not disappearing. "My samba will turn out like this . . . ," sang Jackson do Pandeiro. Indeed, transnational genres like rock and reggae are themselves revitalized through these encounters.

Part of the dynamism of contemporary popular music is a result of the continual reinterpretation of the local through the global and the global through the local. For MPB artists, miscegenation and cannibalism are just two of the discourses through which they interpret cultural change. To the extent that these ideologies are central in conceptions of Brazilian national identity, they seem to be in tension with the urge to be a "universal Brazilian" as expressed by Fernanda Abreu, or to be a "citizen of the world," as affirmed by Milton Nascimento. However, this contradiction is the essence of MPB; it is what MPB, since Tropicália, is about.

Notes

1. See Hermano Vianna, *The Mystery of Samba: Popular Music and National Identity in Brazil* (Chapel Hill: University of North Carolina Press, 1999).

2. Press kit, publicity office of Fernanda Abreu, 1998, cited next in text as "press kit."

3. I thank Gage Averill for drawing my attention to Abreu's use of the word "organic" here.

4. Philip Galinsky pointed out to me that the original meaning of the "beat" in *mangue bit* was the English term "bit," as in data bits, not a local version of the English word "beat" (in northeastern Portuguese "bit" and "beat" are pronounced homonymously, /biti/).

5. Chico Science & Nação Zumbi, *Afrociberdélia* (Sony Latin, 1996). Text by Braulio Tavares.

6. *American Heritage College Dictionary*, 3rd ed. (New York: Houghton Mifflin, 1993).

7. Charles A. Perrone, *Masters of Contermporary Brazilian Song: MPB 1965–1985* (Austin: University of Texas Press, 1989), 103.

8. It is an interesting change from the previous generation's fear of the destruction of the world with the press of a button.

9. Ethnomusicologist Veit Erlmann applied Baudrillard in his analysis of world music, writing that "value, in the viral stage, develops from pure contiguity, from the cancerous proliferation of values without any reference point at all. In this stage, the forces and processes of cultural production are dispersed and cut loose from any particular time and place, even if local traditions and authenticity are what the products of the global entertainment industry are ostensibly about." See Veit Erlmann, "The Aesthetics of the Global Imagination: Reflections on World Music in the 1990s," *Public Culture* 8 (1996), 475.

10. Gage Averill, "Haitian Music and the Global System," in *The Reordering of Culture: Latin America, the Caribbean and Canada*, ed. A. Ruprecht (Ottawa: Carlton University Press, 1995), 353.

11. Larry Crook, "Black Consciousness, *Samba-reggae*, and the Re-Africanization of Bahian Carnival Music in Brazil," *the world of music* vol. 35, no. 2 (1993), 95.

12. Marcelo D2, *Eu tiro é onda* (Sony Music Brazil, 1998).

13. Michelle A. Stephens, "Babylon's Natural Mystic: The North American Music Industry, the Legend of Bob Marley, and the Incorporation of Transnationalism," *Cultural Studies* vol. 12, no. 2 (1998), 163.

Contributors

Charles A. Perrone is professor of Portuguese and Luso-Brazilian literature and culture in the Department of Romance Languages and Literatures, as well as an affiliate and concentration coordinator of the Center for Latin American Studies at the University of Florida.

Christopher Dunn is assistant professor at Tulane University, where he holds a joint appointment in the Department of Spanish and Portuguese and in the African and African Diaspora Studies Program. He is also an affiliate of the Roger Thayer Stone Center for Latin American Studies.

Caetano Veloso is the author of *Verdade tropical* (1996) and is a Brazilian recording artist. He resides in Rio de Janeiro and Salvador, Bahia.

Liv Sovik is adjunct professor of communication at UFRJ, the Federal University of Rio de Janeiro, Brazil.

John J. Harvey was musical director at radio station WTUL in New Orleans and is a doctoral candidate in Latin American literature at Tulane University.

Idelber Avelar is associate professor of Latin American literature at Tulane University.

Livio Sansone is director of the Centro de Estudos Afro-Asiáticos, associate dean for research at Faculdades Cândido Mendes, Rio de Janeiro, and professor of anthropology at UFBA, the Federal University of Bahia, Salvador, Brazil.

Milton Araújo Moura teaches sociology and holds a doctorate in communication from UFBA, the Federal University of Bahia, Salvador, Brazil.

Piers Armstrong is adjunct professor in the Departament of Letters and Arts at the state university of Bahia, Feira de Santana, Brazil.

Osmundo de Araújo Pinho is a research associate at CEMI, the Center for Studies of International Migration, and a doctoral candidate in social anthropology at UNICAMP, São Paulo state university at Campinas.

Antonio J. V. dos Santos Godi teaches at the state university of Bahia, Feira de Santana, Brazil.

Ari Lima is a research associate of S.A.M.B.A. (Social Anthropology of Music in Bahia) at UFBA, the Federal University of Bahia, Salvador, Brazil and a doctoral candidate in anthropology at UNB, the Univeraity of Brasília.

Larry Crook is associate professor of ethnomusicology, affiliate of the Center for Latin American Studies, and codirector of the Center for World Arts at the University of Florida.

John Murphy is associate professor of ethnomusicology at Western Illinois University.

Frederick Moehn is a doctoral candidate in ethnomusicology at New York University.

Copyrights and Acknowledgments

Index